RIT - WALLACE LIBRARY
CIRCULATING LIBRARY BOOKS

OVERDUE FINES AND FEES FOR ALL BORROWERS

- Recalled = $1/ day overdue (no grace period)
- Billed = $10.00/ item when returned 4 or more weeks overdue
- Lost Items = replacement cost+$10 fee
- All materials must be returned or renewed by the duedate.

SERIES ON TECHNOLOGY MANAGEMENT – VOL. 2

THE KNOWLEDGE ENTERPRISE

IMPLEMENTATION OF INTELLIGENT BUSINESS STRATEGIES

J FRISO DEN HERTOG

MERIT, Maastricht University and Altuïtion bv, 's Hertogenbosch, The Netherlands

EDWARD HUIZENGA

Altuïtion bv, 's Hertogenbosch, The Netherlands

ICP

Imperial College Press

Published by

Imperial College Press
57 Shelton Street
Covent Garden
London WC2H 9HE

Distributed by

World Scientific Publishing Co. Pte. Ltd.

P O Box 128, Farrer Road, Singapore 912805

USA office: Suite 1B, 1060 Main Street, River Edge, NJ 07661

UK office: 57 Shelton Street, Covent Garden, London WC2H 9HE

British Library Cataloguing-in-Publication Data
A catalogue record for this book is available from the British Library.

First published 2000
Reprinted 2001

THE KNOWLEDGE ENTERPRISE
Implementation of Intelligent Business Strategies
(Series on Technology Management — Volume 2)

ISBN 1-86094-136-2

Printed in Singapore.

Preface

After fifteen years, knowledge is back on the political agenda. During the no-nonsense period that is behind us, firms and institutions have learned to focus on the market. Quality has become the subject of continuous attention and focus. Bureaucracies have been dismantled. Lean is in fashion. Now, on the threshold of the turn of a new century, we are becoming aware that inexpensive and rapid delivery of products and services is not sufficient to be able to, at least, maintain our economic position. In countries with an open economic order, it is impossible to put up barriers against the outflow of activities that can be performed in other countries and companies more cheaply and better. Under such circumstances we will have to rely upon our own strengths to deliver products and services which others are unable to deliver at the same time. Thus, the knowledge factor is now the focus of business strategy. Concentration on core competencies ('doing the right things') and a drastic increase in the effectiveness of knowledge work ('doing the right things right') have become priorities on the strategic agenda of the firm. This holds true not only of the trade and business community, but for the public sector as well.

The development and exploitation of the knowledge factor requires investments in the knowledge infrastructure. Without substantial investments in education and public and private R&D, the future of the firm as a knowledge enterprise is no more than an illusion. More important, however, is the way in which knowledge processes are organized. Knowledge processes are not so much concerned with the application of new organizational techniques, but with an essentially different way of organizational thinking. This book is about this new view of the organization. The firm is regarded in this vision as a knowledge system which faces risky choices: the knowledge enterprise. The starting point of this study is that the success of the knowledge enterprise fully depends on the ability of organizations to innovate. Yet the source of organizational innovations are seldom found in organizational theory. Innovations ensue (Daft & Lewis, 1993) from the organizational experiments continuously carried out by managers in actual practice. Nevertheless, there are also significant tasks for organization scientists, which are concerned with the analysis, integration and transfer of experiences and theoretical underpinning. This is also the division of tasks that has been the basis of this book. The innovative work has been performed by seven Dutch market leaders in industry and the service sector. The authors are responsible for the analysis and synthesis. In so doing, they have tried to fine-tune their analysis to the knowledge stored within the organization sciences.

The writing of this book was quite a (knowledge) enterprise in itself. Throughout this enterprise, we have been able to rely upon the active support of many people:

- the firms which have opened their doors to us: AVEBE, BFI, DSM Andeno, Gist-brocades, HAK, Pink Elephant, Moret Ernst & Young, Nationale Nederlanden, Raychem, and Stork;
- our sponsors: the Ministry of Economic Affairs, the Dutch Foundation of Scientific Research, the European Commission (DG V), and MERIT;
- the colleagues and students who have read and commented upon the draft version, more specifically: Rob Janssen Duyghuysen and Boudewijn Struijk (Adviesgroep KOERS), Ton van Reeken and Riemer Fokkema (University Maastricht), Ed van Sluijs (GITP), Jeroen Nijland (Ministry of Economic Affairs); and finally,
- Corien Gijsbers, our logistic and editorial anchor woman.

Thank you all very, very much!

Friso den Hertog and **Edward Huizenga**

Contents

PART I
THE KNOWLEDGE THEORY

Chapter 1

The Knowledge Enterprise

Managers are expected to divide attention over an increasing number of important matters. Throughout the past ten years, managers in most organizations have invested a great deal of time in the improvement and streamlining of processes. Market focus, quality, flexibility and slimming down have been among their daily activities. Throughout Europe and North America, this has undeniably led to a number of distinct results. Quality and productivity have been improved in the 'no-nonsense' era. We are doing things quicker and faster using fewer people. At the same time, a gradual and creeping reversal is taking place which remains unnoticed to many managers. In the years to come, competitive advantage will be determined increasingly by the way in which firms deal with the knowledge factor. Price and quality have become preconditions for market entry. The future of firms will depend more and more on the ability to convert knowledge into good currency. Firms will have to evolve in this process into a 'knowledge enterprise'. This chapter concentrates on the risks of our preoccupation with quality, cost and market focus. It addresses the factors that contribute to the increasing knowledge intensity of business management. Finally, it sketches the challenge that is ahead of us: competition on the basis of knowledge.

Two years ago, business units were introduced by Firm A. The functional lines that were at the basis of the firm's organization from the Executive Board to the shop floor were replaced by market- and product-centred lines. The switches were reversed in virtually every department of the organization for the benefit of the market. Inroads were made even into the sanctuary of the corporate R&D laboratory, turning it into a support department. New creative ideas were expected to come from the market place. Now, at the internal quality award two years later, not one manager among those present would dare to throw doubt upon the accuracy of that decision. The president of the enterprise enthusiastically lists the results achieved: a cost reduction of 8 per cent and an increase in volume of 7 per cent, ISO certificates in modern frames in the hallway, higher scores in the customer surveys, and decreased absenteeism. Everybody toasts to the successes. The managers are grouped according to the new business set-up, rather than the way they used to stand together on such occasions: manufacturers with manufacturers, marketers with marketers. Still, after a while they go and have a chat with their old mates, and less positive stories are recounted. The R&D people observe that the market does not generate new ideas. They have done service work more than anything else in recent times, which has led to lots of cost-saving and quality-enhancing measures. Yet there was no challenge from the market. The marketers have taken these improvements almost as self-evident givens, but something is bugging them too: they are no longer bothered by stubborn developers who cannot be put off their ideas no matter what. There has come an end to the times where they were surprised by resourceful innovations that were sometimes invented in the illegal margins of the business.

Tour Operator B is urgently looking for a purchaser with a great knowledge of South-east Asia. The purchase group in question has been tampered with a huge turnover in recent years. This did not create too many problems initially, because it was possible to extend ongoing purchase contracts. Recently, however, Firm B has been in trouble and the lack of highly adept purchasers is felt. New active policy and new alternatives are required once again: new destinations are becoming popular, and the well-known suppliers provide too little value while asking too much money. A head-hunter is called upon, who asks a phenomenal fee yet comes up with two good candidates after a long search. But the personnel department is in for a surprise: the first candidate works for another business unit of the same firm, while the second left the firm after a serious conflict a year ago.

Firm C has made a radical shift in production. The organization has been made more compact to a great extent, 'lean production' being the slogan of the organizational change process. Compared to eastern competitors, the plant employed too many indirect people. All those not directly needed for production were made redundant. The ratio indirect/direct personnel was reduced from 4 to 10, to 2 to 10. The maintenance of breakdown-sensitive machinery was integrated with operation, which did not cause too many problems initially. The experienced maintenance engineers were called upon to teach them the tricks of the trade. The production teams seemed to manage quite well in their new jobs. The production staff were ardent about their job extension. Machine up-time even improved because defects were fixed more rapidly. But then the older experienced engineers were sent away with their redundancy money. As a result, machines sometimes stand idle for days. The production teams are capable of handling the problems they are familiar with, but are increasingly confronted with new unknown technical problems. The know-how they need to be fed with continuously has dried out.

Knowledge Escapes from Attention

Today's organizations are facing a gradual, creeping, but at the same time fundamental and irreversible change. The danger of creeping changes is that one gets used to them, just like one gets used to traffic jams. Traffic jams become a little longer every day. And one day we won't even remember that there was a time they did not exist. Business travellers have adjusted to the creeping discomfort. They possess a wireless phone, and it won't be long until standard lease cars are equipped with personal computers including modems and faxes. They are busy people, who cannot afford to do nothing. So they adapt. When people have to spread their attention, they tend to ignore certain signals. That's what people have in common with frogs (Van de Ven, 1988): when frogs are thrown in a pot filled with boiling water, they jump out. But when they are put on the stove in cold water, they will slowly boil to death.

Thus, Firm A starts to be aware that the formation of self-managing business units does not only have positive sides to it. The supply of new ideas that may be the base for tomorrow's business is running dry. This will be reflected in the portfolio of R&D projects within two years' time. Projects are increasingly tailored to today's business. There doesn't seem to be one single manager who dares to risk his neck for projects with a 'high risk/high reward' profile. The firm is becoming aware that if nothing is undertaken, the supply of knowledge will dry these new opportunities. This implies three things:

- The firm should invest more in long-term knowledge development;
- The knowledge potential within the firm should be utilized more effectively;
- It is imperative that the firm develop knowledge synergy with other firms and make use of the knowledge available at universities and other public research institutions.

Firm B has learned how to generate a higher turnover using fewer specialists. The tour operator has found a strong niche in the market for trips to the Far East. The purchase team has learned how to work efficiently to the extent that when a few team members left the firm, the remaining group members managed to cope with the work, and the firm is proud of that. But when substantial changes in the environment present themselves, the departure of one individual shows that a bomb is ticking away under the lucrative market niche. The firm discovers that the supply of new talent cannot be left to coincidence. Talents should be nurtured and kept up in a strongly fluctuating market. Rather than personnel *work*, where one looks for a sheep with five feet, this requires personnel *policy*, which ensures the knowledge advantage of the firm. "Human resource management" is the term used for this in the 1990s.

'Lean production' is particularly a matter of counting and cutting for Firm C. Slimming down by a quick and effective diet rather than exercise and training. The financial result is expressed by a denominator: revenues divided by cost. Increasing revenues takes time, resources, and energy. Counting and cutting is an easy way out. The management of Firm C, without thinking about the consequences, has taken refuge in what Hamel and Prahalad (1994) refer to as *denominator management*. The firm is in trouble after the first wave of technological innovations. The capacity to process and internally transfer new production know-how has been kicked out. Machines stand idle for hours, which costs lots of money. Fresh blood from the labour market will solve this problem only in the long run. It will take at least two years for someone to be familiar with business-specific knowledge. With a lot of effort two maintenance engineers are found who are willing to return to the firm for two more years. But even they will have to become acquainted with the knowledge about the new systems.

What do these three examples show? They show that due to our focus on customer demands, quality procedures, cash flow and internal streamlining of processes we threaten to overlook one crucial factor: the *knowledge factor*. The knowledge not only needed to keep our processes going and to improve them continuously, but also the knowledge required to safeguard our position in the future. Knowledge that can be used to explore new opportunities and keep competitors at a distance.

Why is the Knowledge Factor Important Right Now?

Isn't it true that knowledge has always been a self-evident factor in company policy? Of course, knowledge is a self-evident factor in many firms. It's for that very reason that the Dutch business and trade community invests more than 4 billion guilders in training. It's for that very reason that large companies such as Philips and Unilever have protected their prestigious R&D laboratories for such a long time, and governments underline the importance of knowledge infrastructure. (In Northwest Europe, more money is spent on fundamental research than in Japan.) It's for that same reason that the average company has carried along its overweight in terms of staff capacity for so long. Knowledge has long been such a self-evident factor that nobody was talking about it. However, there are three reasons why the knowledge factor should be given priority on the policy agenda of firms and institutions.

The Speed and Complexity of Knowledge Development are Increasing Rapidly

Ten years ago, it was possible in a medium-sized firm to quickly localize the most important changes. Projects had a start A and an ending B. They took place in Departments C and D. The project applied Methods E and F, and used Specialties G and H. The postal services shifted to the electronic reading of postcodes, and newspapers got to be edited electronically. Bicycle firms introduced an electronically steered induction welding technology for the production of bicycle frames. Department stores started to sell insurance policies, and chemical paint companies water-based coatings. It was fairly easy to describe the knowledge required to do these things. Additionally, it was not difficult to ascertain when the introduction of new knowledge could start and when this knowledge could become productive.

If we look at our business processes, it seems as if there is no beginning and end to the changes that our organizations are facing. Change projects continually merge into one another. Innovation has become a continuous process: nothing is constant, except change itself. It's not only the time boundaries that merge into each other. The knowledge used by organizations is increasingly composed knowledge. The number of specialties rapidly increases, and these specialties must somehow be linked as one goes on. The development of products, services and processes is no more than the responsibility of a few departments in the firm. Each specialty adds its own know-how. The list of indicators for the speed and complexity of the knowledge development is different for every individual organization. Whether we work in a hospital, insurance company, or pharmaceutical company, the results of the analysis is the same time and again: things are going quicker and they are becoming more complex.

Metamorphosis

In some companies, this development takes place as a true revolution. Firms that were known as being 'low tech' five or ten years ago have undergone a metamorphosis that only few people would have believed possible. A striking example of such a firm is the Dutch subsidiary company of the American garbage disposal firm BFI. BFI has developed since 1987 into a market share leader in the service sector in the Netherlands, with an annual turnover of 650 million guilders. In 1997, the Dutch BFI subsidiary was taken over by the French SITA. Its market leadership developed not only in a process of constant acquisitions, but is based mainly on the way in which knowledge was added continuously at every level — each function and each region. 'Making sure the garbage cans are emptied adequately' was the core of the business eight years ago. Entrepreneurs were able to benefit from the distinct growth of the market with a strong focus on customers, much effort and enthusing leadership. Management was 'management by driving around'. The entrepreneurs drove around in their cars to solve problems. There were no personnel policy and no reward system, no commercial department, price control and automation plans. These entrepreneurs were steering on intuition rather than numbers. In the early 1990s, however, it became clear that trees don't grow into the sky. When a number of firms were taken over, their results appeared to be a big problem, which was obscured by the substantial property it had built up in the past years. More serious, however, was the lack of transparency of the business processes in this environment-sensitive sector. In the sector as a whole, this lack of transparency had led to lapses. The authorities had no intention to tolerate these any longer. This implied that transparency, quality and process control became critical conditions for the legitimization of the sector. Additionally, the authorities tightened the rules, and it became clear that future growth was impossible without paying attention to services with a higher added value. The firms were not able to benefit from the strongly developing technologies.

For six years, BFI Nederland invested in virtually every area of knowledge:

- Money flows have been made transparent. Controllers were recruited and new administrative tools were introduced to make costs and profits visible and substantiate targets.
- Information technology has become a priority, focusing on an integral approach to the entire business process, with routing being the hard core.
- Professional personnel policy has been introduced paying attention to careers, assessments, training, internal consultations, work and health, and rewarding policy.
- Investments have been made in training programmes, particularly for the middle management. Most of these training programmes are based on the principle 'train the trainers'. Middle management are expected to transfer the newly acquired knowledge about such matters as safety, quality and health to their own organization. Meanwhile, this has led to fewer accidents, less damage, and lower absenteeism.
- A commercial office and field service has been set up in order to give shape to relation management and develop new services.
- A legal department replaces the lawyers that used to be called in *ad hoc*. The legal knowledge relevant to this sector is now anchored in the firm itself.
- The technology of garbage disposal has been made pivotal. At the central level, a technology group has been established.

Within six years' time, the firm changed from a conglomerate of hardworking garbage disposers into a cleverly operating professional firm capable of taking responsibility vis-à-vis the economy and society. Remarkably, the central staff (40 versus a total of 2,100 employees) has not become top-heavy. The principle was that knowledge should be carried as low in the organization as possible.

Today's Challenge is To Be Found in the Exploitation of Knowledge

The customer struggle in Europe and the United States of America is no longer about quality and price first. Price and quality have become conditions for entry in a lot of markets. They are the conditions under which existing products and services can be sold. In other words, they are the defensive weapons used to protect a firm's market share. The use of defensive weapons is becoming increasingly difficult for western companies. Due to low wages in Eastern Europe and Central Asia and craftsmanship in Eastern Asia, ground must be conceded continuously. Thus, television plants move to Poland, the data entry of banks is transferred to India, and Dutch shrimps are peeled in Morocco. A recent example is the transfer of reference works on CD-Roms, which European publishers subcontract to firms in India.

Competitive advantage and growth require unique products and services. The weapon of attack is the added value that other firms and institutions cannot deliver. In Europe, such added value does not come from raw material (with the exception of the natural gas reserves and North-sea oil) or from unskilled labour. Rather, more than ever, the added value will come from exclusive knowledge in the future. Knowledge that is continuously in motion and difficult to imitate. Hence, innovation of goods, services, and processes will become the only remaining source of differentiation capacity for Western firms (Andreasen *et al.*, 1995; Wijers, 1994). There are several ways to build up such capacity:

- The integration of products and services;
- The shift of bulk products (and services) to specialties;
- The purchase of process knowledge;
- Renewed interest in radical innovation;
- Globalization.

The Firm as a Hi-Tech Service Provider

'Not only do we deliver products, we also provide our clients with clear-cut solutions. We've become problem solvers.' Using similar phrases, firms indicate a revolution in the way they think and behave. The value added to the client's value chain by the supplier is what counts: the advantages experienced by the client in his or her own (business) household. This implies that the supplier must be able to get under the client's skin, so to speak. The supplier's own product know-how must be combined with the client's process know-how. For example, cattle feed firm Hendrikx Voeders not only supplies cattle feed, it also gives advice about the design of stables. And Van Lanschot bankers are concerned not only with banking, but equally with such important target groups as physicians and lawyers to help them with their bookkeeping. One of the Dutch producers of hydraulic systems, Hydraudyne, has its engineers involved in the development of driving simulators sit in regional buses for months in order that they learn about the profession of a bus driver. DSM Andeno (a producer of pharmaceutical intermediates) demonstrates its possibilities at the client's in order for the client to anticipate the power of his supplier when developing his own products.

The Firm as a Specialist

Closely linked to the first tendency is the shift from bulk to specialties, particularly in firms that are highly sensitive to economic fluctuation. Specialties are products and services with a high added value that are supplied in small amounts according to customer specification. This tendency is strongly increasing in the raw material industry. Firms like DSM Andeno, AVEBE and Gist-brocades (Chapter 4) opt for this strategy because it makes them less susceptible to economic fluctuation of bulk products. This strategy implies that innovation becomes a continuous process. Before starting a substantial upgrading, the development of the next version of the product or service has announced itself. This route is increasingly followed in the services sector. Examples are the insurance company that specializes in insuring dangerous industrial transports, the bank that develops into the home banker of physicians and lawyers, and the IT firm that has acquired a reputation in the graphical industry.

The Firm Opening Up New Horizons

Throughout the past ten years, a great deal of firms have worked hard to target the development of new products and services to the market place. They were forced to increase the development speed, enhance the quality of products and services, and gear directly for today's customer demands. In so doing, attention has shifted from the radical 'novel' innovation to incremental innovation. It is becoming clear now that this development has tipped too far to the defensive side of things. Firms should be concerned not only with today's market, but with tomorrow's market as well. Today's hits are usually based on yesterday's breakthroughs. This was the conclusion at Gist-brocades (Chapter 4) of an internal business group comparison. This insight is slowly (too slowly in many firms) gaining recognition in firms that wish to (continue to) be in the forefront. Hamel and Prahalad (1994) speak of *Strategy by Stretch*: firms gear for targets that challenge its employees to accomplish what is virtually impossible. There is hardly one sector of industry in which similar major challenges are lacking:

• The automobile industry: the economical car;
• The chemical industry: 'ecologically-sound' processes and products;

- Information technology and the electronic industry: integration of data, image and sound.

Smaller firms, too, can take large steps. It's not only the small advanced pioneers ('high technology start-ups') that, not impeded by bureaucracy, force breakthroughs which are impossible in large firms. Thus, exporting to a neighbouring, bigger country may be a large step for a small furniture firm. Equally, the use of pure natural raw materials can be a revolution for a small-sized food producer.

The Firm as a Supplier of Know-How

The production potential arising in Eastern Europe and Asia not only presents a threat, it also offers a new opportunity for the high-wage countries, i.e., the export of product and production know-how. For example, it is becoming more and more difficult to translate the Dutch knowledge of agricultural high technology into profits on the basis of Dutch production. However, there exist vast opportunities for this know-how in terms of worldwide export. The suppliers in Dutch market greenhouse horticulture increasingly concentrate on the export of complete production systems.

The Firm as a Global Player

Globalization means that knowledge-intensive products are sold and produced worldwide. But it also means that marketing and R&D are diffused more and more in global terms. Global presence has the following advantages:

- Being able to develop in a knowledge-intensive environment;
- Being able to produce in the most productive environment;
- Being able to sell in the most consumptive environment.

Such global diffusion places astronomical demands upon the utilization of the knowledge factor. The knowledge flow between R&D, marketing and production is vulnerable in every organization, even more so in firms hindered by both organizational and geographical boundaries. The global player must invest additional resources in his or her organization to keep the free flow of essential know-how going.

The Knowledge Factor Places High Demands on the Organization

'We must do more using fewer resources.' This is briefly the meaning behind the concept of 'leverage of resources' introduced by Hamel and Prahalad (1994). Europe and the United States have an enormous potential of knowledge, but make bad use of the potential. This is largely an organizational problem. Many organizations are still dominated by functional concentration, where department boundaries are classified according to type, based on a vertical principle: chemical analysts with chemical analysts, purchasers with purchasers, developers with developers. In the compartmentalized organization, horizontal processes require a high degree of control, which has four consequences:

- it takes too long for new ideas to be put into good currency in the market place;
- it costs too much time and effort to align functional units;
- the quality is below customer expectations because responsibilities are left to other functions;
- the firm loses track of the market.

Inherent in this model of organization is a view of the labour factor as being on the cost rather than the asset side, where people are exchangeable units that can be recruited to fill vacancies, or, alternatively, made redundant in the context of high-gear productivity enhancement.

Most firms and institutions try to break through the dominance of the functional organization (Cobbenhagen *et al.*, 1994). Increasingly, priority is given to horizontal processes, which bring the market back in sight. This organizational streamlining is given shape at the business level in the business unit, where a direct link is made between the three basic functions of the organization: marketing, R&D and production. This strongly decentralizes the decision making about the course to be followed in a business. At the project level, multidisciplinary teams and strong project leadership are used to try to break the walls erected between the functions. Personnel work becomes *personnel policy* (human resource management) in that perspective. People are carriers of the unique knowledge and skills that serve as a source for each improvement and innovation, assets rather than costs. Research among 62 Dutch firms (Cobbenhagen *et al.*, 1994) has revealed that innovative frontrunners have progressed further in this streamlining process than members of the pack in the same market. However, a great deal of firms have hardly made the first steps in breaking with compartmentalization.

Additionally, the introduction of new market-oriented horizontal structures, such as the business unit, is no panacea. The business unit is not the ultimate answer to all organizational problems. New solutions bring with them new problems. This becomes clear especially in firms that have played a pioneering role in the transfer of responsibilities to the business unit. A basis for and prospect of long-term knowledge development threatens to be lost, putting the boundaries of the business under pressure once again. Not only the boundaries between the business units of one single company, but also those between companies. This demonstrates that the exploitation of the knowledge factor requires new organizational solutions that are not affected by the arbitrary boundaries put up in organizations.

The developments outlined above force us to take the knowledge factor seriously. They force us to view the organization as a system in which knowledge is developed, processed, transferred, used and supplied. Where investments in knowledge are made to gain a deciding advantage in the market.

The Knowledge Enterprise

Effective managers and professionals in organizations have developed the capacity to 'read' situations (Morgan, 1986). At the back of their minds they think out various scenarios and their associate action patterns. They are aware that new insights arise by reading the situation from a different perspective. They are open-minded and flexible, and are able to postpone judgement as long as the image in their mind is incomplete; and they are aware that new insight into a situation does not arise until they look at problems through a different pair of glasses. This book offers that very new pair of glasses: the view of the knowledge entrepreneur.

Five Basic Elements

Similar to the management of cash and materials flows, the firm chooses a system approach. In this perspective, the firm can be understood as a knowledge system. However, the concept of 'knowledge system' is already being used in a more narrow sense — in the area of information technology. For this reason, the authors of this book have chosen to use the term 'knowledge enterprise'. (Thus, the concept of knowledge enterprise covers more than the usual 'knowledge management'.) Entrepreneurship means movement: setting and keeping an organization in motion based on a vision; making choices by weighing opportunities and risks; making better choices by learning from one's own and other people's experiences; and supplying adequate organizational tools to utilize opportunities and reduce risks. These are the basic elements of the knowledge enterprise.

The Vision

How does one become a knowledge entrepreneur? By being aware that knowledge matters, that strategic objectives can be reached only when they *can* be reached. By understanding that competencies of the organization are the basis for its differentiation capacity, for its identity and for its reason to exist. This insight gives a sense of urgency for change and movement. The present chapter has particularly focused on this aspect.

The Knowledge Ambition

'What do I want to be good at and what do I want to be better at?' The result of this choice is the *knowledge ambition*: 'Doing the right things'. When defining the knowledge ambition (Chapter 2) of the organization, competencies will be named and assessed. What are the current competencies? How important are they for the organization? What are the core competencies that enable the firm to distinguish from others? Which are the firm's enabling competencies, essential in order to create added value, and which are exchangeable? The knowledge ambition shows the focus of knowledge development, which indicates what must be done to achieve a knowledge objective, because stagnation means lagging behind. This focus also shows the limitation of the competencies that really matter, which might imply that some competencies must be given up.

Knowledge Development

Visions and ambitions are important, but make no sense unless they can be achieved effectively. This also holds true of strategic objectives, and, equally, the knowledge enterprise. Knowledge must be developed, maintained, transferred and used: 'Doing the right things right.' Insight into the process of knowledge development and diffusion in the organization is indispensable. What is important is the working of the organization as a knowledge system, the strategies of knowledge development, and the different types of knowledge flows. Chapter 3 will focus on these issues.

The Learning Organization

Knowledge development is a learning process *per se*, which is anchored in the organization. Individuals, groups, and business units can be viewed in that learning process as carriers of knowledge. In other words, knowledge development is a function of the learning organization. This has three important implications. First, knowledge development is irretrievably linked with the structure and culture of the organization, which largely determine a firm's capability to turn investments in knowledge into good currency in the market place. Second, knowledge development can never be separated from business development. The past of an organization leaves its mark on the future. Thus, the supplier of bulk products that wants to shift to specialties with a higher added value will long be haunted by the structure and culture of mass manufacturing. Third, knowledge development within organizations can never take place in isolation from its environment. These three 'contextual' features of knowledge development make it extremely difficult to imitate best-practice cases. It's just like school: you don't learn anything by cheating (except cheating). That is the reason why the practical examples in Chapter 4 have been written with another intention: to provide insight into the transition process that firms have to go through when realizing their knowledge ambition. This insight helps when we try to learn from our own actions. It enables us to reflect on the choices we make.

The Tools

In order to redesign the knowledge enterprise one needs tools (Part 3). First, instruments of analysis (see the Appendix) to be able to categorize and assess competencies and to map the knowledge flows. Such an analysis provides the point of departure for the redesign, which distinguishes three types of tools:

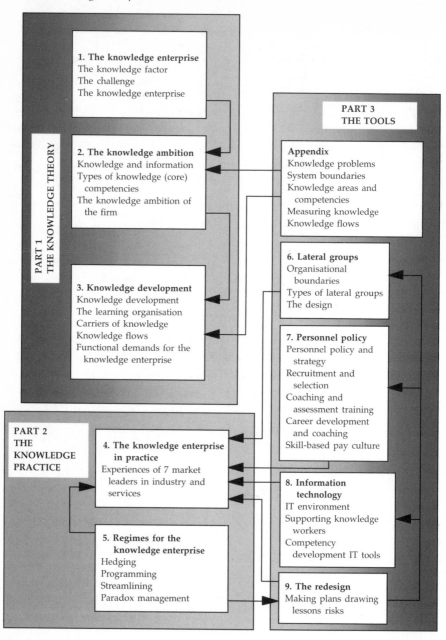

Figure 1.1

- Organizational lateral linkages (Chapter 6);
- Personnel policy (Chapter 7);
- Information technology (Chapter 8).

Remarkably, the separate design instruments are not new or unique *per se*. The toolkit of the knowledge entrepreneur is filled with well-known management instruments. The difference lies in the use and combination of the tools. The last chapter presents a practically phased model as guideline for the redesign.

Chapter 2

The Knowledge Ambition

What knowledge does the firm possess? What knowledge is vitally important for a firm's competitive advantage today and tomorrow? What knowledge should be better exploited? In which fields of knowledge do firms want to catch up, or take a lead? All of these questions are concerned with the starting point of the knowledge enterprise: the knowledge ambition. 'Doing the right things' or better: 'Knowing the right things' is the slogan when the direction must be determined and choices need to be made. This sounds logical, but 'knowledge' is an abstract and comprehensive notion. The knowledge enterprise presupposes that we are able to determine what knowledge is. It is different from the concept of 'information'. It must moreover be possible to code knowledge. Coding (or 'ordering') means that different types of knowledge can be named and provided with characteristics.

That is what this chapter tries to do. After defining the concept of knowledge, knowledge is split up into several areas. Knowledge areas focusing on the performance of certain tasks and the production of added value are referred to as 'competencies'. This division can take various forms. In this chapter, we will first choose a division based on three sources of knowledge:

- functional knowledge: knowledge developed within disciplines or subject areas;
- operational knowledge: knowledge based on experiences in actions;

- contextual knowledge: knowledge gained in a certain environment.

A second division addressed is into explicit and tacit (or implicit) knowledge. Tacit knowledge is not written down, but built up and stored in the brains of people. This particular type of knowledge seems to constantly escape attention in organizations. Tacit knowledge is embedded in the culture of an organization. It is a vehicle for efficiency and creativity as well as a brake on change. 'Core in-competencies' are created when holding on to obsolete implicit knowledge. The knowledge enterprise which steers only for explicit knowledge is heading for destruction.

Formulating the knowledge ambition implies that choices be made between competencies. It is possible thus to determine the strategic importance of different competencies. For that purpose, we introduce the distinction between core competencies, enabling competencies and exchangeable competencies. Subsequently, we will focus on the extent to which knowledge can be measured and purchased. Finally, we will describe the steps that will lead to the formulation of the knowledge ambition.

What is Knowledge?

Knowledge is a self-evident concept and therefore difficult to define. The definition of knowledge in philosophy (epistemology) is a subject that has kept entire schools of philosophers busy ever since antiquity (see Box 2.1). The difficulty that emerges again and again is that each definition of a self-evident concept such as knowledge requires words that must themselves be defined. Thus, the question "Do we know what knowledge is?" is a tautology, because the word 'know' presupposes knowledge. Before one knows it, one keeps turning around in circles. The authors of this book have chosen a pragmatic approach. Concepts are linked to a concrete content or application as much as possible. In so doing, it is much easier to make clear what we are talking about. For example, knowledge about export rules within the

Box 2.1. True or false?

Do the things around us really exist and can we, people, learn to know these things? Does something like an absolute truth exist, isolated from our own thinking? These are simply put the three main questions that philosophy has been concerned with since ancient times. In addition to ontology, epistemology is the philosophical basis of science. Without realizing this, philosophical considerations play a substantial role in the way in which we see the world around us. Our thinking about organizations is punctuated with them. Dominant in our rational way of organizing is the vision that organizational processes can be viewed objectively and measured. Concepts like 'organization', 'market', and 'management' are realities in that view (or in philosophical jargon: 'entities'), whose properties such as 'quality', 'added value' and 'effectiveness' are measurable. However, sometimes we take a side-road from this positivist or realistic main road of organizational thinking without being aware of it. Those are the moments where deep-rooted concepts threaten to lose their sense of reality and things are not what they seem to be. People talk about management, but think about power. The market one speaks of appears to be nothing else than a list of old clients, and quality care a bureaucratic ritual. We discover what Scott-Morgan (1994) calls 'the unwritten rules of the game': the unconscious of the organization. It's the feeling that we have sometimes when we return from a meeting: 'For God's sake, what are they talking about? Everybody uses the same words, but is talking of something different.' Implicitly, we are led at that moment by the reverse of positivism: subjectivism. Reality as we see it is no more than appearance in this perspective. It is no more (to use the words of Dostojewski) than 'a story told by an idiot'. In the daily practice of the manager, we recognize another perspective of knowledge: the pragmatic perspective. A statement is true in that perspective because it is a useful statement. A lot of management approaches derive their value from this usefulness. They 'work' in practice. The question as to whether they are 'true' in a positivistic sense is less important in this vision.

European Union, the upgrading of new chemical products, the insurance of hazardous transports, and the set-up of a marketing plan for cigarettes in a restrictive market. But even pragmatics cannot escape from answering the underlying philosophical questions, because 'no philosophy' equals an implicit philosophy. Yet, pragmatics are driven by the question (Box 2.1) what use a concept, model or argument has for actions in practice. They accept that useful concepts, models and arguments do not fit in philosophical frameworks for one hundred percent.

Knowledge, Information and Data

The meaning of the word 'knowledge' can be clarified when comparing it with two other concepts: data and information. Knowledge and information are not synonymous, nor are information and data. There does, however, exist a relationship between these three concepts. Data is the direct consequence of observations, for example when a supermarket records the number of Heineken beer bottles sold on Saturdays using a scanner and bar codes. This data leads to information once the data is categorized and a meaning is attached to it, or, to return to our example, when a computer is used to ascertain the inventory, or when a comparison with other warm Saturdays and other brands show that Heineken is on the increase. Knowledge does not arise until predictions can be made: if Situation A occurs, Measure B is required to obtain the desired Results C. When the temperature rises, take more Heineken bottles in stock. Knowledge can be viewed in this sense as a collection of information and rules (algorithms) that can be used to fulfil a certain function. In the above example, this function is making decisions on the basis of a prediction with the purpose of making a maximum profit. This function is fulfilled within a specific process, for example in the purchase and sales process of a supermarket. A process can be regarded as a collection of inputs and outputs and the transformations whereby inputs and outputs are converted into outputs.

Carriers of Knowledge

Knowledge does not float around in the air. There is always a *carrier of knowledge*. The most important carrier of knowledge is man himself, as an individual or as a group: human knowledge (Boersma, 1995). Additionally, knowledge can be carried by material hosts:

- Hardware (machines, chips): mechanized knowledge;
- Software (programs, information systems, expert systems): automated knowledge;
- Documents (hieroglyphs, books, magazines, journals, websites videos, CD-Rom disks, and so on): documentary knowledge.

Products can also be seen as carriers of knowledge. Firms and craftsmen put their knowledge in their products, whether these are grass mowers, train wagons, or chocolate chip cookies. Thus, a large number of firms disassemble the products of their competitors in order to get hold of their design and production knowledge. In organizations, there is a mix of human and material carriers of knowledge. For example: the manager and his or her management information systems, the operator and his or her CNC machine, or the cook with his cookbooks. The organization can even be seen in this perspective as a very complex carrier of knowledge, in which virtually every combination of knowledge carriers is to be found.

Knowledge Areas

The Heineken example above focused on a simplified type of knowledge. Also, the process is relatively simple. The decision to purchase can be made on the basis of the limited number of parameters, such as expected temperature, past sales figures, and current inventory. Computers can easily cope with a similar process of decision making. Knowledge in firms usually concentrates on more complex processes, such as:

- The design of a production process;
- The use of new materials;
- Materials management in a plant;
- Re-education of personnel;
- Market exploration for a new product;
- Reporting to shareholders;
- The set-up of an environmental programme.

Elements of Knowledge, Areas of Knowledge, and Competencies

Different types of knowledge are used in the above-mentioned processes. The use in business processes determines the importance of knowledge. A first step in the set-up of the knowledge enterprise is naming the types of knowledge relevant to an organization. Similar to a library, this requires a principle of classification (or 'coding'). The smallest unit of knowledge we distinguish is the *knowledge element* (Figure 2.1). This might be compared to a book in a library. Knowledge elements are more or less complete modules, such as the knowledge about techniques of market analysis, re-education methods, or about the environmental norms used by the authorities.

Knowledge areas are sets of mutually linked knowledge elements generally based on logical connections. Knowledge elements build further upon other knowledge elements, thus leading to hierarchical structures of knowledge elements. Knowledge of elementary mechanics is vital for a full understanding of nuclear physics. Equally, a cook is able to prepare a delicate soup only when he knows how to make a good stock. Knowledge areas are often determined historically, or by social conventions, for example, disciplines at school, or the classification of technological sciences according to the UNESCO BSO code.

Competencies (or 'capabilities') can also be understood as knowledge areas aimed at fulfilling a function in an organization. Concretely: the design of a product, cost control, or the maintenance of machines. In

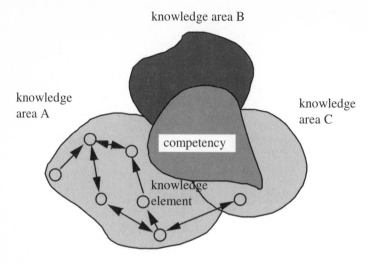

Figure 2.1. Knowledge elements, knowledge areas, and competencies.

more abstract words: creating added value, enlarging the competitive advantage, or enhancing flexibility. Competencies are generally composed of combinations of subsets of other knowledge areas. Thus, the software firm that is frontrunner in the market with its software packages for the administration of salaries must have:

- knowledge of its clients' salary systems;
- knowledge of development in legislation;
- knowledge of software.

Table 2.1 shows a number of examples of knowledge areas from various types of organizations. It also shows the link of the competencies with the basic processes in the organization.

Some knowledge areas specifically belong to one single business process, for example, in Table 2.1 in the case of logistic automation in retail. Other knowledge areas are relevant to different business processes. For example, information technology touches upon virtually all aspects of the insurance company, and knowledge of fermentation processes can be the basis for an entire firm.

Table 2.1. Examples of knowledge areas and competencies.

Firm	Knowledge Area	Competencies	Basic Processes
A. Insurance company *products*: policies for persons, through intermediaries	Information technology	– On-line processing of 'standard' policies and claims – Insight into the risk portfolio – Control of the claim settlement	– Implementation (risk acceptance and damage assessment, service to intermediaries) – Financial control – Financial control
B. Engineering firm *products*: flight simulators	Hydraulic systems	Tailored supply of high-quality and high-tech systems	– Product development – Marketing – Production
C. ICT firm *products*: graphic design systems	Graphic production processes	Offering complete solutions to clients	– Marketing – Servicing
D. Retail firm *products*: car parts	Logistic automation	Optimizing stocks	– Materials management
E. Tour operator *products*: holidays	Asia as destination	Purchasing hotel rooms	– Purchase – Marketing
F. Biotechnology firm *products*: antibiotics	Fermentation	– Producing current antibiotics in large amounts against low prices – Developing products for patients with allergies to the antibiotics most frequently used	– Production – Product development – Process development

Three Types of Knowledge

The knowledge area is not an absolute measurement, but a practical instrument that can be used to classify knowledge in an organization. A knowledge area is to be compared with a row of shelves in a library, or a directory in a personal computer's desktop. Despite the availability of a number of tools (see the Appendix), the organization maps its own knowledge areas. This set-up of the organization's cognitive map might be compared to the way in which a personal computer user organizes the memory of his computer. The point of departure may differ for each company. For organizations, a division according to the source of the knowledge basis is important. The following division serves as a practical point of departure:

- functional knowledge;
- operational knowledge;
- contextual knowledge.

Functional knowledge is based on a certain area or discipline. Within R&D these may be scientific or technological areas such as organic chemistry, micro-electronics or metallurgy. At the level of the organization, various functions can be distinguished, for example marketing, accounting, personnel policy, and IT. In some firms, functional knowledge coincides with product know-how. Thus, knowledge of property and travel insurance can be considered as being functional knowledge. Central to functional knowledge is *know what* and *know why* (Kogut and Zander, 1992). This type of knowledge is often anchored in a firm's functional department, where a knowledge area has become a *knowledge domain*. Thus, personnel recruitment is a knowledge area that belongs to the domain of the personnel department. The functional departments ensure that this knowledge is kept up to date, used and diffused inside the firm, and they update their own stock of knowledge by the supply from function-orientated organization in their environment: faculties, sections, and institutes of universities, and professional organizations.

Operational knowledge is primarily based on action. Expertise is developed on the basis of experience, for example in the introduction of TQC, the performance of turn-key projects, the acquisition and integration of firms, or the development of products. The acquisition of operational knowledge is particularly 'learning by doing'. *Know how* is central to operational knowledge. In the development of operational knowledge, project groups and operational units have an important role to play. In professional servicing (for example, in finance, automation or engineering) the contact between the firm and its client is a highly intensive one.

Contextual knowledge arises by operating in specific environments. In most cases, this is concerned with knowledge in a specific market. For example, Van Lanschot bankers are familiar with the customer-specific knowledge of professionals like physicians and lawyers, and DSM Andeno works closely together with the producers of antibiotics. Contextual knowledge may also be concerned with the institutional environment: the law in France, the role of trade unions in Australia, opportunities for subsidies, and the legal import limitations. In addition, contextual knowledge is strongly linked with the culture where products and services are supplied: the culture of a country, but also of target groups in the market and of organizations. Contextual knowledge particularly focuses on *know where* and *know when*. It is mainly developed in the domain of groups and departments that interact directly with the environment of the organization: marketing and sales, purchase, field service and personnel department.

This division may have a strategic meaning for organizations. Stork (Chapter 4, see Figure 2.2) is guided by the principle that product innovation should depart from two fixed points, for example the presence of the required functional and operational knowledge. New contextual knowledge can be gained from these two fixed points. Innovation then focuses on the new application of an existing technology in market B, for which experience had been gained in market A. When, according to this vision, new knowledge is required in two fronts, the risk of failure is too high.

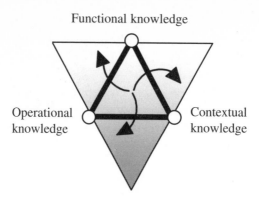

Figure 2.2. Stork's knowledge triangle.

Box 2.2 illustrates the working of this guideline, which is highly similar to a basic principle of mountaineering. A mountaineer has four possibilities to find support in a sheer cliff: two hands and two feet. When moving upward or downward, only one of theses supporting points (one hand or one foot) can be freed for the movement to be made, otherwise the risk of falling is too high.

Firms A and B operate with a markedly similar set of functional knowledge. They both try to introduce a new approach (operational knowledge) in the market place. Firm B tries to nestle in a certain application market following the introduction of a new product, and benefits from the contextual knowledge it has gained in the market place. Firm A is chasing itself. It must make continuous investments in order to become familiar with a certain context.

Explicit and Tacit Knowledge

The knowledge stored in a library, a personal computer, or a patent has one common characteristic: they are all concerned with explicit knowledge, knowledge that can be stored one way or another,

Box 2.2. Running back and forth.

Firm A (Cobbenhagen *et al.*, 1994) designs complex technical installations and possesses a unique combination of three technological skills. These functional competencies serve as the development base for new applications. However, the market approach is lacking a clear focus. Operational knowledge is gained in industry X, which takes a lot of time and effort, because the firm must become familiar with the knowledge of the application environment (the context). A lot of experience is gained, but the gains are practically nil. Before the project is completed even, a shift is made to industry Y for a comparable application. Turnover and coverage are sacred. In the new project, a new investment is needed in contextual knowledge. When a lucrative follow-up order is finally placed in industry X, the most important experts are stuck in a project in industry Y. Moreover, the application in industry Y is very different in character and requires investment in operational knowledge as well. As a result, the organization lacks the breath to develop routines, and personnel do not have the time to hold on to their competencies and rebuild their reserves. They are running back and forth.

Firm B is highly similar to Firm A. It also develops complex technical systems on the basis of a unique combination of technical competencies. The firm pursues a similar strategy, but implements it differently. A new application is developed in conjunction with a number of good clients (lead users, or launch customers), which requires the investment of a large amount of money. However, the firm does not get involved in this trajectory until it has made a thorough analysis of the market and the discovery of a market niche. The new application is tried out in practice and all efforts are set to landing closely related orders or even repeat orders. One single team is put to work on the first two or three projects so that a lot of the problems can be solved using a routine. The firm enters the learning curve and is able to reduce costs and enhance quality. A large reservoir of employees is made familiar with the product design. When followers appear in the market place that have also learned the 'trick', the firm leaves the market and searches a new application area for its own core competencies. The strength of Firm B is that it has developed a strategy used to lift learning experiences over projects. This is possible only in the case of perfect project management and a continuous open relationship with the management team. Firm B was in the same position as Firm A was ten years ago. In a development process of 10 years it has mastered technical as well as organizational competencies.

separate from a human knowledge carrier, and which can be transferred through books, websites, user manuals, computer programs, CD-Rom disks, and so on. In the case of tacit knowledge, a human being is the one who carries and transfers knowledge. This distinction between explicit and tacit (or implicit) knowledge (Nonaka, 1994; Polanyi, 1966) is relevant to virtually all aspects of business, for example, to the way in which:

- The maintenance engineer inspects a production machine;
- A salesperson explores the needs of a client in a converzation;
- The head of personnel tries to picture a candidate's personality in an interview.

The maintenance engineer possesses both explicit knowledge in the form of inspection guidelines, and tacit knowledge gained from experience. Equally, the salesperson and the head of personnel will probably have a checklist of subjects they can throw into the converzation. However, they will be led to an important degree by the unspoken (implicit) ideas at the back of their minds.

Economists that are concerned with technological development use a similar distinction: that between embodied and disembodied knowledge. Embodied knowledge refers to concrete knowledge, the knowledge stored in material: patents, software, expert systems, archives and equipment. Remarkably, disembodied knowledge is the knowledge stored between the ears of human beings. The transfer of tacit knowledge is difficult, because 'we can know more than we can tell' (Polanyi, 1966, p. 4). This type of knowledge is transferred, for example, by craftsmen who teach apprentices the tricks of the trade. One learns the trade by performing it while being supervised by somebody who is good or better at it (Box 2.3). Thus, tacit knowledge is largely a product of learning by doing. Socialization (Nonaka, 1994) plays an important role in the transfer of knowledge. Without realizing it, our behaviour

Box 2.3. 'Do as I do, talk as I talk ...'

The transfer of tacit knowledge is the thread in a classical novel from Dutch literature: Lijmen/Het been. The author of this book, Willem Elsschot, puts the shady business man Boorman on the stage, who calls himself the director-general of the World Journal. Boorman has singled out the deadlocked office clerk Laarmans in a pub. He has made Laarmans his apprentice and wants to retrain him to be a businessman (Elsschot, 1980, p. 271):

'This is what I propose: I will make you my apprentice and will give you some title. Let's say secretary or general editor. Think of a title yourself that you like, but especially one that will be to our clients' liking. I don't care whether you are married or not, nor what you been up to until today. But you must do as I tell you. As I tell you... And not only must you do as I tell you, you must also do as I do, talk as I talk, and be silent as I am silent.' Thus, Boormans teaches Laarmans, who is given a new name 'de Mattos', how he can get rid of troublesome clients who want to cancel their contract (p. 299): 'De Mattos, watch out for the telephone. It would be best not to answer it at all, then they will soon get tired of calling up. People never order anything from me by telephone, and if I receive a phone call, it is only to try and annul a made deal. And when they have witnesses, as I tried that night with Korthals, and you answer the phone... Well, it's not deadly yet, otherwise a registered letter would also do, but still one can never tell. Given the chance, I would not even own a telephone, but a World Journal without a telephone makes people suspicious. Let them call until they are fed up, and if they complain about it later, we will put the blame on the girls from the switchboard. Ah, monsieur, cette administration, ne m'en parlez pas. And meanwhile, a couple of days have gone by, you understand?'

in an organization is formed by the implicit norms imposed on us by other people.

Another way of transferring tacit knowledge is by converting it into explicit knowledge, also called 'articulation' (Hedlund, 1994). This is tried in the design of expert systems, for example. By accurately following and analyzing the behaviour of experts and extensive interviewing, it is tried to elicit their tacit knowledge (know-how) and make it available to others through information systems. In that way, the master-apprentice relationship can also be simulated using a computer system. Examples are a business game, or the simulation of a control room in a chemical plant. Anyway, the question is whether the conversion of tacit into explicit knowledge is always advantageous for the firm in question. Along with the transferability of knowledge (Kogut and Zander, 1992), the imitability also increases. The internal processes of knowledge exchange in Japanese firms (Hedlund, 1994, Box 2.4) appear to be difficult to imitate due to the heavily tacit character of the internal knowledge transformation.

Box 2.4. The Japanese and the western model of knowledge transformation.

Japanese firms seem to differ essentially from western firms (Hedlund, 1994, p. 80) in the way in which they acquire, process and supply knowledge. Japanese firms mainly acquire explicit knowledge (EK), for example in the form of patents and products. The internal transformation process thrives on tacit knowledge (TK), whereas in the output the emphasis is on explicit knowledge. The knowledge process is thus as follows: EK ➔ TK ➔ EK. Western firms acquire a more complex set of explicit and tacit knowledge. They transform that knowledge in a strongly mechanistic and explicit way, where division of labour and exchangeability of staff and parts have an important role to play. In the end, they supply a richer mix of explicit and tacit knowledge. This can be schematically represented as follows: EK + TK ➔ EK ➔ EK + TC.

Organization Culture

Tacit knowledge is largely based on the formation of routines, the automatic actions that we have learned and are self-evident to us to the extent that we are no longer aware of them. For example, the standard way in which:

- A salesperson addresses a client on the phone;
- A purchaser attempts to dispute a reduction;
- The maintenance engineer deals with a machine fault;
- The CEO browses through the quarter figures.

Together, such routines are part of the organization's culture. Routines are based on an implicit logic, 'the unwritten rules of the game', as Scott-Morgan (1994) calls it. This logic departs from the values that are relevant to the organization, and encompasses the argumentation that supplies norms for behaviour which will lead to fulfilment of the organization's values. The implicit logic can be compared with the operating system of a personal computer, and the routines with the daily operations we perform using the personal computer. Routines enable us to solve numerous problems, without actually thinking about them. In other words: they provide the efficacy in the actions we perform. However, routines may abrade, when the external circumstances change, or when new solutions and new rules present themselves. This is something, for example, that firms which have only just started with the exportation business, do not discover until after some time. They discover that the self-evident, business-like way in which they negotiate contracts in the home market does not work in another country. There, the handshake and contract may not get a real meaning until mutual confidence is gained after long-term 'dating'. Another example is the machine plant which bases its cost leadership on maximum machine efficiency. The moment the firm addresses advanced flexible technology, it may stumble over its own deep-rooted efficiency routines (see Box 2.5). The old implicit logic is overtaken by technology, but continues to steer people's behaviour. Or in the personal computer metaphor: the new application program is not compatible with the old control system. In this way, a competence becomes an 'incompetence' (Dougherty, 1994).

In such situations, new routines must be learned, and old routines unlearned. Not only behaviour is relevant here, but particularly the unwritten rules ('the implicit logic') that steer behaviour ('the routines'). In such a case, a 'change in culture' must be set in, which refers to the most concise definition of organizational culture: 'the way we operate around here' (Graham, 1984). In this perspective, it is obvious why changes in culture are so difficult to realize. Changes in behaviour

Box 2.5. Learning and unlearning routines.

Machine plants try to make maximum use of their production machines; machine downtime should be minimal. Traditionally, high machine uptime is achieved, among other things, by planning production in such a way that minimal adjustments are needed for other products or batches. The routine in which large batches are given priority is based on this argumentation, but it becomes obsolete once flexible production systems (FMS) are introduced. The very advantage of these systems is that adjustments can be performed much faster and easier. Firms might be expected to do their utmost to exploit this advantage as soon as possible after introducing this costly technology. In practice, however, one sees that they tend to stick to old routines. This was revealed in a study (Jaikumar, 1986) comparing the introduction of FMS in Japanese and American firms. Although the systems that were applied in both countries bore a strong resemblance, the introduction strategies were strikingly different. The American firms held on to the old routines: they continued to give priority to large batches and avoided adjustments as much as possible. The variety of products was limited. In contrast, the Japanese firms were using the systems for the purpose they were meant for: flexible production for a large variety of small batches with a lot of adjustments. They developed new routines in order to exploit the advantages offered by the system. This proficiency becomes visible in the difference between the average machine uptime in the Japanese (84%) and the US (52%) firms.

are not successful until a new logic is anchored in the way people think.

'Serendipity'

In contrast to the above, another part of tacit knowledge is not or seldom based on repetition or routines. This knowledge has a creative, inventive and intuitive character. People use it when they are facing new phenomena and are able to make a mental leap. When doing so, they make a new link (analogy) between two phenomena or processes that do not seem to have anything to do with each other. This is referred to as serendipity in the English literature, and 'Neue Kombinationen' in German literature (Schumpeter, 1975).

This type of tacit knowledge is the motor for innovation. For example, an analysis made at Philips during a company-wide turnaround operation (the 'Centurion programme') showed that most of the major market breakthroughs in the past were based on innovations initially labelled as failures. They were not used for the purpose for which they had been developed. Their success did not show until the innovations were applied in other products. Sony's walkman (Box 2.6) is another case in point. A similar mental leap can also take the form of 'reversal'. Reversal takes place when a problem facing customers with a certain product or service is re-built into an advantage in another product or a new service. An example is the 'full package' offered by insurance companies nowadays. Until recently, the insurance policy rather than the customer was the primary organization principle for insurers. Most insurance companies did not possess computer files integrating data relating to all ongoing policies of one specific client. Thus, the client was landed with an abundance of superfluous paperwork. The integrated package or family package is now presented as a 'new' product which offers many advantages to the consumer.

The development of this creative and intuitive tacit knowledge cannot be forced on an organization, but what one can do is to create

Box 2.6. Product innovation by 'serendipity'.

In the 1970s, a team of electricians at Sony supervised by Mitsuro Ida were working on the development of a small mobile stereo cassette player that was to be given the name "Pressman". As a first step, a mono recorder was designed, to be followed by the development of a stereo version. By the end of 1978, it looked as if the team was not going to be successful. Eventually the group succeeded in assembling the stereo circuits on the Pressman chassis (length 13 cm, width 8.5 cm, less than 3 cm in height), but there was no room left for the recording mechanism. The Pressman was no more than a stereo recorder which could not be used to record sound. The product seemed to be failure. Nevertheless, the engineers involved did not throw away the prototypes. They used the recorders to play their favourite music at the workplace. Several months later, the development lab was visited by Masara Ibuka, founder and honorary director of the company. When seeing the failed product, the quality of the sound struck him, and an idea sprung from his mind. At another department in the same building, Masara Ibuka had just been introduced to the engineer who was designing light-weight mobile headphones. 'What if we combine these two products and leave out the recording function? Couldn't we make a successful product out of that? A product that can only play music?'. This was a heretical thought in the world of tape recorders. Headphones were not a part of the product, they were merely an accessory. Ibuka's mental leap made an end to that way of thinking. (Ketteringham and Nayak, 1987)

conditions in which creative thinking is given more opportunities. A creative climate can be stimulated by:

- recruiting creative minds and 'dissenters';
- rewarding creativity;
- focusing on external developments ('gatekeepers');
- bringing together people that seldom meet professionally;
- reflecting upon one's own actions (why did things turn out right or wrong?)

Consequences for Control

Tacit knowledge is an essential part of the human capital in knowledge-intensive organizations. Tacit knowledge, however, also confronts the organization with control problems. A lot of organizations in the west focus their policy on matters that can be measured or expressed in time and money. They steer primarily on numbers and intangibles are often ignored. Disembodied tacit knowledge is one of such entities that are hard to measure. In difficult times, such organizations tend to cut the expensive knowledge workforce. It's relatively easy to get rid of knowledge, which quickly shows the savings made by the organization. It's far more difficult to estimate the costs this cutback will bring with it in terms of lost opportunities. As a complication, competencies can be rapidly abased while it may take years to rebuild them. Other organizations try to solve this control problem by 'personifying' knowledge: they steer on individuals by labelling them as 'the good guy' or 'the bright girl' that the firm should hold on to regardless of the cost. Another strategy is to hedge a knowledge sector in the firm (e.g., the corporate R&D lab) from regular business. The department is hedged (see Chapter 5), and the firm follows the philosophy of hope: eventually it will lead to important discoveries. In recent years, lots of knowledge-intensive companies have come to recognize that new styles of management and communication must be developed which gives tacit knowledge its due. Modern personnel policy (human resource management) has an important role to play here (see Chapter 7).

Which Competencies Belong to the Core?

Some knowledge areas are more important to the organization than others. Thus, some knowledge areas (or 'competencies') provide the foundation of the firm's existence. They are the source for the development of new products, services and processes. Hamel and Prahalad (Prahalad and Hamel, 1990; Hamel and Prahalad, 1994) speak of *core competencies*. These are the unique competencies which distinguish the firm from other firms. Core competencies alone do not suffice for a firm to function. Other competencies with a less unique character are needed to bring products and services into the market timely and against a good price. Thus, a transport company that distinguishes from other firms on the basis of its advanced logistics and telecommunication should also possess a sound administrative system as well as a strong sales function. We call these *enabling competencies* (Leonard-Barton, 1995): the competencies that a firm should possess in order to operate effectively and create added value. Finally, there are competencies that can be *exchanged* among companies ('outsourced') fairly easily, without losing much added value or strongly affecting its competitiveness. In a transport company, for example, this may be knowledge of truck maintenance, security, or the cleaning service.

Core Competencies

Within highly developed economies, it is no longer possible for firms to be competitive by doing things better, quicker and cheaper. Serving existing markets does not suffice for firms that take their market leadership seriously. In the future, competitive advantage will be possible only by doing things that others *cannot do*. Firms should base their strategy on the unique knowledge and skills they possess. Within the firm, the powers must be bundled to develop these core competencies in such a way that they cannot be imitated or copied. Core competencies enable the firm to create markets.

   This is briefly the message which has been successfully disseminated by Hamel and Prahalad since 1990 in their books and articles. Firms must seek the core of their abilities and determine what is needed to take and keep a decisive lead. Hamel and Prahalad demonstrate that the success of large Japanese companies such as Honda and Sony are based on that very strategy. Thus, the development and manufacturing of engines for a variety of products is a core competence at Honda. At Sony, the ability to reduce products to the smallest possible size (miniaturization) is considered a core competence. Core competencies are identified by subjecting the most important competencies of an organization to the three following tests:

- A core competence must enable an organization to provide its clients with a real advantage;
- A core competence must provide the firm with a unique competitive advantage;
- Core competencies must be the basis in various businesses of the firm for new products and new markets.

In recent years, this approach has been followed by numerous firms throughout Europe and the United States. The analysis of core competencies during the recent 'Centurion' turnaround programme at Philips was the starting point for the new business strategy. In addition, the concept of core competence seems to be useful also to smaller and medium-sized companies. The words 'new' and 'unique' are related to the market in which one operates rather than the world market. For example, the supply of a broad range of freshly made sandwiches in the UK or The Netherlands may be the core competence of a fast food chain.

The strategy of core competencies has made a significant contribution to the management of the knowledge enterprise in a very short time period. Hamel and Prahalad have made managers aware of the strategic importance of the knowledge available within the organization. They have made them aware of the need to make choices for the developments that really matter in the future. Hamel and Prahalad have given a strongly technological meaning to the concept of 'core competence'. Meanwhile (Cobbenhagen *et al.*, 1994), its meaning has been broadened to include organizational and market-oriented core competencies. It is argued that a strongly technological knowledge base does not lead to any worthwhile results unless a firm possesses a smooth organization as well as an effective marketing function.

The concept of core competence should not be confused with 'core activity'. Core activities primarily focus on the added value of activities in the *existing* market. Activities that do not lead to sufficient added value today, or might be purchased in an improved way, are hived off. The future market is hardly relevant here.

Enabling Competencies

Core competencies determine the future success of the company. Enabling competencies (Leonard-Barton, 1995) strongly determine the success of the company today. They are usually connected to the most important stages in the value chain (Porter, 1985), such as marketing, R&D and production. Other firms also possess these competencies. In that sense, they are irreplaceable, but not unique. Enabling competencies do not distinguish a firm from others, but provide the necessary conditions to enter the market and create added value. Thus, an insurance company cannot do without knowledge of actuarial mathematics, or a dairy factory without a thorough knowledge of quality. Without such know-how it is impossible to bring a policy or a dessert on the market. But the policies or desserts are none the better than those of the competition, because they too must master this necessary knowledge. The second characteristic of these competencies is that they are often highly entwined with the firm's core competencies.

This is a result of the continuous exchange of (usually tacit) knowledge needed to bring products and services onto the market that yield a profit. The product development department will involve the production department in a chemical firm in its projects in an early stage in order to anticipate upgrading problems. A hospital having brain surgery as a core competence is almost unthinkable in that sense without an advanced nursing department.

Entwining may also be based on the impossibility of trading the core competencies in isolation from the enabling competencies. For example, pure R&D ventures (firms having only R&D and, hence, pure core competence) are found only in areas like pharmacy, where patents and licenses can be well protected and traded. Consequently, in most sectors enabling competencies cannot be exchanged, or only with much difficulty.

The decision to keep a competence inside the firm and label it as 'enabling' is made in practice on the basis of the following criteria:

- The firm can do it better and cheaper;
- The competence is concerned with 'competition-sensitive' know how;
- Enabling competencies are strongly rooted in core competencies;
- Outsourcing leads to the destruction of capital and social problems.

Exchangeable Competencies

One category of competencies is exchangeable: the know-how that can be outsourced to other organizations without it having direct consequences for the rest of the organization. This may be knowledge that can be replaced by other knowledge without crucial consequences. The most straightforward examples of exchangeable knowledge are concerned with such activities as security, catering, salary administration, and 'factoring'. The boundaries between enabling and exchangeable competencies, however, differ per firm. For example, a number of pharmaceutical firms keep the chemical plant in which the active substances are manufactured inside the firm, whereas the assembly of active substances and additives (the 'pills plant') are subcontracted. Such shifts are also found in the services sector. For example, a large part of the standard work in insurance companies (risk acceptance and damages assessment) in knowledge systems are shifted to intermediaries. At the same time, the development of these knowledge systems is taken in the firm's own hands.

Can Knowledge Be Purchased?

In general, building knowledge is a time-consuming effort. Additionally, the development of knowledge is risky because one is never sure whether oneself *can* actually gain the knowledge that one *wants* to gain. It might be worthwhile to consider purchasing this knowledge. Four main types of purchased knowledge can be distinguished:

• Outsourcing;
• The purchase of patents and licences;
• The take-over and recruitment of personnel;
• Acquisition.

Outsourcing is mainly concerned with the transfer and purchase of knowledge, based on the price and quality of a complete (half) product or service. The knowledge that is implicitly related to these products or services is then hived off for the greater part. This is possible when the knowledge is exchangeable and not intertwined with the core competencies and enabling competencies. The most important preconditions for outsourcing are:

• The product or service will become cheaper;
• The quality of the offered product or service offered is better;
• The quality can be adequately determined;
• There are reliable suppliers that the firm is not or will not become dependent on;
• The transaction costs are low;
• No competition-sensitive information is released;
• Capital destruction is low;
• No large social problems will arise;
• Entwining with the firm's own competencies is low.

Throughout the past ten years, most firms have investigated the possibility of outsourcing. The supply of services has greatly increased during that period. This holds true especially for services that many firms can make use of, such as security, catering, leasing and factoring. Outsourcing has not proved a panacea for a wrong cost structure, particularly in the case of goods and services that are a vital part of the firm's own end product or service. Dependency of one single supplier may even contribute to the downfall of the corporation.

Another form of acquiring knowledge is by *purchasing patents and licenses*. In that case, the firm purchases the right to use the knowledge of others. The advantage of this is that the firm obtains access to new and tested knowledge and technology within a very short time lapse. Additionally, the firm does not have to pay the full price for the development of knowledge. However, there are also a number of drawbacks to this strategy (Roberts and Berry, 1988). First, the knowledge must be shared with others, which implies a considerable limitation to develop unique and imitable products and services. Second, the firm will continue to be dependent of the firm selling the license. The right to use knowledge alone does not build up competence inside the firm.

With the *take-over* and *recruitment of personnel* a firm does not only purchase a workforce but knowledge as well. Of special importance are the knowledge workers (Drucker, 1994, p. 8); '(those) who know how to allocate knowledge for productive use...'. Characteristic of knowledge workers is that they are the owners within the organization of the production means: their knowledge. Recruitment and selection of personnel is receiving more and more attention in most knowledge-intensive organizations (Chapter 7). The management is increasingly aware that it can not only fill vacancies, but also that new knowledge can be 'recruited'. When taking over the personnel of other firms, it should be noted that new norms and values are also 'imported' into the organization.

The purchase of an entire company, or *acquisition*, is a fourth way of purchasing knowledge. This may be viewed as the counterpart of outsourcing. In the case of outsourcing, part of the organization is sold, and the products and services are purchased. In the case of acquisition, a new part is added to the organization and the products and services of that part of the organization are sold. Acquisitions are performed for various reasons. Important arguments for acquisitions include rapid access to the market and rapid increase in the production volume. In some knowledge-intensive sectors of business, such as the pharmaceutical and the chemical sectors, information technology, accountancy and electronics, acquisition is seen as the only possibility to rapidly provide the firm with new core competencies. The build-up of core competencies takes more than 8 or 9 years in these sectors, in some firms even as long as 15 years. An acquisition can be arranged in a few weeks' time. However, knowledge acquisition can also be hazardous. Being head of a firm whose market is unknown and whose competencies one does not master may prove very difficult. Additionally, cultural differences and differences in industrial relations and labour conditions may be serious obstacles to achieving the synergy desired. When integrating a knowledge acquisition, the knowledge enterprise is an absolute top priority.

Measuring Knowledge

Managers want to measure. Without the weekly balance sheet, the company manager feels naked and hopeless like a snail that has lost its house. It's a total disaster when the monthly results sheet is not on the division management's desk before the last Wednesday of the month. Managers presuppose that input and output can be measured. Adequate action is possible only when deviations from the norm can be ascertained. Comparison with the management of cash and material flows seems to fall short here. Is it possible at all to measure knowledge? Does the existence of continuation of the knowledge enterprise depend on this precondition? We will try to answer this question below.

We Can Measure More Than We Think

First, although it is far more difficult to measure knowledge than a flow of goods, there are numerous possibilities to obtain a better and clearer picture of the factor knowledge. We will go into one of the most important approaches here, which can be depicted in a simple system model as shown in (Figure 2.3).

The input, output, and throughput of knowledge can be measured. For example, investments in knowledge can be measured as *input*. Such investments are concerned with both the knowledge areas and the use of knowledge. Remarkably, only a limited number of firms keep a record of such indicators. Our own research (Cobbenhagen *et al.*, 1994) showed that only half of the 62 Dutch medium-sized firms was able to estimate its own level of R&D investments. A second important way of measuring input is by measuring employee competencies. An increasing number of knowledge-intensive firms keep a record of the competencies of individual employees. They maintain an electronic or other type of data file, in which the present and desired knowledge and experience is kept up to date in what is called a 'skills map'. A third method of measuring input focuses on the knowledge purchased by firms, for example patents and licences.

The measurement of *output* concentrates on the use made of the knowledge when achieving company objectives, rather than on the knowledge itself. Indicators for this are the following:

• The percentage of turnover or profits that is presently achieved with products and services brought onto the market throughout the past five years;

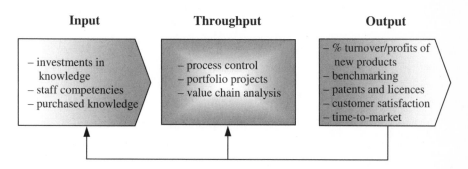

Figure 2.3. Input, output and throughput measurements.

- Benchmarking: comparing the strengths and weaknesses of a firm's own products and services with those of competitors;
- Counting patents and licences;
- Measuring customer satisfaction;
- Time-to-market.

These indicators are particularly useful because they tell us something about the profits from knowledge. For example, the first indicator is highly suited to give the factor knowledge priority on the policy agenda. A great deal of firms use this indicator to compare business units, which is the starting point for a good discussion. However, the indicators are indirect, because they are related to the use made of the knowledge rather than to the knowledge *per se*. The use of knowledge is determined by many other factors, such as organization, financial scope, and business strategy. In addition, in most firms a time lapse of several years exists between the measurement of the eventual result in the market and the actual development of knowledge. In this way, they assess yesterday's knowledge.

The third approach focuses on the firm's *present capabilities*: what can we do now, what are we capable of in terms of knowledge development? In other words, what can be measured in the knowledge flow ('throughput') between input and output? One way to examine this is by looking at the degree to which a new business process is controlled. Roger Bohn (1994) describes eight stages of development for the control of an advanced production process, from complete ignorance about the certain phenomenon to absolute mastering of the process. This method requires the analysis of a concrete business process (a production process or a logistic process). This approach is not appropriate for complex knowledge areas that feed a series of processes.

The analysis of the portfolio of development projects is a second way of measuring current 'knowledge work'. This method was strongly advocated by Arthur D. Little consultants (Roussel *et al.*, 1991) and is now widely accepted in the strategic policy of most large knowledge-intensive companies. The first step in such an analysis is to make a list of relevant knowledge projects within an organization. These projects are subsequently assessed by internal and / or external experts as to a number of different dimensions, including:

- the reward expected;
- the risk;
- the novelty of the market;
- the novelty of the technology / knowledge;
- their cost;
- the time it takes to complete them.

On the basis of these estimations, the portfolio of development projects can be graphically represented in different types of 'Boston matrices'. One of these is the risk / reward matrix as shown in Figure 2.4.

Such a portfolio analysis may show, for example, that increasingly few 'High Risk / High Reward projects' are performed. Portfolio

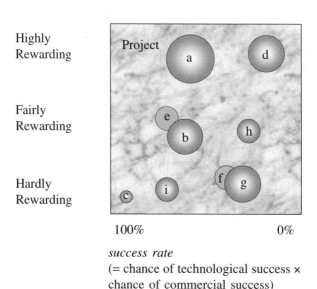

Figure 2.4. The risk / reward matrix.

analyses can be applied in a similar way at the level of knowledge areas.

Portfolio analyses are important, in the first place, for ascertaining a company's strategy. The current course can be made visible by looking beyond ongoing projects. Making this course explicit may lead to some very surprising results from the outset. The current course can be compared with the course one would like to or should follow.

The portfolio analysis is equally important for making decisions about individual projects. It enables the firm to assess what a new project adds to the existing portfolio. The same holds true of the analysis of the value chain, where the starting point is the complete production chain the firm belongs to. In this way, the firm can pinpoint the exact spot in that chain where a (knowledge) investment is expected to produce benefits. An example is the investment in the development of new potato variety by AVEBE, a Dutch manufacturer of starch. This investment in the beginning of the chain allows for a substantial increase in quality at the end of the production process.

Box 2.7. Knowledge managament at Skandia.

Skandia is a Swedish insurance company that operates on an international scale. In recent years, the firm has developed quite a reputation for its progressive knowledge strategies. It is the contention of Skandia's top management that their intellectual capital is as important as its financial capital in providing truly sustainable earnings. This axiom led the firm to develop a method for describing its human capital, structural capital and customer capital. Skandia's 'knowledge manager' Leif Edvinsson explains that the intention is to try to devise adequate valuation indicators that could at the same time serve as management tools for a service company. The approach is meant both for external reporting and internal management. The firms tries to reveal the hidden values which are left invisible by traditional accounting for the benefit of auditors, analysts and accountants who need more accurate ways of assessing the future value of companies, and in particular the value of intellectual capital. The company's own managers have an even greater need for such indicators both for operational efficiency and because the investment policy of knowledge-based service companies majors on intangible investments in customer relationships, information technology, networks, and employee competencies.

The language of this project sounds like accountancy, but the measures are not accountancy-derived. The pay-off from intellectual capital investments will not be visible in financial accounts for some time, and it will then be difficult to disentangle from the pay-off on any other assets. A little taxonomy and glossary is unavoidable in order to prevent misunderstandings.

Intellectual Capital Glossary

Intellectual capital
The sum of structural capital and human capital. Defined by Thomas Stewart (1997) as 'something you cannot touch but still makes you rich'.

Human capital
The competence and capabilities of the employees.

Structural capital
Databases, customer files, software, manuals, trademarks and other elements of the organization's capability: everything that remains when the employees go home. Structural capital can be owned, human capital cannot.

Customer capital
The value of the company's relationship with customers, part of the structural capital.

Organizational capital
All of a company's structural capital except for its customer capital.

Innovation capital
Capacity to innovate by differentiating products and staying ahead of competitors through process improvement. An example is finding ways to use information technology to share employee knowledge and experience and to transform it into structural capital.

Process capital
Operational capacity

Intellectual properties
Information in which a company has rights against all the world. Property is a relationship, not a thing. An asset is a thing.

Intangible assets
Assets of the company, such as good will, which have a money value but no physical presence. In sum, the difference between what the company would cost to buy and the book value of its identifiable, tangible assets.

Measuring is Useful; Thinking and Communicating about Knowledge is Far More Important

Measuring does not bring about a change. It can be a starting point for change (see Box 2.8), but also a ritual that may be an obstacle to change. Thus, a great number of strategic analyses and benchmarking reports produced by staff departments are mothballed. Additionally, there is a risk that attention is focused on the knowledge which can be easily measured: the explicit knowledge in well-paved knowledge fields. The well-known metaphor from the *Stories of A Thousand and One Nights* applies here. If someone comes home late at night and finds that he has lost his key, he won't be looking in the place where he is most likely to have lost it, but in the light of a torch, because that's where he can see better. Effective changes do not come about in the knowledge enterprise until the moment there exists consensus across organizational boundaries; consensus about the relevance of knowledge fields and about the methods to be used to achieve the knowledge ambition.

It is impossible to reach full consensus about all aspects of the knowledge enterprise. The point is to recognize the overall lines, the strategic intention and the common starting points that allow for cooperation. Full consensus about everything is not even desirable in the knowledge enterprise, because it also deadens the source of creativity.

Box 2.8. Say what you have to say.

A business unit manager in the food industry: 'In the past, thick reports were written in this company about the future of the business and the role of technology. But despite all of this documented knowledge about our own company, we have not been able to set things right. Marketing and development have bombarded each other with writings. The business units did not listen to corporate R&D and vice versa. Everyone had his or her own vision of our future. This has changed. For one year now, we have been talking with one another. This has gradually led to a common vision of the change of our business. Of course we use all kinds of tools, such as the portfolio analysis and the analysis of the value chain. But the essence is that developers, sales people and producers talk "from their belly", so to speak. That they actually communicate what they have to say. That process is really a change in culture.'

Knowledge Should Also be Utilized Effectively

Measuring knowledge is like grading papers. 'A' grades don't necessarily guarantee success in the labour market. Equally, a high output and stock in terms of knowledge is no guarantee for a high company turnover and profit. Transferring knowledge in advanced products and services is equally — if not more — important as the stock of knowledge *per se*. This skill, as a number of analyses have shown (Andreasen *et al.*, 1995, Hamel & Prahalad, 1994), seems to be further developed in Japan than in European countries. Japanese firms are more capable in many areas to use knowledge more effectively. They do more using less. Hamel and Prahalad (1994) speak of 'resource leverage' in this context. The R&D budgets (in percentage of turnover) of many Japanese companies are lower than those of comparable European and American firms. Their output in terms of new products, however, is higher. The above-mentioned study among 62 medium-sized firms in the Netherlands (Cobbenhagen *et al.*, 1994) demonstrates that the real difference between frontrunners and 'pack members' in terms of innovation is the way in which they organise their innovation processes (Box 2.9).

Box 2.9. Organizational conditions.

An R&D manager in a pharmaceutical company: 'We are well aware that knowledge development in our line of business is often difficult to plan or measure. This does not mean that we don't try to measure. What we do, is measuring afterwards. We steer knowledge development in three different ways. First, each marketer and researcher is familiar with the mission we try to achieve using knowledge. We want to be the best anti-histamines producer on the basis of core competencies developed here. Second, we map the progress of knowledge development: we don't merely focus on successes, but also on the projects which appear to be running in a dead-end street. Third, and this is the essence of managing a company, we try to create organizational conditions that enlarge the *chance* of success. To begin with, the recruitment and selection of scientific talent is not a formal procedure in our firm. It is a policy priority that directly involves the top management of our R&D laboratory. Second, the internal organization is expected to be as little of an obstacle to free communication of ideas as possible. The organization *should* never be a problem. Thus, organizational boundaries are put in perspective to a large degree. They exist, but minimal value should be attached to them with a view to cooperation. Third, we have an active policy when it comes to the communication of experiences. We organize, on a frequent basis, all kinds of internal professional meetings, whose purpose is that our knowledge workers learn from each other. The discovery that a certain knowledge route leads to a dead end may be more relevant in that perspective than a success story. Although such a message is "bad news", it is bad news that may save other people unnecessary work. In any case, it means that you're creating a climate in which open and free communication does not result in negative repercussions.'

Front-running companies distinguish from pack members from the same sector by better horizontal communication and horizontal steering of knowledge processes.

The Knowledge Ambition Formulated

Starting point for the knowledge enterprise is the definition of the knowledge ambition. The following aspects are relevant to this definition:

- Form and content of the document;
- The target groups for which the document was written;
- The iterative approach;
- The dialogue;
- The division of current and new competencies;
- The assessment of competencies;
- The formulation of knowledge objectives.

1. Form and Content

The knowledge ambition indicates for the firm in its entirety:

- The competencies the organization possesses;
- The relevance of the current competencies to the firm;

- The competencies the firm must (further) develop in order to achieve the strategic objectives; and possibly:
- The competencies that can be cut back or sold.

The knowledge ambition is at the basis for determining the functional demands (Chapter 3) that should be placed on the organization of the knowledge enterprise. The knowledge ambition is formulated in a five to ten-page document which should be clear and transparent to all those involved. It is not a planning document, but a mission statement which tells what binds the members of the knowledge enterprise. The knowledge ambition gives them a sense of direction, the challenge, the stretch of the current business objectives.

2. Target Groups

The document is formulated for four different target groups:

- Management and staff responsible for achieving the ambition;
- Clients that address the firm on the basis of its competencies (particularly relevant to supplier or business-to-business relationships);
- Investors that are looking for knowledge development objects for their portfolio;
- Potential partners in knowledge development.

It may be obvious that the form of the document can be adapted as to details for these different target groups. The firm will not, probably, keep its cards to its chest in every single area. In general, however, the basis will have to hold up. That is an indication of the quality of the ambition document.

3. The Iterative Approach

When formulating strategic plans, we are used to placing the activities needed for them in a fixed, logical order. First, the environment is explored, which serves as a self-inspection. On the basis of the developments in the environment possible scenarios are formulated. These scenarios are compared to the internal state of affairs, thus indicating 'gaps' between what is desired and reality. The gap analysis leads to the choice of the most fitting scenario and the definition of change objectives. In this sequential approach, tasks are usually split up into sub-tasks, which are subsequently divided into the existing parts or sub-parts of the organization. Rosabeth Moss Kanter (1983) speaks of a 'segmented approach' in this connection. In such an approach, the knowledge ambition is a derivative of the firm's strategic objective.

When defining the knowledge ambition, we strongly advise against the use of a similar approach for two important reasons. First, in doing so, the knowledge ambition, and hence the firm's competencies, are understood as a derivative of the strategic objective of the firm. Yet, competencies, and core competencies in particular, are at the same time the breeding ground for the firm's strategic positioning. Thus, it shouldn't just look from the outside to the inside, but the other way around as well. What the firm *can* do determines to a great extent both its opportunities *and* its limitations. This means that the approach will have to possess a strongly iterative character. One might view the business strategy (Figure 2.5) as a wedge which can be used to 'stretch' the current competencies and the knowledge ambition. The current and desired competencies are linked to one another, so to speak, by an elastic bandage. The business strategy can reach further as the distance between current and desired competencies is stretched. However, it takes an effort to stretch the current competencies to the desired competencies. The power exerted to achieve this is dependent on the urgency and scope of the new business strategy.

The above explains the dynamic link between market pull and technology push. An example from the services sector will illustrate this. A medium-sized tour operator has made the strategic choice for products with a higher added value. Two new market segments are considered as being part of this strategy: adventurous trips to Africa and Asia, and active holidays (mountaineering, scuba diving, cycling,

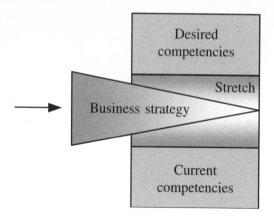

Figure 2.5. The linear and iterative approach.

and canoeing) in Eastern Europe. When looking at the firm's own know-how and experience, the first segment appears to be too ambitious. The firm lacks the know-how about local conditions, language proficiency, and knowledge of the risks that might present themselves underway. The second segment seems feasible, because the firm had previously gained experience with cultural and winter sports holidays to Eastern Europe. The firm knows the environment and employs a number of people that speak the relevant languages fairly well. Additionally, it does not seem to be too difficult to recruit skilled sports guides. The choice for this option leads to the question inside the firm whether or not Eastern Europe can be extended to include a broader segment. It seems possible to develop into 'the' tour operator for Eastern Europe on the basis of two starting activities. This example demonstrates that the business strategy should initially be limited due to a lack of competencies (about Asia and Africa) that can be stretched. In a next step, the business strategy can be broadened when there is a possibility for stretch in another knowledge area (Eastern Europe).

A second objection to the sequential approach is that it leads to segmentation and compartmentalization. When a definition of the knowledge ambition breaks up tasks according to the existing organization culture, it is very likely that the firm does not make any progress whatsoever. There is a risk that departments and other section of the firm will try to protect their own knowledge domains. Attempts to connect these with one another usually result in patchwork.

4. The Dialogue

The knowledge ambition is an instrument used to move the organization into the right direction. This places demands upon the quality of the knowledge ambition itself, but quality alone is not sufficient. Broad support across the organization is needed to convert paper intentions into concrete behaviour. Bringing together the right expertise in a small think-tank is not enough. Converting ideas into action places demands upon communication, which are paradoxical in nature. A diversity of ideas must be tapped, which is expected to lead to a clear focus eventually. The established interests of groups and individuals will come up for discussion, while the basis and consensus are preconditions for success. In other words: decrees from the top are equally useless as endless rounds of participation. The *dialogue* is therefore the most appropriate form of involvement for the development of the knowledge ambition. 'Dialogue is where parties exchange views about paradoxical situations, each having the intention of modifying their position before the views and evidence presented by the other. Each participant is open to being influenced by the other' (Stacey, 1993, p. 105). The dialogue is a type of communication (Senge, 1990; Gustavsen, 1991) for a team in which:

- The common end objective is put first;
- Contrasts in opinions and interests are accepted as being normal;
- The knowledge needed is brought together;
- Openness is put first;
- Factors of hierarchy and power are eliminated to the farthest extent possible.

It is not sufficient that conflicts and hidden agendas are put on the table. Arguments and debates *per se* do not imply an intention to change. The *dialogue* is a type of communication in which this intention is inherent.

In a large organization, one might think of dialogues among and between three groups:

- The *management team*, which indicates the frameworks and takes the final decisions;
- An *inner circle* of highly qualified knowledge workers and managers from different business units, functional departments and management echelons that carry the process;
- A larger *outer circle* in which ideas can be expressed and comments given.

In the inner circle, a number of different roles must be fulfilled:

- *Leadership*: a member of the management team must continuously safeguard the translation to the business strategy and the communication to the rest of the firm;
- *Expertise*: insight into one's own competencies and fine-tuning to the latest development in relevant subject areas (functional knowledge);
- *Lateral thinking*: making connections between different knowledge areas;
- *Looking outward*: picking up external knowledge developments ('gate-keeping') and market developments;
- *Opposition*: a continuous counterbalance is needed for the people that supply the knowledge: the internal knowledge users (for example: developers versus marketers).

It may be of importance to involve clients or external experts in this process, particularly in the case of firms that are strongly internally orientated, or where certain departments possess a knowledge monopoly internally.

5. Categorization and Assessment of Competencies

When formulating the knowledge ambition (see the Appendix for a practical approach), competencies are identified and assessed. The division according to core competencies, enabling and exchangeable competencies can be combined with the division according to functional, operational and contextual knowledge. While the former division states focus and priority, the latter provides insight into the possibility of translating competencies effectively into profitable business.

In some organizations, the division of technological core competencies does not lead to many problems, because these can be described in accepted and explicit terms. Thus, in (bio)chemical firms the technological competencies are reflected in (bio)chemical transformation processes, for example fermentation (Gist-brocades, see Box 2.10), and asymmetrical synthesis (Chapter 4: DSM Andeno). In the IT sector, servicing companies usually refer to a limited collection of (mostly tested) technologies, such as a new program language (JAVA), program environment (ORACLE), program strategy (object orientation), program package (SAP), or configuration (client server systems).

Box 2.10. Core competencies in three firms.

Functional and operational knowledge

The following excerpt has been taken from a brochure made by Gist-brocades (*Gist-brocades, your partner in technology*, 1996, p. 5): 'Microbiological production technology [...] is the collective term for a number of technologies used by Gist-brocades. It allows us to competitively produce fermentation-based products. In essence, it constitutes our first core competence. It enables the carefully controlled selection and cultivation of micro-organisms such as yeast, bacteria and fungi. A special feature is the capability of upscaling laboratory culture to pilot plant and commercial, large-scale fermentation. Pilot plants are available for both in-house innovation and co-development projects with customers. They provide flexibility for translating laboratory findings to small industrial scale, scaling-up research findings on processes and testing for reproducibility. They are also fully automated: process parameters are available on-line, with specially developed software handling of the most sophisticated processes. This naturally involves specialized engineering work and dedicated systems control. After the completion of a full-scale fermentation, the product is recovered and the by-products may also be put to good use: they may be converted into other products or recycled. What is finally left over is processed to minimize environmental impact. The desired end-product may be the live micro-organism itself (for example bakers' yeast) or products made by it during the fermentation (e.g., enzyme or antibiotic).'

Operational knowledge

The IP/Informatica Projectgroep B.V. is a strongly growing Dutch IT firm with an annual turnover over 110 million guilders. On its Internet pages (http:www.IP.groep.nl) the firm makes clear that the firm's competence focuses on the support of organizations in the implementation of their core process. IP recognizes the superiority of these organizations' knowledge about their own core process. Emphasis is placed upon the way in which the service is implemented as well as on the relationship with the customer. The TOKIO model provides the direction. Far less specific is the firm in its web pages about the characteristics of its customers.

Contextual knowledge

L + T is a Dutch IT firm (part of Pink Roccade) employing 200 people. In its company profile, the firm mainly accentuates its role as 'information partner for the local authorities'. The firm's slogan is: 'Information technology: a matter of empathy'.

In other words: the technological competencies are mostly defined on the basis of available technologies. The customer knows what knowledge the firm possesses and the firm knows which knowledge must be built up, maintained and further developed through training and recruitment. In the case of an existing and tested technology, it is more difficult to indicate with which competencies the firm distinguishes from its competitors. This distinction is sought in the servicing IT firms (Box 2.9) mostly in the way in which the services are provided. In other words, the technological competencies are viewed as enabling competencies, and the operational competencies are viewed as core competencies. In that case these operational competencies must be made explicit: "This is the way we work, and we do it better than our competitors because ...'.

When competencies are strongly intertwined, it is much harder to categorize and assess competencies. This is particularly the case in the professional services sector, where functional, operational, and contextual knowledge are often a complex tangle. In that case, it is inevitable that the firm make a kind of map ('cognitive map') of its own competencies. 'Cognitive mapping' (see the Appendix) can be a useful instrument for this. Subsequently, the assessment of competencies is mainly a matter of reaching consensus, based on such factors as:

- the novelty of the knowledge for the firm and the sector;
- the success rate in the market;
- the ability to distinguish;
- exchangeability;
- cost/benefit ratio.

Assessment scales are useful to make the estimations in the roup visible, but can never be used to replace the common judgement (consensus) in the group. The same holds true of the portfolio approach (Roussel *et al.*, 1991, see the Appendix), which is used in industrial and engineering firms. This approach chooses the portfolio of R&D projects, or high-quality client projects as starting point, which are seen as carriers of knowledge. Systematic comparison of these projects gradually leads to an image of the firm's own competencies.

6. Formulating Policy Consequences

The final aspect that needs to be considered when defining the knowledge ambition are the policy consequences. These consequences can be very far-reaching, particularly when the core competencies are formulated in another wording. In a short time period, this is possible only by selling company parts and/or the acquisition of other firms. As an example, Gist-brocades (Chapter 4) decided to withdraw from the field of industrial enzymes in 1995. The firm concluded (Annual Report 1995) that market leadership was the only possible way of being sufficiently profitable in the long run. A precondition for achieving market leadership was a large and permanent investment in new knowledge, which went beyond the firms' financial base. Once co-operation in this area with other firms appeared unrealistic, the firm decided to sell the division and invest the money thus made available in the development of the other core competencies.

In most cases, however, what is needed is not a fundamental and direct change of the core competencies, but gradual expansion. Thus, a basic objective of many IT firms is to apply themselves to object-oriented programming and fourth-generation programming languages. The knowledge ambition briefly states the most important ways of achieving this objective:

- Personnel policy (Chapter 7);
- The organization (Chapters 3 and 6);
- Information and communication technology (Chapter 8).

The set-up of new development projects that fit in the knowledge ambition and may or may not be implemented in cooperation with other firms (see Box 2.10) may serve to make the new lines more visible.

Box 2.11. Knowledge management and co-operation.

Stork (see also Chapter 4) is a large Dutch engineering firm, employing more than 18,000 people and operating on a world-wide basis. A lot of Stork's development projects are carried out in co-operation with other firms and (semi-)public knowledge centres such as TNO. Stork is also a very active participant in innovation programmes supported by the government, such as so-called 'cluster projects' and 'innovation-focused research programmes' ('IOPs'). In Stork's annual report of 1995 we read: 'The cornerstone of the technology and innovation policy are: knowledge management and co-operation. An example of co-operation is the cluster project aimed at the automation of pig slaughter lines. The first results of this project are expected to reach the commercial stage in 1996.

Another cluster project, for visual detection systems, will also introduce its first products into the market in 1996. A cooperation agreement has been reached with Elbit/EVS, a leading Israeli firm in the area of vision systems. In addition, an IOP project 'vision editing' has been initiated, as well as an IT-mechatronics project in which Stork will cooperate with TNO and the University of Amsterdam.'

Chapter 3

Knowledge Development

The knowledge needed by an organization changes constantly. Knowledge that is not maintained, becomes obsolete and evaporates. The vehicle of knowledge development must be continuously kept in motion. This holds true of virtually every aspect of business. Thus, knowledge development is a fundamental process of the organization. The strategic task of firms and institutions is to increase the effectiveness of that process, in other words, to do more with fewer resources ('leverage of means'). As a precondition, firms need to have insight into the different strategies available to develop knowledge. The organization can be viewed as a 'learning system', where the organization acts as a carrier of knowledge. Apart from continuous change, constant movement is an essential characteristic of knowledge. Knowledge flows, from one development department to another, from developers to users and back again, from unit to unit, from the market place to the inside of the organization. Knowledge flows do not follow rigid bureaucratic channels. Knowledge flows form a dynamic system that can be compared with a river delta. This chapter will illustrate the main flows of the 'knowledge delta'. Using the insight thus gained we can draw a map of the organizational bedding of knowledge which shows what flows are clogged up and which curbs should be cut off.

Knowledge Development

Knowledge is not developed according to a single fixed pattern. A variety of development patterns can be distinguished, which are often implicit. At the start, one tries to set out lines, but once the knowledge development process is running, it tends to be forgotten. The working method has become self-evident. This changes when the knowledge development leads to a dead end, or when one does not succeed in speeding up the development of knowledge. At that moment, one starts looking for strategies to get the development going again. This is where insight into the different strategies of knowledge development proves its value.

The Ripple Strategy

The ripple strategy is based on the above-mentioned perspective. As most models presented here, the model builds on the work of Arnold Reisman (1988). Starting point for his model is the most rudimentary strategy (see Figure 3.1).

The dark circle represents the knowledge field controlled by the organization at time T1. This knowledge is based on one specific theory, discipline, technology or approach, and is developed from one place or central location in the organization (a 'knowledge centre', see Section 3.3). Examples are:

- direct writing by an insurer;
- a coating process using a 'powder coating' by a manufacturer of bicycles;
- the automation of a logistic process;
- the design of concrete construction elements using CAD systems.

The firm uses the well-known route, which we might call 'Model A'. Knowledge is developed in this strategy in incremental steps along one single line, during which process the model is refined and

Domain of
problem characterics

Figure 3.1. The ripple strategy (Reisman, 1988, p. 216).

improved. In abstract terms, this means that a model is developed concerned with n + 1 dimensions from the perspective of a model that explains the working of *n* dimensions. In this incremental development, one gradually gets a grip on the phenomenon. Progressively, it becomes clear what the relevant factors are, how they can be measured, what their influence is, and how they can be influenced. Knowledge is developed here in the eight stages described by Bohn (1994, see the Appendix). The initial route (Model a) is not abandoned. It is closely related to the expertise in one knowledge centre, or one knowledge domain. An example is the continuous improvement of process control by the process technology department of a food-producing firm. The ripple strategy is mainly a safe strategy: there are few risks and coordination efforts are minor. Quality is the most important product of this approach. When a major change presents itself in the market or the technology, there is a risk however that one will linger in the well-known track too long. Additionally, there is the danger that one becomes too isolated from business developments within the rest of the organization.

The Strategy of Flow-Wise Accumulation

In most firms, innovations evolve from a combination of different knowledge centres rather than from one single department or knowledge centre. Similar to a relay race, projects are handed over from one knowledge centre to the other. The project flows through the firm, so to speak, with each centre adding its own knowledge (Figure 3.2). The knowledge gradually grows during this process.

This strategy is commonly used in the traditional way in which products and services are developed, for example in an insurance company where the marketing department launches the idea for a new insurance policy. The product concept is described by the marketers, they subcontract a consumer survey, while the actuaries calculate the policy premiums and the communication department designs a campaign.

Procedures concerning the issuing of policies and the assessment and processing of damage claims are determined by a product group.

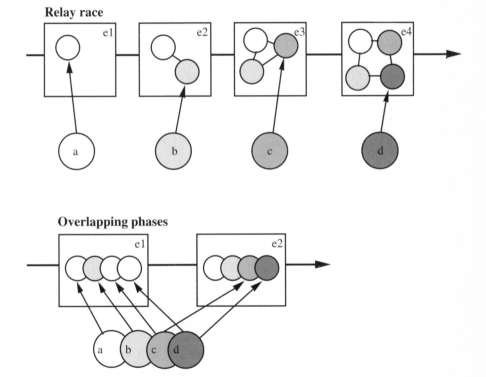

Figure 3.2. Flow-wise growth.

The insurance intermediaries are subsequently informed about the new product by the department of external information. Finally, the field service feeds back the field experiences with the new policy to the marketing department. Each station adds knowledge to the end product in the making from its own Model (a, b, c, etc.) The advantage of this strategy is that it is clear for each 'station' what the previous station produced in terms of ideas and requirements. The major drawback is that the downstream stations are dealing with product specifications that cannot easily be changed at that stage. The problem which may arise between the Development and Production departments is classical. Development works on a product within the boundaries of its own domain. The moment (as in the example of the chemical firm in Box 3.1) the specifications are printed on paper and handed over to Production, it seems that the product can be manufactured only with huge efforts or with differing degrees of quality. This is the key problem of the relay race approach: the risk that the baton falls to the ground after the transfer and the firm is out of the race in one stroke.

Box 3.1. Interface problems.

The developers of a chemical firm succeed in making a new product on a laboratory scale which offers major advantages for clients in addition to the existing products. The clients seem to be prepared to pay a good price for it. The developers hand the recipe over to Production, who are facing an enormous problem in upscaling the product. Time after time, the recipe is adapted, and each time Production is unable to achieve constant quality. Tens of millions worth of test runs are spent. Eventually, the firm is thinking of throwing the towel in the ring. In a last effort to get the lucrative product out of the plant, a team of developers, process engineers and production assistants lock themselves inside the plant for a week to find out what it is exactly that's going wrong. At the end of that week it seems that the new product places much higher demands on process control. An investment of 400,000 guilders resolves the problem.

That is the reason why firms increasingly shift to a working method in which development phases deliberately show little overlap. In other words, upstream knowledge centres cooperate with downstream centres at an early stage. Thus, they are better able to anticipate the impact of their choices downstream. In addition, the downstream stations can start their contribution to the whole chain sooner. In this strategy, the firm intentionally invests in the knowledge of the interfaces ($a \times b$, $b \times c$, etc.) between the functional knowledge domains. The risk that the firm is unpleasantly surprised is reduced and total throughput time (time-to-market) can be drastically shortened. Preconditions for such a working method is that upstream stations fulfil an active role in the communication with later stations, and that later stations are prepared to work on the basis of preliminary and incomplete knowledge and information. The multidisciplinary project group is an organizational instrument (see Chapter 6) that can be used to steer this into the right direction. It is imperative that the project leader be held responsible for the development trajectory from a to z. This approach is also referred to as the 'rugby approach' (Takeuchi and Nonaka, 1986): it is a team sport in which the ball is continuously played around. This also means that the ball can be handed back if necessary. The same line of thought is followed in 'concurrent engineering' (cf. Clark and Fujimoto, 1991).

Recently (Nonaka and Takeuchi, 1996, p. 211), a third development strategy has been recognized: 'American football'. Combining the relay race and the rugby approach, this strategy was followed in the development of the Nissan Primera in Japan. At the start of the development process (predevelopment) the multidisciplinary teams work very closely together. Once a common denominator is found the different functional teams start working in parallel. This approach tries to prevent functional departments from 'giving in' too much and thus adding too little knowledge to the product.

There also exists an external variant of the accumulation strategy, which is adopted (see Chapter 4: DSM Andeno) when the supplier nestles in the client's knowledge development stages. In an early stage, the knowledge workers of the supplier attempt to convince the client of the value that their Model a adds to the client's Model b. In the dialogue with the client, the knowledge from Model a can be adjusted in such a way that it fits within the client's Model b. For knowledge-intensive products and services this also implies that the specifications resulting from one's own Model b are adapted to the possibilities offered by Model a. The supplier no longer starts from the accurately described client specifications, but has its own development overlap with the client's. One might also refer to this as a rugby approach, because the ball is played round constantly.

Box 3.2. The relay race and rugby approaches.

The figure below (Takeuchi and Nonaka, 1986) illustrates the time gain of the rugby approach versus the relay race approach. The horizontal axis represents the development time. The vertical axis illustrates the efforts of the departments ('stations' or 'knowledge centres') in a development project. In the relay race approach, a department does not start an effort until those of the previous departments are completed. In the rugby approach, the efforts not only overlap, but most departments also continue to be involved in a project from beginning to end.

Sequential

Overlapping

Overlapping

Development time

The Embedding Strategy

The embedding strategy (Figure 3.3) brings different Models (*a* and *b*) within a broader framework. The Models *a* and *b* remain recognizable for the greater part. In other words, no major changes take place fundamentally.

The strategy is applied mainly in the coupling of information systems and integration of products and services. Thus, within Management Information Systems (MIS), links can be made between cost administration (a) and quality assessment or stock control (b). The advantage of coupling systems is the improvement of the control function. In our example, the firm is able to ascertain whether minimization of 'inter-stocks' has a negative impact on quality. As a second advantage, information is far more accessible: one is able to look into each other systems. Another example is the development of a 'family insurance package' in the insurance sector, in which the models on which the separate policies are based do not need to undergo much change. Products and services are also integrated in the industry sector: the customer not only purchases a software package, he also buys a course to teach him how to work with it as well as

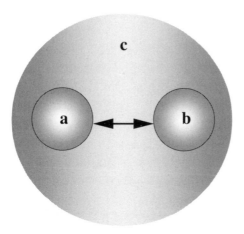

Figure 3.3. The embedding strategy.

support by way of a 'helpdesk' for possible problems that can present themselves after purchase.

This strategy may have major advantages for both supplier and customer. The transactions between client and supplier are simplified. The customer only needs to turn to one address for a range of products and services. He or she is no longer overwhelmed with heaps of policies, but instead receives one integrated policy. Additionally, the supplier learns to get to know his customers better and he can add more value to the product. Remarkable in this context is that insurance companies used to possess complete files about insurance policies, but not of their customers. In recent years, not only products and services, but also the information flows are integrated, which brings the customers in the picture in many firms. The customer is becoming a relation. For the organization, this means that the function-oriented attitude must usually be abandoned in exchange for a market or product orientation. This is what happened at the general insurance division of Nationale Nederlanden (Chapter 4). Under the umbrella of a market-oriented team, this insurance company operates both from the perspective of Model a (risk acceptance) and Model b (damage assessment). Although the firm continues to make use of the same pure insurance knowledge, it thus creates a new perspective of the client and the environment.

In the case of MIS, the coupling of systems provides a better information supply. A precondition for such a strategy is, however, that the systems in which the Model a (for example: quality control) and b (for example: cost control) are embedded are designed in a such a way that the Models a and b are not somehow affected. That is to say: the user must be able to continue to work according to Model a or b. This is usually the problem in actual practice when applying the embedding strategy. Old subsystems cannot generally be converted in a new information structure without problems. Adjustments are mostly required, because they do not fit in the new structure for one hundred percent. A field of tension may arise between the opportunities of the new system and the specific user demands.

Moreover, some users will not like the idea of other people looking over their shoulders. This may lead to time-consuming discussions about procedures, because one does not like to talk about content itself.

The Bridge Strategy

This strategy aims to come to new combinations starting from two clearly different models. To use a metaphor from chemistry: the reaction of two different molecules creates a new molecule with new and unique properties. In other words, the Models a and b do not continue as separate entities as they did in the previous strategy, but instead, are merged in a new Model c (see Figure 3.4)

In science and technology, this strategy leads to the creation of new disciplines, for example in biotechnology and mechatronics. New subject areas are created. Firms adopt a bridge strategy when clearly differing core competencies are mixed. This usually happens in the case of strategic alliances and joint ventures, or internal ventures between divisions or business units. The build-up of a new core competence is extremely costly and time-consuming. This also holds true of the bridge strategy itself. Totally different disciplines must start a dialogue with and learn how to understand each other. The bridge strategy is risky, but may also lead to high rewards (high risk/ high reward), because the resulting knowledge is unique in character. Examples of the bridge strategy are the ventures between Gist-brocades

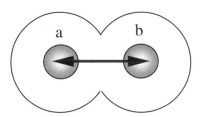

Figure 3.4. The bridge strategy.

and DSM Andeno (Chemferm), and between DSM Fine Chemicals and the Japanese Tosoh ('Holland Sweetener'). Critical in the bridge strategy is to find the right internal or external partners. Partners must complement each other and should not stand in each other's way in the market place. This requires a high degree of trust and 'commitment'. Moreover, it is necessary in general to create a new common organizational entity, because otherwise the new model threatens to be eaten away by the existing management structures. Within the company one finds special 'business development units' which serve as 'delivery rooms' for new business units. The bridge strategy is also followed in the services sector. Thus, accountancy firms advise their clients not only about their administrative organization (a), they also provide appropriate automation solutions (b) which are directly concerned with external accountancy (c). This approach is more than a sum of the three activities and leads to far-reaching changes in each of the three functions (or models). These changes become visible in the shifts in the accountant role: from verification to consulting.

The Transfer Strategy

In the transfer strategy, a useful *element* of Model b is integrated in Model a, whether this be a technology, knowledge of the market, or organizational knowledge (see Figure 3.5). This integration usually takes place on the basis of an analogy.

Thus, methods used by banks for the control of the money flows are based on the 'Just-In-Time' (JIT) approach from industry. Public authorities try to translate the organizational model of the business unit to their own context in the form of 'result-responsible units'. Electronics firms such as Philips fit adaptations of its high-tech products developed for professional equipment into consumer products later. Original transfers are sometimes far-fetched in both a literal and a figurative way of speaking.

The transfer strategy can be applied in two directions. One can either try to find a new application field for available knowledge, or

Figure 3.5. The transfer strategy.

new original knowledge for a known application field. The former is the case in the JIT example, the latter in the detection technology of the HAK firm (see box 3.3). The JIT example is fairly straightforward, the fundamental thought is simple. Which does not mean to say that the implementation is simple. Adaptation to the new context may take some doing. The second example is far more creative and original because the solution is not at all straightforward. The word 'serendipity' is relevant here. In general, one might state that the transfer strategy is simpler when a firm, as in the Philips example, controls both knowledge areas (a and b) itself.

The Learning Organization

Knowledge development within organizations is by definition a learning process. The organization can be viewed from that perspective as a 'learning system', a system that will function better on the basis of experience. Economists primarily think of scale effects here: a firm learns by constantly repeating certain activities and measuring output. They thus create routines. Routines supply efficiency. Economists illustrate this scale effect in the learning curve (see Figure 3.6).

Box 3.3. US defence technology in the glass conserves industry.

The Dutch HAK company is a market leader in the area of glass-contained vegetable and fruit conserves. At first sight this seems to be a low-tech rather than high-tech industry. However, quality and food safety is a highly critical given within the food and beverage industry. For example, no product-foreign components, such as glass splinters or such like, are allowed to be packaged in the glass containers.

Until recently there existed no detection equipment to track product-foreign components in a filled, closed and conserved container. Therefore, the management of the firm took the initiative to have such an apparatus constructed. The firm searched for technologies that would allow for a highly accurate degree of detection. HAK ended up with advanced X-ray detection and image recognition techniques that were initially applied by the US defence industry in the design of cruise missiles. In the automobile industry, these techniques had been previously used for the inspection of welding connections. An Italian firm made a first prototype detection apparatus on the basis of knowledge derived from both these sectors (defence and automobile). HAK is the first firm in The Netherlands to make use of this system.

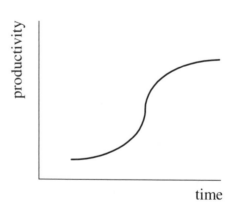

Figure 3.6. The learning curve.

Table 3.1. A comparison of knowledge development strategies.

Strategy	Possibilities	Risks	Conditions
Ripple	– Continuous improvement – Quality – Cost control	– Generally low – When major changes in technology or market present themselves, the risk exists that one continues to work in the same direction – Isolation from other knowledge centres inside the firm	– Motivation to critically look at one's own processes continuously – Adequate process information – Closed control loop (see section 3.2)
Accumulation	(Inherent in all development processes) – Integration of functional knowledge – Time-to-market – Market orientation	– Jamming and interface problems – High coordination burden – Too much conformist behaviour	– Overlapping phases – Multidisciplinary teams – Rugby approach – Project management from A to Z
Embedding	– Coupling of systems, products and services – Simplified access for clients and users – Improved control by coupling of information	– System embedding is too complex – Loss of autonomy	– Consensus about points of departure – Accepting central management – Integration of tasks
Bridge	– Unique new knowledge by combination of core competencies – Basis for new generations of products and services – Shared development effort	– High control burden – Technical risk (can it be made?) – Economic risk – Rejection by the environment – Difficult communication	– New managerial forms – One must learn to speak each other's language – Clear commitment from the top
Transfer	– Exploiting available knowledge in a new context – Creative findings which may provide a unique market position	– Technical risk – Economic risk – Lack of knowledge – Internal resistance	– One must gain and diffuse sector-foreign knowledge in a relatively short time span – Support from the top

Table 3.2. Learning by doing, using and failing.

Learning by	Examples
Doing	*The organization consultant*: 'We are really familiar with the TQM process now. Our company has supervised its implementation in 14 firms.'
Using	*The marketer*: 'Not only do we deliver our machines at the client's, but we also ensure their adequate implementation. Our engineers continue their relation with the client, not only to provide service, but also to learn from their experiences with our equipment. The field service and our development are one team. The knowledge thus gained can be used in new machines.'
Failing	*The strategic planner*: 'A year ago we listed our market breakthroughs during the past 20 years. Remarkably, most cases were concerned with the application of knowledge from a product or project that had previously failed. Apparently we are able to convert failures into successes.'

Thus, we see that the introduction of a new product in a plant, or of a new service in the market, will lead to a decrease in cost price per unity as the volume increases. In this vision, learning is first of all 'learning by doing'. It supplies the operational knowledge that was discussed in the previous chapter. In the case of innovation, however, one may also learn from the use made of products, services and processes (Hayes and Maidique, 1985).

Finally, failures are an almost unlimited source of learning experiences. As a precondition, however, one must be prepared to talk about these failures openly. Some firms (Box 2.8) have managed to make this into an art. Other firms need a big shock (Box 3.1) to look at themselves critically. This is an argument to assess new products and services not only on the basis of their success in the market place, but on the basis of new knowledge as well.

Control Loops

It is essential in every learning process to consider the effects of one's actions. Measuring effects leads to reflection: reflection on the question as to why an action leads to good or bad results, and 'how' the action can be steered in order to achieve better results. The advantage of the systems approach is that it enables us to make a link with the management of organizational processes. In the systems approach, the control loop (Figure 3.7, Argyris, 1976) is the simplest representation of a learning process. A system (a department, business unit, or a team, a work station, or a machine) is expected to produce a certain output (c). This output is the result from transformation (b) of the input: the means that are added to the system (information, materials, money). The output is measured (d) against a norm determined in advance. Deviations from the norm can be fed back to the input (a), which can then be adjusted.

This simple system model forces us to check to see whether or not the most important condition for learning behaviour in control loops (De Sitter, 1994) is fulfilled: the control loop must be *closed*. As an example, let's have a look at the complaints filed by customers of an insurance company to its general insurance department. A first step is ascertaining the possible cause for the complaint: uncertainties about the policy conditions of a specific insurance. The second step is giving a signal to the unit responsible for formulating the policy conditions. The effect of the action that is subsequently taken (rewriting the policy conditions) is to ascertain whether the number of complaints ('deviations from the norm') are actually decreasing. It may be clear that the control loop does not function when one of the links is missing, for example, a general insurance department that fails to take action after receiving the complaints, or a policy developing department which does not reformulate the conditions. This leads to an important principle for the design of organizations (De Sitter, 1994): *unity of time, place and action*. It is essential in learning processes that as little as possible time goes by between the moment of action (transformation of the input), the measuring of output, and steering of the action. The working of the control loop is reinforced by keeping and integrating, measuring and steering the action at one organizational locus and in one single task as much as possible. As a second example, take the upscaling of a chemical process (Box 3.1). The quickest way of upscaling a chemical process is when one multidisciplinary upscaling team (unity of place) measures the effects of upscaling experiments as quickly as possible (unity of time), leading to a possible steering action (unity of action).

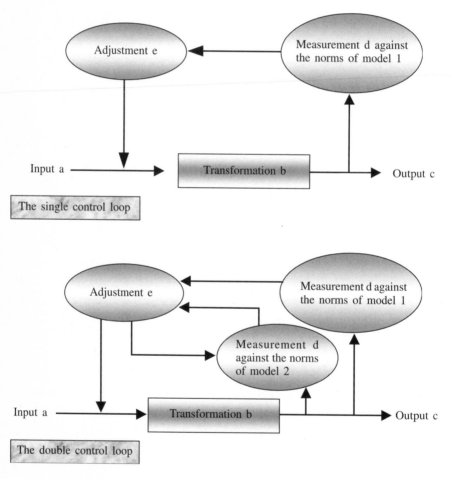

Figure 3.7. Learning with a single and a double control loop.

However, in actual practice, organizational learning processes are generally more complex in nature. They require a double rather than a single control loop. The cause can be read from the learning curve. There comes a moment that the energy put in system improvements no longer equals out the effect of that improvement. According to economists, that is the moment that the marginal equals cost. If one wants to achieve better results (lower costs, better quality or higher turnover) new solutions are needed. The system must be looked at from different perspectives. Put differently: by developments in technology or in the market place it may be necessary to apply different norms to assessment of the system. An example has been given in Box 2.5. Due to the introduction of a new technology, the flexible manufacturing systems (FMS), the old norms have become obsolete (machine downtime). Only by steering on the basis of new norms (flexibility and variety) can the learning process be revived again. This leads to a higher level learning process: learning with a double control loop (see Figure 3.7).

Communication

In terms of knowledge management, the learning organization model is of great relevance for another reason. Apart from formal information systems, people play an important role in the control loop. When these people fail to inform, warn timely and support one another, there is a risk that the control loop is not closed. This brings us to communication within the organization. The learning organization requires sound communication. Partly, communication within an organization is hindered by a great number of obstacles. Thus, communication between the various organization functions in a firm often goes via long (hierarchical) detours. Lateral thinking (see Chapter 6) and the effective use of information technology (Chapter 8) may help to cut these detours. But even project teams, steering and work groups installed across organizational boundaries often fail to contribute to good communication. For example, members of such groups may withhold information, keep their cards to their chest, or fail to commit themselves to the group's objective. The discussion in the group fails to become a dialogue, because the members allow their own interests to be dominated above the interest of the group, they have a hidden agenda. Sometimes, communication is aggravated because each of the various functions represented in one team continue to speak their own incomprehensible jargon. Additionally, a lot of experts do not possess the skills needed to function in a group.

Good communication in a team is a precondition for a learning organization, but it is also a learning process itself. The model for good communication is increasingly sought in the dialogue (cf. Chapter 2).

The development of dialogues might be considered a form of organization development. New structures (lateral management teams, project teams, technology councils, and so on) are brought to life in the dialogue. The need for dialogue development is felt in every knowledge enterprise sooner or later. Mutual trust is a prerequisite.

Box 3.4. Fear of failure.

Firm A develops and manufactures complex scientific machinery. The development department consists of different functional groups that make parts for the products. These groups supply the parts, and complex technical systems, to one another. It is essential that these parts fit each other precisely. For these reasons, the specifications of the parts have been laid down in detail in the design. The groups are constantly facing complex technical problems when these parts are designed. It often happens during the development process that a small change in the specification of other parts quickly clears up the problem.

However, the groups compulsively stick to the specifications they received. They tend to cover themselves: 'At least we have complied with the specifications.' They are afraid to be caught for mistakes by others to the extent that it is not until the last moment, when practically all problems are solved, that they start to communicate with the other groups. Yet it's their fear of failure that causes the product development process to last extremely long.

The Organization as a Carrier of Knowledge

Individuals play an important part in the knowledge enterprise. They are the most important carriers of knowledge in the organization. The tacit knowledge they have acquired over the years makes knowledge-intensive companies vulnerable, because knowledge workers can be exchanged only to a limited extent. It is extremely difficult in general to fill the gap in a specific knowledge area. The role of the individual is often strongly felt when breakthroughs are made in the established knowledge. Radical changes in the knowledge enterprise are often based on the imperturbable work of a pioneer, a whiz-kid, who will hold on to his own ideas no matter what. These pioneers are not always understood in the organization. Because there is no room for their new ideas, the real go-getters leave the company to start their own business. That is how the computer firm Apple came into existence.

Nevertheless, such breakthroughs do not thrive on pioneers alone. The pioneer's ideas do not take root until they are vigorously propagated into the organization. This role is called 'product champion'. Additionally, radical breakthroughs, which are usually time-consuming and swallow up money, require protection from the top management. This is the role of the knowledge entrepreneur (or 'Godfather') who believes in the idea and is prepared to cover the risk because he is confident that it will lead to new opportunities. Finally, the significance of the role of the 'gatekeeper' is recognized in most knowledge-intensive firms: the man or woman who follows external new developments and introduces promising developments in the organization.

Thus, innovation does not thrive on one single person. A variety of roles must be fulfilled, even when radical and creative developments in knowledge are concerned to which the individual pioneer is central. In other words: knowledge development in a firm or institution is practically always a collective effort. This holds true by definition of knowledge development which is based on the input of various individuals, functions, and organizational units. Knowledge development is mostly teamwork, and the organization can therefore be viewed as a collective carrier of knowledge. This collective character can take three forms.

Firstly, the total amount of knowledge of the organization must be *more than the sum* of the knowledge of separate knowledge carriers. Not only do two people know more than one, two people also know more than two. The combination of knowledge leads to new knowledge. Suppose a new marketer is recruited who has set up a new distribution method in Sector A. When the marketer co-operates with the salesman in the firm who knows Market B inside out, the possibility arises to adapt this new method of distribution to Market B. We have called this the transfer strategy. Characteristic of the organization is that knowledge is closely intertwined with other knowledge. Knowledge of individual carriers or groups of knowledge carriers is seldom standing by itself, but is generally found in combination with other knowledge. It is these very combinations that produce effect. Thus, knowledge of quality management does not provide better quality unless it is combined with production knowledge. These combinations produce clusters of knowledge, which even for a small firm can be highly complex. Much of this knowledge has a tacit character. In addition, the knowledge elements are intertwined and highly specific (idiosyncratic) of the organization, the product or the service, process and the market of the firm. This is what makes it so difficult to copy the internally available knowledge of an organization.

A second characteristic of organizational knowledge is that it has a *common character* for a large part. Knowledge is transferred in an organization, which can thus be shared. Basically, the common stock of knowledge within an organization is freely accessible to all of its members, which is an advantage of an organization compared to market relations (Kogut and Zander, 1992). This enables the firm to deal with knowledge efficiently; it is not necessary to reinvent the wheel again and again. Practically all of the instruments mentioned in this book are used for the transfer and storage of collective knowledge, ranging from training programmes, automated knowledge databases, handbooks, lateral groups, to electronic mail and job rotation. There is one danger here (Kogut and Zander, 1992): as knowledge within the organization is easier to transfer (made explicit and codifyable), this knowledge can also be more easily copied by rival firms. Quality certification is a fine example here. If the procedures for garage A are laid down adequately, it is not difficult at all to introduce these in an adapted form in Garage B.

Finally, the organizational character of knowledge is reflected in the way in which this knowledge is embedded within the *structures and processes* of the firm (see also Chapters 5 and 6). Knowledge areas are covered by organizational units or combinations of units: the knowledge centres.

Knowledge Centres

Knowledge is developed and used within the organization at virtually every workplace. The knowledge development in organizations, however, is not divided in a homogenous way. Knowledge is concentrated in a number of places. We call these concentrations *the knowledge centres* of the organization: a knowledge field where they are the experts. For example, Shell speaks of 'focal points', groups that can be addressed for specific problems. They focus on functional knowledge for a significant part, which is related to a basic function of the organization:

- Marketing and sales: knowledge of the market place;
- R&D: knowledge of products and technologies;
- Process engineering and production: knowledge of production processes;
- Administration: knowledge of money flows;
- Personnel and organization: knowledge of people.

These knowledge centres pick up, process and transfer knowledge within the organization, or to its customers. To this end, they are equipped with skilled and experienced staff as well as material devices, such as measuring equipment, information systems, organizational manuals, client panels, documents, journals, and knowledge databases. Usually, they are also responsible for training in order to maintain the functional knowledge. The concept of 'critical mass' is often used in such knowledge concentrations to indicate that the knowledge centre is able to fulfil its tasks only when sufficient knowledge is concentrated in one point. This 'point' is generally a collection of human knowledge carriers: a department, a project team, or an informal group within the company. However, the domain of the knowledge centre is mostly shared with other departments or groups. For example, a marketing research department can be viewed as a centre for market knowledge, but the domain of market knowledge is shared with the sales and field service departments. Knowledge centres have the following characteristics:

- A specific knowledge domain which results from the centre's assignment or interest;
- A concentration of human and material carriers;
- Frequent interactions (informal or formal) within the centre;
- A mechanism to transfer the knowledge gained within the organization in its entirety.

Within the decentralized organization we find the same type of knowledge centre (such as marketing, MIS, quality control) within different business units. They are each other's mirror image, so to speak (Galbraith, 1994). One might speak of *local* knowledge centres with their own knowledge domain. Thus, the knowledge domain of a business unit is generally determined by the specific knowledge of the market place, the application of specific technologies in products, processes and services, and the organizational knowledge required to develop, produce, manufacture and provide and sell products and services. Box 3.5 lists the most important knowledge centres of a small IT firm.

Box 3.5. Knowledge centres in a small firm.

The core activity of OCC, a firm employing 28 people, is to sell a self-developed software package for salary administration. Four knowledge centres can be distinguished in this firm:

The *software development group*, which builds and re-builds the system, but also closely follows new technical developments (operating systems object-orientation). The group also ensures the development of the internal systems storing the group's own knowledge of software and content matter;

The *content experts*, who make sure that salary-specific matters (for example, changes in the law) are directly processed in the available packages. Together with the programmers they are part of the same team. The content experts and programmers use a scenario for the adjustment of the software packages;

The *helpdesk* in the sales department, which knows everything about clients' problems and needs; the helpdesk has a self-developed electronic handbook to which each new problem with its solution is added;

The *management team*, which does not only run the firm, but also possesses a specific skill which determines managerial activities: personnel policy. Accurate data concerning the most relevant facts about and agreed upon arrangements with staff are kept up to date in an electronic database by the staff and their bosses.

Knowledge Flows

Knowledge becomes valuable for an organization when it is used effectively. However, the route between the development of a new idea in a knowledge centre and its use is usually a long one. Other knowledge centres and carriers of knowledge must add to the knowledge.

A marketer is on to a market niche. Based on his knowledge of the market place he is able to make a rough draft of a new product, which he must first discuss within his own knowledge centre (a marketing group): does it fit in the portfolio, what are the expected risks and profits? Subsequently, an initial market exploration is carried out in order to test the draft in the market place. This is followed by product development, which makes a rough sketch of the product, and later process development and production, which check to see if the product can be manufactured. It is not until planners and calculators have provided insight into time and funding that the management of the business unit is able to give a go-ahead for the product and process development. Each link in this process adds value to the initial idea. Of course, it is also possible that value is destroyed, when somewhere along the line it is decided to cancel the project. Or the project may be temporarily mothballed due to lack of funding, but it may also be dismantled, for example by discontinuing the team of knowledge carriers or spreading it over other knowledge domains. Whatever the case, this example shows that knowledge in organizations does not obtain value until it is transmitted from one knowledge centre to the other.

Each group or department adds valuable knowledge to the product or service on its way to the customer. This value is converted into good currency at the end of the line, when the customer pays for it. In other words: the knowledge is transported in a value chain.

Comparison with a production chain, however, does not in general do justice to the complexity and dynamics of the processes in which knowledge is developed, transferred and used. Let's use a metaphor to get a grip on this complexity and dynamics: the metaphor of a *river delta*. Knowledge from various highly located sources flow to the market through the river and its branches. Yet the tides ensure that the salt water of the market place flows into the delta at fixed times. Once every couple of years, new ideas and new knowledge sources are responsible for flooding and changing the banks. Not only is knowledge continuously moving, the beds of the flow are also changing constantly. The 'flows chart' of the knowledge delta must be adapted on a regular basis. However, a number of main flows can be found in each organization which have eroded over time. These are the main flows that link the knowledge centres. A few of these have canalized, they are the navigable formal water ways with locks

Box 3.6. Knowledge in the value chain.

Any one organization is part of a value chain (Porter, 1985). For example, raw materials are purchased by suppliers and converted into half-products, which are then distributed by other firms. The firm uses the half-products to manufacture products, which reach the final consumer through wholesalers and retailers. Value is added in each of these stages. A value chain can also be distinguished inside the firm.

In doing so, the primary process (from purchase through production to the market) is traditionally chosen as the main axis, and the other activities (for example, product and process development) as 'supporting side-axis'. Most value is added along this main Axis a in the form of labour and capital. For the analysis of the organization as a knowledge system, however, the other chain is even more interesting: the Axis b which emphasizes innovation and knowledge development. The analysis of the value chain may lead to interesting discoveries. Starch producer AVEBE (Chapter 4), for example, discovered that it was able to reach a high cost saving in its own manufacturing process by investing in research on new potato varieties for its potato suppliers.

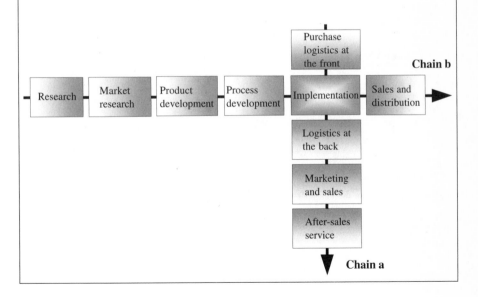

and bridges which may be responsible for long delays. Other flows have a far less predictable character; they are difficult to navigate, they burst their banks, or they may run dry.

It is essential within the knowledge enterprise to keep a good flows chart. Not only to plot effective courses of navigation, but also to visualize the water ways that must be deepened, canalized or provided with better concrete. Figure 3.8 illustrates the knowledge flows in and around a large software company. The firm is part of an international company. It possesses a New Technology (NT) unit, which translates new technological signals into services that can be sold. This happens on the basis of direct cooperation with 'lead users' and NT groups classified under the divisions. The flows chart of the knowledge enterprise distinguishes five main flows as follows:

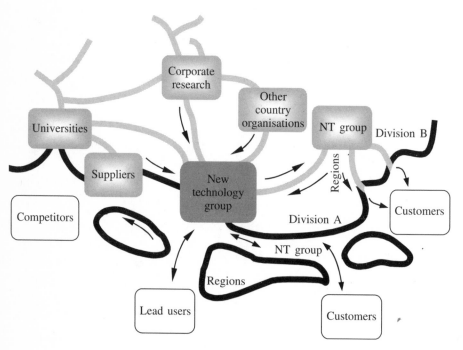

Figure 3.8. The knowledge delta.

The Vertical Flow

The vertical flow is concerned with the flow of knowledge between the centre of the organization and its periphery, for example that between:

- the corporate organization and the divisions and business units;
- the local points of sale and headquarters;
- production firms and the production division management;
- the production teams on the shop floor and the management.

Vertical flows of knowledge are hierarchical and possess a strong power component by definition. These flows are specially developed in bureaucracy (Mintzberg, 1979). Policies are delineated high up in the hierarchy and disseminated to the lower echelons. Investments in vertical information systems (Galbraith, 1973) ensure improved central assessment of what's going on locally. The first-generation Management Information Systems (MIS) are based on this argumentation. The information that must be collected locally is derived from the central need for information.

Vertical flows can be identified in two types of firms. First, in organizations that base their management on *standardization* of their products and services. Exemplars are not only McDonald's, Safeways, and Boots, but also public organizations such as Inland Revenue and ministries. Mintzberg refers to these organizations as 'machine bureaucracies'. The second type of firms, the 'professional bureaucracies' are characterized by the dominance of *functional structures*. The functional departments at the various levels (for example, production engineering, IT department, administration, and marketing and sales) form the bedding for the upward and downward knowledge flows. Most larger companies (see Chapter 4) have tried to take a distance from this organizational model in recent years. In the public sector, universities and hospitals can still be regarded as the perfect examples of this type of organization.

The Horizontal Flow: Right Across Functions

In the horizontal flow, knowledge flows move from one organizational function (for example, marketing) to the next (for example, purchase) and often back in a reverzed direction. Horizontal knowledge flows in compartmentalized bureaucracies tend to run into walls that separate the functional knowledge domains. For that reason, the majority of modern organizations have created facilities that promote the progress of horizontal transport of knowledge. The necessity to operate more customer-centred and develop processes, products and services more rapidly has contributed to this. The introduction of self-managing units (business units), matrix structures, project management, and multidisciplinary teams (see Chapter 6) provide the channels for these horizontal flows.

The Horizontal Flow: From Business to Business

Because company entities, such as the business unit, became more autonomous, the basic functions (marketing, R&D and production) are more closely linked both to each other and to the business. As a result, preconditions are created for improved knowledge flows across functions. A common domain is constructed: the business. However, the boundaries of this new domain also bring with them limitations for the knowledge flows between the business units. There is a risk that one loses sight of such matters as knowledge synergy between the units, long-term knowledge development, and the preservation of the critical mass of the decentralized knowledge centres. In other words, the old horizontal flows from the functional organization must be scooped out again or canalized.

The Geographical Flow: From Branch to Branch

Geographical spreading of production and sales branches is a well-known given. Geographical spreading imposes high demands upon the knowledge flows, even more so when such knowledge-intensive business functions as R&D, engineering and marketing are spread. Market leadership is an important factor here. A great deal of firms strive to underpin their position as market share leader by focusing on core competencies and core business. They take over firms in order to increase their sales and production potential for core business. These acquisitions are then partly funded by hiving off business that does not belong to the core. Thus, Gist-brocades (Chapter 4) sold its interests in industrial enzymes and reinforced its position for products as yeast and antibiotics. The net effect of this shift is the expansion of the number of foreign sales and manufacturing branches. However, the focus on core competencies implies at the same time that a higher value and hence more knowledge is added to products and services. Salespersons and manufacturers are expected to possess more knowledge than previously. With branches located at a large geographical distance, this is no *sinecure*, as starch producer AVEBE (Chapter 4) experienced. Managing knowledge flows is an absolute necessity to keep the business together.

External Flows

Intensifying the exchange of knowledge with surrounding knowledge centres is a general trend in organizations. Managers are becoming aware that an extrovert attitude and outward view has major advantages. A great number of companies must free themselves from the 'not-invented here' syndrome when doing so. For example *suppliers* and *customers* work more closely together than they used to. They participate in each other's product and process development chains, enabling them to add more value with knowledge. Specialists working for customers are thus becoming colleagues with whom they cooperate on a daily basis.

Moreover, companies choose increasingly for strategic cooperation when developing products, services and processes. This cooperation particularly focuses on developments that individual companies are unable to cope with, and on developments in which companies complement each other. *Outsourcing* may lead to efficiency and reduction of the management burden. In general, exchangeable competencies are given up. Finally, companies try to benefit more from the (fundamental) knowledge developed in *universities*.

External knowledge flows always require special arrangements. This holds true even of outsourcing. When knowledge is purchased, sufficient knowledge of purchasing must at least continue to be available. For each 'knowledge import' flow the organization must possess sufficient *absorbing capacity* (Cohen and Levinthal, 1990) to select relevant external knowledge and translate it into its own business situation. It may be advantageous to gradually build up a knowledge network around the company, which enables firms to look into each other's kitchen on the basis of trust. The advantage of this is that the firms can build further upon existing relationships in the case of new developments. In some sectors, for example the dairy sector, firms can make use of the services provided by public or commonly funded knowledge institutes such as MIT or the German Fraunhofer Institutes. For creative, not quite straightforward ideas, the firm continues to be dependent on its own experts who have a particularly sensitive antenna for weak signals: 'gatekeepers', who set about to gain fresh ideas outside. The search for a new detection technology at HAK (Box 3.3) would have come down to nothing without that special feeler.

Functional Demands

What functional demands should the organization fulfil in order to achieve the knowledge ambition? The answer to this question is the third step in the knowledge enterprise. The functional demands are the point of departure for the next step: the redesign. The use of knowledge management tools makes no sense unless one knows what should be improved in the organization. This is not possible until the current situation is mapped and compared to the situation that is desired in order to be able to achieve the knowledge ambition. In other words, the functional demands are formulated by means of a gap analysis, a comparison of 'IST' and 'SOLL'. We will illustrate this approach using a strongly simplified example.

An Example

A manufacturer of exclusive office furniture employing 70 people wants to manufacture products with a higher added value. The firm decides to carry out total design projects for entire office buildings. This is possible because negotiations are ongoing with a large company which is very much taken with the firm's products and is inclined to design the entire new head office according to the style of the furniture manufacturer. The decision is moreover compatible with the core competencies of the firm:

- Designing exclusive furniture;
- Supplying small batches according to customer specification;
- Knowledge of demands placed on furniture in an office environment.

The Knowledge Ambition

Another implication of this choice, however, is that the core competencies and the enabling competencies must be stretched and expanded. The knowledge ambition defines the following new competencies:

- The design of projects;
- The management of complex projects at the customers' premises;
- Efficient and timely delivery of project orders in addition to the normal (product) order;
- The development and maintenance of relationships with customers.

The firm largely possesses the functional and contextual knowledge to enter into the new challenge. Yet does the same hold true of the operational knowledge?

The Knowledge Flows Chart

The next step in formulating the functional demands for the redesign is to map the knowledge enterprise (the knowledge 'system'). In so doing, four elements must be identified:

- The knowledge centres (where is knowledge developed, brought in, or gained?);
- The knowledge flows (from where to where does the knowledge flow?);
- The most relevant control loops (where does feedback take place?);
- The knowledge development strategy (how is knowledge developed?).

This leads to the knowledge flows chart in the furniture firm illustrated in Figure 3.9. The firm's current knowledge is concentrated in three groups (sales, designers and manufacturing). These groups cooperate only when this is absolutely necessary. Knowledge development is based mainly on the ripple strategy. The control loop between sales and manufacturing is closed, the one between sales, customers and designers is hardly closed. Nor is that between the designers and the factory.

The Gap Analysis

Keeping in mind the knowledge ambition, the gaps between IST and SOLL are indicated, which serve as a basis for the definition of the functional demands. The knowledge flows chart is filled in on the basis of the following questions:

- Which knowledge centres require reinforcement?
- Which knowledge flows need to be intensified?

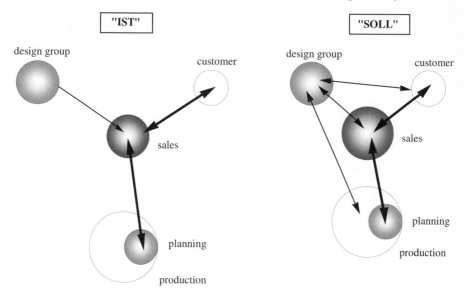

Figure 3.9. The knowledge flows chart.

- Which control loops should be closed more tightly or shortened?
- Is a new knowledge development strategy needed?

On the basis of the knowledge flows chart the firm checks to see whether or not it can deal with the knowledge ambition. This analysis shows the following gaps:

- The designers operate separately and will have to function as a team; designs must be embedded in a broader concept;
- The designers do not take into account manufacturing consequencs in their design, but will have to do so in project work;
- There is a lack of project managers in the sales department;
- Designers and (project) salespersons are not accustomed to working together; there is a lack of feedback from the market;
- The logistic knowledge and tools are lacking in order to adequately guide product and project orders together through the manufacturing process;

- Sales, design groups and manufacturing deal with today's business, but seldom discuss tomorrow's business;
- The customer does not come into the picture until the furniture is sold.

Functional Demands

The functional demands are formulated on the basis of the gap analysis:

- A powerful design centre which is able to depart from system conception, communicates with sales and the customer, and anticipates production opportunities;
- Reinforcement of the logistic competence and information flows across the firm;
- Knowledge and information must be pumped continuously between sales, manufacturing and the design group;
- Expert project management must be built up within the sales department.

   Once the knowledge ambition and functional demands for the organization are written down, a large number of managers will ask themselves whether they have made the right strategic decisions. When looking back at what the organization is expected to yield, isn't it just a bridge too far? This question is a realistic one in the example given above. The furniture manufacturer will have to transform into a professional service provider in a very short period of time. The opportunity offered by the customer should not be wasted. Adjustment of the ambition appears to be a logical reaction in that case. Yet the philosophical question remains: 'Isn't it true that innovation comes about by neglecting warnings?' To which cynics will immediately add: 'But doesn't the same hold true of major failures?' What the entrepreneur should do is make a choice (s)he believes in and for which (s)he can enthuse the organization.

PART II
THE KNOWLEDGE PRACTICE

Chapter 4

The Knowledge Enterprise in Actual Practice

This chapter presents seven company case studies, which serve to illustrate the development of the knowledge enterprise in seven Dutch market share leaders in the service and industrial sectors: AVEBE, DSM Andeno, Gist-brocades, Moret Ernst & Young, Nationale Nederlanden, Pink Elephant, and Stork. The working method followed in this study is briefly outlined. It is not our intention to present best-practice cases. In fact, real change cannot take place by copying best practice. Organizational innovation is predominantly a learning process that requires inspiration, insight and recognition. This implies lateral thinking: thinking beyond the boundaries of one's own organizational domain.

Lateral Thinking

Practice is the richest breeding ground for organizational innovation. A firm deviates from existing patterns because its management is facing a problem that the available solutions won't fix. It was like that in the past, and it is still like that today, whether we are talking about self-managing teams in the coal mines of Durham, JIT at Toyota, BPR at Ford, or benchmarking at Rank Xerox. To organization scientists, these first crucial experiments were the starting block for theorizing and developing tools to bring the theory into practice. Practice is also the most important vehicle for learning. By bringing new ideas into practice one actually *learns* to bring new ideas into practice. The lessons drawn from one's own mistakes are the affluence of the organization. One should cherish them as inalienable property. However, learning from one's own experiences is generally a long-lasting and painful process. Managers who are convinced of the need for change tend to look for ways to shorten the change trajectory. They look at firms that were there first. Their motives for doing so are different. First, they want to take over imitable practices. Why bother inventing something that others have already done? The second argument is that other people's experiences show where the pitfalls are to be found. These risks are an argument for some managers to refrain from action and leave things the way they are. But the most important argument to pry in a frontrunner's kitchen is to become convinced that a specific organizational innovation really works. To gain cogency for a new policy. It is not surprising, therefore, that the best practice is the peak in each management conference.

Yet *can* best practice be copied? Part of this question can be answered in the affirmative: it is possible to copy innovations based on explicit knowledge. The organization can purchase the same database and personnel information systems, implement intranet, establish technology councils, and set up training programmes based on the same pattern. The heart of the change, however, generally lies in the implicit knowledge which is interwoven with the organization itself. Firms have a different *past history*. Some firms (for example Stork and AKZO Nobel) are the result of the gradual integration of various firms. The culture of fairly independent operating companies was quite strongly felt even before business units were being created. Other firms (DSM, Gist-brocades, and AVEBE) were initially bulk producers with a distinctly centralized culture. In recent years they have chosen for a strong decentralization in order to better serve special markets.

Knowledge and organization can also be interwoven as a result of the *specific relationship with the environment*. Thus, developers from DSM Andeno work closely together on a one-to-one basis with the customer's developers. At Nationale Nederlanden, the interface with the customer takes place much more at the implementation level.

Finally, knowledge and organization are interwoven with the *organization's internal design*. One firm (DSM) has a central lab, while the other (Gist-brocades) does not. In addition, there is a difference between firms that belong to a large corporation and the independent firms.

Box 4.1. Real change

> The firm belief in 'best practice' and easily imitable solutions leads at best to the insight that these don't really help. A large number of firms experienced this following the introduction of total quality management using crash programs. This was revealed by a study into innovation management among 62 Dutch firms, carried out at MERIT in 1994 (Cobbenhagen *et al.*, 1994). In this study, frontrunners and pack members were compared in 30 sectors. Curiously, ISO certification was found more among pack members than among frontrunners. One of the important reasons for this was the different way in which firms look at the process of quality control. The majority of pack members tend to view the systems and procedures as objectives in themselves, whereas frontrunners more often recognize that the attitude and behaviour of managers and workers should 'really' change.

These three aspects can be clearly retraced in the seven company cases presented in this chapter. The seven companies can be considered as being frontrunners and market leaders in their own local or even international markets. In other words, they face the absolute need to distinguish from other firms. They must do things sooner than their competitors. It also means that they make mistakes that other firms will also make after them. In this sense, the company cases are not examples of best practice. The development processes that the seven firms have gone through cannot be copied. So why bother to describe these processes along with their problems and solutions? We bother because when forming an image of their firm, managers must be able to look beyond its boundaries. Organizational innovation requires lateral thinking. To use the words of De Bono (1971) 'rather than digging deeper into the existing hole', we acquire inspiration elsewhere. 'Aha-erlebnissen' are often felt when looking into completely different areas, for example when a manager of an insurance company gets to talking with a colleague working for a chemical specialities producer.

By delving into the development processes of other firms one can gain more insight into these processes. No doubt, the firm will come across comparable phenomena in the knowledge enterprise sooner or later. It is essential that it can dissociate itself from that. In order to reflect upon one's own behaviour one should look through another pair of glasses, so to speak, to use a different frame of mind than the one that is generally used. Inspiration to change tack, insight into issues that really matter, and awareness of the pitfalls are more valuable than the rapid implementation of 'canned' success stories. These are preconditions for learning behaviour. It's like cheating at school: it only helps to temporarily pep up a grade. Cheating does not suffice to successfully complete a training programme.

Working Method

The company cases are based on a study commissioned by the European Union and performed by MERIT (Andreasen *et al.*, 1995). We were able to expand this study through the support of the Dutch Ministry of Economic Affairs (Den Hertog, 1996). It was moreover a follow-up to a previous study into innovation management in the processing industry (Den Hertog *et al.*, 1996). Literature survey, exploratory interviews with managers from eight companies, and a workshop with R&D managers from ten companies served as a preparation. In the study itself, open interviews were held with three or four managers per company, who had been involved, in various roles, in organizational innovation processes within their firms. Both the corporate organization and the business unit were involved in these processes. The resulting case reports have been thoroughly discussed with the representatives of the firms in question. A total of 13 market leaders have been approached for this study. Three companies were unable to take part in the research due to internal developments at the time. Three other case reports have been published elsewhere (Den Hertog and Van Sluijs, 1995). For the study, we had been looking for firms in both industry and services (see Table 4.1) which

Table 4.1. The participating companies.

Firm	Status	Products/Services	Number of Employees
AVEBE	Independent, cooperative company	Starch and starch derivatives	2,200
DSM Andeno	Business unit of the DSM Fine Chemicals Division	Chemical components for pharmaceutical products	725
Gist-brocades	Independent company	Yeast, antibiotics and related specialities	6,200
Moret, Ernst & Young	Part of Ernst & Young International in federative terms	Accountancy, tax and organizational advice	4,200
Nationale Nederlanden	General insurance section of NN (NN is part of ING)	General insurance policies	2,200
Pink Elephant	Operating company of Pink Roccade	Life-cycle management of computer centres	1,100
Stork	Independent company	Industrial (manufacturing) systems, engineering	18,000

clearly recognize the significance of knowledge synergy and the development of competencies. For a detailed description of this approach, see Den Hertog (1996).

AVEBE: Focusing on the Value Chain

AVEBE is one of Europe's market share leaders in the starch industry. The firm processes potatoes into a broad range of starch products and derivatives. AVEBE's products are retraced as raw materials in (animal) food, paper, pharmaceutical products, textiles, and adhesives. AVEBE is a cooperative company and property of its suppliers, the potato agriculture. The firm was established in 1918 with the aim of providing its suppliers with their own market channel for the supply of potato starch. Originally, AVEBE is a bulk producer with a leading position in the starch market. The basis for this position is the knowledge about starch, starch derivatives and process know-how. However, AVEBE's playing field has fundamentally changed in recent years. Competition has become harder partly due to the emergence of substitutes (corn and wheat). The margins for bulk products are low. Rules concerning health care and the environment have become more stringent both at the national and European levels. In addition, the firm will gradually have to anticipate declining European agricultural subsidies.

AVEBE initiated a far-reaching transformation process four years ago to be able to stay on course. The firm is developing into a technologically advanced and market-centred company. This transformation implies another orientation towards the market: the 'functionality' of a product and added value will be more important than the price per ton. The introduction of business units, which became formal on 1 February 1995, is an important step in this development. The restructuring has required AVEBE to carry through extensive cost reductions. Although the strategic importance of the R&D function has been left untouched, fundamental changes have been initiated in focus, organizational anchoring and steering of the R&D function. These changes are both directed at serving today's business and at providing the basis of tomorrow's business. The following contribution, which underlines the integral character of the change process, focuses on this transformation. A new strategic focus on the environment is useful only when it addresses the structure and culture of the firm in its entirety.

From Bulk to Functionality

In the past, the future of AVEBE seemed to be self-evident: the firm enjoyed a powerful position in raw materials with a self-evident raw material: potatoes. Cost leadership was the self-evident business strategy. Powerful R&D and engineering were self-evident parts of that strategy. Production, with its impressive machinery, was the iron heart of the company. The culture of the firm was bulk-centred and cost-centred, which was reflected in a conservative, risk-aversive and introvert climate. To put it differently, in the bulk industry one must ensure that the 'kettles continue to be full' and that production kept on going with as few interruptions and changes as possible. Experiments with new products are viewed in such a culture as inopportune disturbances of ongoing processes, particularly in the case of products manufactured in small quantities. This bulk culture was reflected in the firm's structure, for which the functional focus was the point of departure.

Thus, AVEBE was run until the early 1990s by a management which was primarily represented by the main functions (marketing, production and finance) rather than the business. Production held a powerful position in top management, which was also reflected in the influence of branch managers. This functional division applied to the organization from the top management to the shop floor. R&D was centralized in this set-up. In this culture, the words strategy, marketing, and product innovation hardly had a real meaning. Plans were operational plans, marketing mainly meant sales, and innovation was product improvement. Early in the history of the starch industry in the north of the Netherlands, it was recognized that market leadership can be kept up only on the basis of exclusive know-how.

In the early 1990s, however, it became clear that the future of AVEBE had lost its self-evidence. A number of market segments corroded. The margins were small, also due to the emergence of substitute raw materials such as corn and (especially) wheat. AVEBE had to compete against true bulk-purchase prices by rival firms. Meanwhile, its competitors had also provided themselves with 'exclusive' knowledge. In addition, AVEBE had to adjust to the increasingly stringent rules at the national and European level in the area of health and environment. It was impossible to safeguard the future of the firm with cost reductions alone. This required more: a new strategy, and a new company culture and structure.

In 1993, the firm adopted a strategy which focused on the following objectives:

- Maintenance of market share in Europe;
- The development of new market places with existing products (Eastern Asia in particular);
- Widening the raw material position with a view to increasing sales;
- Substantial and continuous improvement of stages in the existing complete value chains;
- Producing new products with a high added value.

These objectives mark the transition from a pure bulk producer and cost leader to a firm where the *functionality* of the products comes first. Functionality means that the client is interested in 'what he can do with the product' rather than 'what the product costs'. Central are the profits yielded by the product in the customer's process.

Box 4.2. AVEBE.

AVEBE produces starch and starch derivatives. Its most important markets are: (cattle) feed industry, the paper industry, the textile and adhesives industries, bore-rinsing machines, and the pharmaceutical industry. The turnover of the firm was 1,214 millions of guilders in 1994–1995. The net company profits amounted to 22.7 millions of guilders in 1995. The firm employs around 1,500 people in the Netherlands and between 600 and 700 abroad. During the 1993–1995 period, AVEBE carried through a far-reaching cost reduction programme in which jobs were lost. AVEBE invested 28 millions of guilders — 2 per cent of net turnover — in R&D in 1995. The firm has four business units each having a known market:

- Food and Pharma;
- Paper;
- Technical Applications;
- Starch and Cattle Feed.

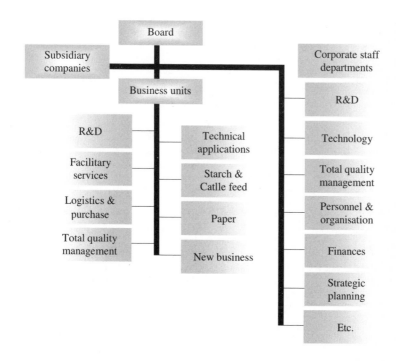

A fifth business unit has been established for a market which is as yet 'unknown': New Business. R&D is decentralized to an substantial degree. Fifty out of a total of 140 R&D workers are active in the business units, and 90 of them in the corporate research department. Twenty percent of the total R&D budget is designated for innovative and explorative research.

AVEBE's core competencies focus on 'the production and processing of starch and resulting side-products into starch derivatives and other starch products'. The most relevant disciplines applied for this are organic chemistry, chemical analysis, biotechnology, and process technology. AVEBE encompasses eight production centres in six countries, and sales organizations in 14 countries.

Organizational Innovation

The new strategic objectives require a new organization. Functionality implies that the firm should be able to get under the customer's skin and develop effective cooperation patterns with customers. As a logical consequence, the firm has had to transform from an inward-looking and product-centred organization into an open and market-oriented organization.

The most visible change in this process was the introduction of business units. The firm's corporate management was reduced to two persons. Discipline-orientation hardly played a role in the task division between the two of them. Four business units were set up, each of them having a clear product/market profile. Being responsible for the three key elements of business — marketing, R&D and production — these units may rightly be called 'strategic' business units. They made their own strategic analyses and plans, while the board continued an evaluation role. The positions of branch and production managers were relinquished in the new organization. Engineering fulfils the role of service provider rather than having a steering role. When forming the business units, the organization has tried to avoid the existence of 'double functions' as much as possible. The expertise available is used as effectively as possible. Business units are not expected to possess all of the expertise and capacity needed. They heavily rely upon each other and exchange capacity on a regular basis. The role of the corporate organisation has been restricted substantially, incorporating common services and the specialists concentrating on long-term issues — a stimulating rather than a directing role.

Innovation

In the new organization, the business units are held responsible for innovation oriented towards existing markets and technologies. Fifty out of a total of 140 R&D workers have been decentralized to the business units. They are expected to report to the unit R&D managers. The remaining 90 R&D workers both have a stimulating and a mind-broadening task. Little has changed in a physical sense as a result of decentralization. The entire local and central R&D function is still operating in the same location. Little has changed also in their informal contacts. What essentially differs is the way in which R&D is steered. The corporate R&D programme is the result of an intensive brainstorm across all units and functions. Efforts were made to bring a clear focus in the programme and to protect the long-term R&D from day-to-day pressure as much as possible. At the corporate level, the emphasis is on Research, while it is on Development in the business units. Frequent meetings between corporate R&D and business unit R&D focus on the long-term programmes, discussing centrally allocated capacity as well as the 20 per cent of local R&D designated for long-term projects. The corporate R&D department moreover has an important task in linking up with universities and other external institutions. The aim of AVEBE for the coming years is to subcontract research or cooperate with third parties.

The distance between the R&D and marketing functions has been dramatically reduced within the business units. A dialogue has been initiated about strategic issues. Open discussions about the product and project portfolio take place increasingly at an early stage. These discussions are held more and more on the basis of equivalence of functions (marketing, R&D and production). One business unit may be in a more advanced stage than the other. Some units attach great importance to the portfolio and value chain analyses being performed within the organization. In their vision, strategic and operational plans require a broad base in the organization for their implementation. This base as well as consensus about the new direction are considered to be more important than the concrete form of the analysis outcome. It is imperative that marketers, producers and developers understand each other's argumentation and be able to think along with each other. In any case, this will prevent the analysis outcome from disappearing in some drawer like they did previously. At the operational level, the responsibility of project leaders has clearly increased. They are responsible for the entire development trajectory from the moment the project is defined: composing the team, hiring other AVEBE capacity, and upscaling in the factory. The effects of this integral responsibility have become visible in the reduction of the time-to-market.

Interaction between the business units, mainly based on the need to use the capacity and expertise as effectively as possible within a tight budget, is rising. Business managers and R&D managers are thus encouraged to have a look in each other's laboratories. In this process, the business units exchange the outcome of their portfolio analyses, thus showing the innovation course of the business units. This development primarily results in the *exchange* of expertise rather than cooperation efforts with a view to a further common objective.

A fifth business unit (New Business, NB) has been set up for the development of *new business*. It was recognized that this function would come off badly within the existing business units which mainly focus on existing applications in existing markets. Searching, defining and serving unknown markets requires a different way of working. This new way of working is still being developed. New networks have to be built and developed, for example, with trade associations, universities and clients. New Business concentrates both on sectors in which starch derivatives can replace the raw materials used, and on chains in which the use of new starch derivatives may enhance the added value. In this approach, the products that can be applied within the various new markets are particularly attractive. New Business attempts to avoid the risk of fragmentation by focusing attention on the exploration of potential markets as well as assessing technical and commercial feasibility.

Information technology is expected to play a more forceful role in AVEBE's organization function in the future. IT was strongly administrative in character in the past and quite static in terms of laboratory know-how. The development and use of dynamic systems is one of the future tasks at AVEBE. In the coming years, the functionality of IT will be reflected in the value chain of the business unit.

It is recognized that personnel policy can and must be a powerful tool within the new AVEBE organization. Increasingly, Personnel and Organization managers are involved in new plans and projects at an early stage. Training, personnel assessment and planning play an important role here.

Interim Score

The organizational restructuring of AVEBE is a comprehensive process which leaves no single role or position untouched. This process has not finished yet. After adequate preparation, the fundamental structure was established, and the firm is working hard to bring this structure to life. Taking an interim score, most managers appear to view the introduction of business units as a clear step forward, even though it will take some time for the picture of the market, the technology and the organization at unit level to take shape. In any case, the customer has 'come into the picture', not only for salespersons and marketers, but for developers and producers as well. Organizational processes have been streamlined. Responsibilities have been tied more closely to the customer. Additionally, numerous problems that remained opaque in the old organization have become transparent. As a result, the list of issues requiring improvement or new solutions is expected to be long for some time. These new challenges can be summarized as follows:

Firstly, a new balance must be found between *technology push* and *market pull*. Innovation must clearly be more market-centred. At the same time, however, there exists growing awareness that the technological boundaries must be stretched in order for AVEBE to distinguish from its competitors in the future. This leads to a tension between the tendency to protect mind-broadening R&D ('hedging') and the call for more explorative and basic R&D. The latter is mainly concerned with the improvement of process control in production. As a result of the introduction of business units the business demands imposed on production have become clearer and more explicit, which has contributed to improvement in that area. The relationships, procedures and mainly communication between the corporate and unit organizations have not as yet been fully crystallized.

The relationships between the three core functions (marketing, production and R&D) at the level of the business unit have been visibly improved. Yet the introduction of the new way of working to which the concept of 'functionality' is central is not as swift in the *sales organization* as one would wish. The struggle for the customer is won no longer by selling just below competitor prices. Salesmen are expected to play a more active role in tracking and warming up customers for functions that the new AVEBE products can fulfill. 'Sales' is increasingly becoming 'cooperation with customers'. Meanwhile, a great deal of effort is made to inform and train the AVEBE sales organization. In the longer run, the links between the application-centred research and the geographically spread sales functions are in need of improvement.

It is recognized that the new approach also requires another way of communicating, not only between hierarchical levels, but across functions and business boundaries as well. For this purpose the culture change programme MOTOR was set up, ascertaining the *dialogue* as being a norm for communication: communicating on the basis of equivalence, comprehension for each other's stances, and the intention to reach consensus through deliberation. The framework for this new form of communication is anchored in the new structure and begins to pay off within the business units, for example, in the relationships between marketing and R&D. Yet AVEBE is aware that old communication patterns in lots of interfaces have to be unlearned. In line with this observation is the emphasis that the AVEBE management wants to place upon the development of self-managing workgroups in the coming years.

Synergy

The business units are forced to make do with what they've got. They cannot afford duplication, which is a perfect incentive to scrounge with each other. This process has been set in motion. One is interested in the pots put on the stove in the other units and does not tend to hedge one's own activities and build up one's own little paradises. The relevance of synergy between the business units is recognized in the new organization. This holds true especially when direct economic advantage is to be gained through short-term co-operation, for example in the case of using each other's laboratory or in the case of the joint establishment of a production facility in Indonesia. Due to the physical concentration of local and central R&D, a strongly informal cooperation continues to be possible. Yet there are a number of limitations. The various business units make use of the same disciplines (mainly organic chemistry and biotechnology), but most R&D staff have become one with their specific products and technologies to a large extent. This does not only limit their personal mobility, but the mobility of their know-how as well. Bundling and exchanging knowledge across the boundaries of the business units so far has taken place on an *ad hoc* rather than on a systematic basis. When the knowledge domains of the business units and corporate R&D have consolidated, this aspect must be given attention. The cycles of the strategic analysis offer a good point of departure for this at both the corporate and unit level.

DSM Andeno: On Speaking Terms with the Pharmaceutical Top

Business Transformation

DSM Andeno develops and produces intermediates for the pharmaceutical industry. In 1987, the firm, which was until then owned by Océ Van der Grinten, was taken over by DSM. Technological changes in the copier sector compelled the latter to reorient its business. DSM Andeno realized a highly successful transition in a relatively short time period: from manufacturer of repro-chemicals into a flourishing fine chemical/pharmaceutical firm. This transition was based on two factors. Firstly, the breadth and depth of DSM Andeno's core competencies. Second, the take-over was perfectly in line with the DSM strategy which attached great importance to the build-up of fine chemicals. In this way, the firm was able to engage in the development of new products and the exploitation of new markets on the basis of exclusive knowledge. The transition was not realized from one day to the next. For a while there had existed a technological cooperation with DSM concerning the use of the raw material D, L-phenylglycin. Additionally, DSM played an important role prior to the take-over in the development of intermediates for antibiotics. Yet this did not render the successful business transition within DSM Andeno any less impressive. It illustrates the relevance of exclusive know-how in the development of new business.

The continuous development of new knowledge played an equally important role in the new environment. DSM Andeno mainly develops tailor-made products for individual customers. If a customer no longer needs the intermediate after the introduction of a new product, the complete turnover of that specific intermediate is lost at one stroke.

Box 4.3. DSM Andeno.

DSM Andeno is one of the four business units (BU) of DSM's Fine Chemicals Division. This division incorporates three other business units: DSM Special Products, Chemie Linz and Holland Sweetener Company, a 50 per cent joint venture with the Japanese Tosoh. DSM Andeno develops and produces intermediates for the pharmaceutical industry, for example for cardiovascular drugs, antibiotics, and drugs for central nervous system and respiratory disorders. The strength of the BU is based on a relatively broad range of competencies, such as resolutions, bio- and chemo-catalysis, and asymmetrical synthesis. Extremely high demands are placed on its staff, who are expected to measure up to researchers and product developers at every single level. The pharmaceutical industry moreover imposes extremely heavy quality norms on its products. Within the chemical sector, DSM Andeno is a highly evolved specialist. The BU's portfolio is in line with the DSM strategy, in which the development of a powerful fine chemicals division offers opportunities to become less dependent on economic fluctuation. In 1995, turnover was Fl. 320 million (compared to a DSM turnover of more than Fl. 9 billion). In the same year DSM Andeno employed 725 people. Due to the recent acquisition by the fine chemical division of the Austrian fine chemical company Chemie Linz in 1996 the BU has further reinforced its position in the pharmaceutical market. DSM Andeno can be regarded as a flourishing branch of the DSM conglomerate. It has four production locations in the Netherlands (Venlo and Maarssen), Germany, Switzerland, and sales offices in eight countries. In addition, DSM Andeno participates in a number of other firms. In 1995, it founded the biotechnology firm Chemferm in conjunction with Gist-brocades.

DSM Andeno has its own R&D department employing approximately 70 people, who focus on product and process development. For fundamental and long-term research, the business unit can appeal to the

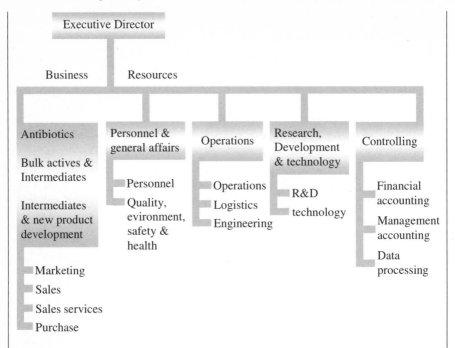

fine chemical department of the corporate (or in DSM jargon: 'Central') R&D lab of DSM in Geleen. Ninety percent of the costs of this department (employing a staff of about 90) are funded by four business units. The contents of this 90 percent is subject to deliberation between the lab and the units. Around 15 per cent of this fine chemical group is set up for bio-organic research for the benefit of DSM Andeno. While the researchers involved also belong to the DSM Andeno organization, the leader of this group is part of both the corporate lab and the business unit. The remaining 10 per cent of the R&D lab are funded from a corporate budget and is allotted for explorative and strategic research.

Time-to-Market

In the 1992-1993 period, the DSM Andeno management ascertained that the factor 'time' was playing an increasingly important role in the pharmaceutical market. The pharmaceutical industry is under enormous pressure to reduce the time-to-market, which is directly felt by the suppliers of intermediates, such as DSM Andeno. The time pressure has other effects as well. DSM operates on a one-to-one basis with its large customers, which implies that it should be able to point out to them at an early stage of product development the opportunities that DSM Andeno can offer. By timely anticipating the customer's problems, DSM Andeno has been able to add more value to the customer's chain. As a consequence of this strategy, DSM Andeno had to speed up its development pace even more than its customers. A forceful impulse had to be given to the internal organization to accelerate development processes.

Additionally, it was recognized that a knowledge-intensive company cannot afford to develop all of the necessary know-how itself. This holds true particularly in a market where the most important trends in knowledge development ('state-of-art science') referred to in the scientific literature offer many insights for customers as well. The business unit should be more open to knowledge development in its environment (including DSM) and get rid of the not-invented-here syndrome.

Organizational Innovations

The organizational innovations at DSM Andeno form a coherent set of measures, which clearly show the market orientation:

From a Functional to a Product-Centred Organization

DSM's organization was characterized by powerful functions until 1993. For example, the development department consisted of separate groups for chemical research, analysis and technology. Only the chemical group was distinctly product-centred. The current organization is more focused on products. As a first step to achieve this, product orientation was introduced in the analysis and technology groups, followed by the integration of these groups into product-centred units. At the same time, the direct administrative relationship between the development departments was redefined. Thus, the development department in Venlo, which used to be a part of the 'Venlo Site', is essentially a part of the business unit at present.

Project Management

The basic dimension of management has rotated from vertical (the function) to horizontal (the product). The project leader is in charge here and responsible for the entire development trajectory including the first production run in the factory. Not only is (s)he held responsible, (s)he also possesses the authority (steering tools) to do so. Project managers are now better equipped and empowered to perform this job. Project leaders are trained within the firm, where much attention is devoted to coaching, training in project management and setting up career paths. The relevance of parallel working in project management is recognized. In other words, groups keep each other informed in such a way that they do not necessarily have to wait for each other in the development chain. Due to the resulting overlap of development phases, the throughput time of the project can be considerably reduced. Additionally, the project leaders meet each other in project leader meetings on a regular basis. These meetings discuss the various projects as well as the learning experiences gained in projects which may be relevant to others. Project evaluation amounts to more in this approach than formal assessment, and is particularly intended to hold on to and transfer learning experiences.

Information Technology (IT)

The introduction of information technology (IT) at DSM Andeno is making progress rapidly. DSM is currently preparing the introduction of the SAP system. The opportunities offered by this system are seized by DSM Andeno to communicate quicker and better and to control projects in both financial and planning terms. The system is moreover increasingly used for storage and retrieval of product recipes and related production knowledge. The objective is to make these accessible to other users within the firm. The systematic storage of knowledge and experience is a recent application of the SAP system. In the maintenance sector, practical knowledge ('the tricks of the trade') stored for general usage by all those involved. In this way, it is also tried to hold on to the know-how of the 'old stagers', in particular, the know-how that would have gone lost after a transfer or pension. To date, the application of IT has focused on the information flows between functions, projects and sites within DSM Andeno itself. A next step will involve linkage with other DSM divisions, to be followed, in 1996, by connecting the local DSM Andeno network to the wider DSM network.

Interface Management

Interface communication between the main functions (marketing, R&D and production) left much to be desired in the past, particularly concerning the interfaces in the business chain. The firm was extremely technology-driven. To put it in black-and-white: the Development department offered product options and it was up to the Marketing department to find customers for these. Additionally, Development often confronted Production with a new product in far too late a stage. This situation has been altered significantly by the introduction of business teams and product teams. The three current business teams (see Box 4.3) consist of: the business managers, the site managers, the product managers, the development manager(s) and the controller. These teams fulfil the function of a management team, setting out the strategic policy for the business, test proposals put forward by the product teams, and cut the knot when this is impossible to do at a lower echelon.

The product team Technology is closely related to the projects. The team recognizes new development needs, opportunities and bottlenecks, monitors projects, and provides input for the technology policy for the business teams. The Technology product teams are composed of the development manager, the product manager, a site representative, and *ad hoc* project managers. This interface management has had, in the first instance, mainly positive effects on the relationship between Marketing and R&D. Meanwhile, the relation between R&D and Production at the sites is also smoother than it used to be previously.

Personnel policy has appeared to be an important tool in the restructuring that DSM Andeno has undergone during the past years. When staffing the new organization, the qualities and potential of the existing staff have been critically considered. The employees of the 'old' organization were invited to apply for the positions in the new organization, which process was not always without disappointment, as was to be expected. In retrospect, it has appeared to be an effective way of turning the organization around. The new organization has continued on the line of personnel development. A systematic follow up has been given to career planning, job rotation, training, coaching, and personnel assessment. The 'skills management' has so far been concentrated on individuals. Long-term training schemes have been outlined, and interviews are held with each employee twice a year, which discuss both past performance and preparation (or 'coaching') for the future.

New Product Development (NPD)

New Product Development (NPD) is an organizational unit which particularly focuses on new applications and innovative customers from the viewpoint of the existing technology. In the early development phase of a product, where DSM Andeno sits at the table with the customer, it must exhibit its know-how and experience and be able to react quickly to the opportunities offered by the customer. In other words, it has to 'nestle' in the customer's development chain. For this purpose, it requires a precocious and decisive team. At DSM Andeno this team is sometimes called 'our lifeline to the future'. NPD incorporates a separate service group 'Rescom', which produces different quantities (varying from several grams to hundreds of kilos) of intermediates in the initial development phases of product development of the customer.

Business development and acquisition have been incorporated at the level of fine chemical division ('Business Group'). The strength of the business units at DSM lies in the clear focus on defined product/market combinations. They know where they stand. Business development is concerned with the responsibility for products and markets that 'haven't made it yet' and go beyond the boundaries of the existing units. That is the concern of the business development unit of the fine chemical division. It is the delivery room for new business, which is expected to play a crucial role in the development intended for the division.

Closer Links with Corporate R&D

The programme of the corporate (or 'central') fine chemicals research group established at DSM (see Box 4.3) is largely (90%) funded out of the business unit budget. The remaining 10%, which is covered from a corporate budget, is designated for fundamental and exploratory research. About 15% of this fine chemical group works on matters that are directly relevant to DSM Andeno. It has been reinforced in recent years due to the increasing importance of fine chemicals to DSM. Emphasis in this group is on research, while it is on development in DSM Andeno's R&D department. For DSM Andeno, it has major advantages to work with a research group that continues to be part of a large and well-equipped research organization. It has access to the knowledge domain of DSM and it is able to profit from the external research relations of the corporation. DSM Andeno's management has a decisive voice in steering part of this research group. Intensive discussions, detachments and participation in each other's projects are important tools for the extensive cooperation with this group. Additionally, the section head has two workplaces: as head of the section, he is both part of the corporate research and of the Rescom/New Products group of the business unit. In this cooperation, the right balance between technology push and market pull must be found. This leads to two apparently contrasting tendencies: although the research is emphasized more than it used to be, it continues on the course of the DSM Andeno business unit rather than plunging into adventures having no concrete connection with the development of the business.

Knowledge Synergy at DSM

DSM's focus is clearly on plastics, where fine chemicals (the pharmaceutical intermediates in particular) are 'the odd ones out'. This limits the opportunities for knowledge synergy, even for the fine chemical division. The synergy with the corporate research group for fine chemicals is evident and well crystallized. However, the potential synergy with other central and local R&D groups is far less obvious, although it is actively sought. At the level of the Business Group, central meetings take place about technology management. The Business Group has its own budget to initiate technology development focusing on synergy with other Business Groups.

The R&D staff of DSM Andeno take an active part in the synergy programme that was set up for DSM as a whole. This programme is steered by a 'Product and Process Creation Council' (PPCC) which represents the R&D management of the business units and of corporate research. 'Technology Exchange Networks' have been established for important areas, where knowledge is exchanged, new knowledge needs are identified and new initiatives going beyond the business boundaries are stimulated. In that approach, senior research fellows (or key scientists) are held responsible for the development of their subject area, and new developments are exhibited and discussed on location in 'tech expos'.

The Future Agenda

The strength of the organizational innovation process at DSM Andeno is that it was initiated at a time when things were going well. Although a need for change (i.e. time-to-market) was distinctly present, the DSM parent company had nothing to complain about. It was courageous to tackle the organization as a whole. DSM decided to follow the difficult route of integral organizational renewal. It has gained most from streamlining the innovation chain, which speeds up the process and leads to better services. A number of issues will be a matter of great concern for the management of DSM Andeno in the near future. At the operational level, these include the interface between R&D and production, and the self-steering capacity of development teams. At the strategic level, the relationship between long-term and short-term R&D will continue to be in constant motion. Knowledge-centred acquisitions continue to be necessary in this process to be able to take major steps within the foreseeable future. The management of DSM Andeno is also aware, however, that acquisitions should not be at the expense of the organizational strength built up throughout the past years.

Gist-brocades: Innovating in a Turbulent Environment

Gist-brocades is one of the many knowledge-intensive companies that have changed their course throughout recent years. In the late 1980s, it became clear that new impulses were needed to tackle the profits which were on an downward movement. Gist-brocades realized that in the market in which the firm operated, market leadership and upscaling were increasingly determinant factors for success. The management recognized that Gist-brocades' portfolio was too broad and diverse. The continuous need for innovation in each of the market segments necessitated clear choices: choices for core competencies. Meanwhile, these choices have been consolidated. A number of business activities have been taken over by other companies, for example the activities concerning industrial enzymes, which were handed over in 1995 to the American firm Genencor International Inc. 'Growing by doing fewer things better than the competitor' is briefly the assignment Gist-brocades has imposed upon itself.

'Better' refers not only to choosing products, markets and technologies, but to directing towards an advanced organization as well. In this context, the firm is focusing on far-reaching decentralization: from the corporate organizations to the four divisions, and from the divisions to the ten business units and what are called 'operating companies'. The transition of the corporate R&D function to the divisions is part of this effort. The conditions are thus created to drastically enhance the innovating capacity of the firm, which is determined both by technological and scientific ingenuity, but equally by the power used to convert knowledge in the market into profits.

At the same time, Gist-brocades has added an important administrative component to the unit organization: a Technology Platform safeguarding long-term innovation across divisions and functions. In other words, the paradox between long and short term, between centralized and decentralized control, between incremental and radical innovation is not eliminated by focusing on one thing or the other. The firm has become aware that it should aim at both sides of the paradox simultaneously. This paradox was formulated by Corporate Manager of Strategy and Technology (CS&T), Ir. J. Roels, as follows:

'The advantage of business units is that efforts made by a large combination of functions are now linked more directly to the outcome. The outcome becomes visible more quickly thus increasing controllability. That is the effect of the choice for market pull. But when comparing business units, we observe again and again that the most successful business units

derive their success from technological breakthroughs in the past. If you take a long time horizon, it's mainly the technology-driven strategies, the real innovations, that now produce a potential for profit. It's an art for knowledge-intensive companies to manage this paradox between the long-term and short-term result.'

Box 4.4. Royal Gist-brocades N.V.

Royal Gist-brocades N.V. is an internationally operating biotechnology concern, whose most important products are the result from fermentation processes. The company is one the world's largest producers of bakers' yeast, penicillin (and intermediates derived from that) and enzymes. Gist-brocades aims for market leadership on the basis of its technological expertise in the area of microbiology, organic chemistry, and process technology. Net turnover amounted to over Fl. 1.7 billion in 1995, net

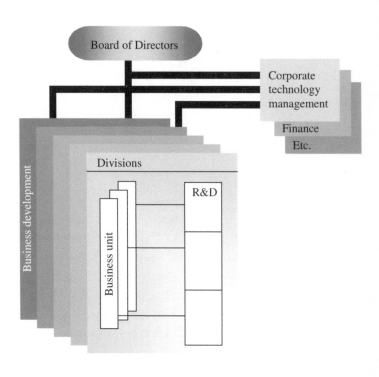

result was 7.8 per cent. In the same year Gist-brocades employed 6,212 staff, 2,141 of whom in the Netherlands. The R&D budget was 4.6% of net turnover. In 1998, the firm was acquired by DSM. One of the basic objectives of this merger is to strengthen their position in the pharmaceutical market.

Gist-brocades' divisions are built up heterogeneously. They consist of operating companies which mainly have a sales or production task as well as business units which are fully responsible for R&D, marketing and production. This heterogeneity is largely a result of the geographical spreading and the take-over and cooperation policy.

Organizational Changes

Decentralization was made concrete in 1994 through the introduction of business units. Arguments in favour of that decision were not much different from those found in many other firms (cf. Wijers, 1994):

- the change from an introvert political organization into an extravert and market-centred organization;
- being able to react to market developments more rapidly;
- reducing time-to-market;
- reducing excess ballast;
- more rapid feedback following results;
- improving the cash-flow.

The business units assumed responsibility for an essential aspect of innovation: the development of new product/market combinations on the basis of the technology available in the firm. In that line of thought, the central lab was given a mainly supportive task. Two years ago, innovation was decentralized even further. The corporate lab was transferred to the four Gist-brocades divisions. The technology managers of the four divisions (DMTs) were thus put in charge in operational terms of the Gist-brocades innovation function. Together with the manager of Corporate Strategy and Technology (the 'CS&T')

and the manager of central facilitative technological unit they are the firm's 'Technology Platform'. This group sets out the firm's technological course and follows the developments of the innovation projects portfolio, which illustrates the focus on technologies and competencies. The group moreover concentrates upon the question into which direction the existing competencies must be broadened or deepened.

Gist-brocades still has a corporate R&D programme which takes up 10% of the firm's total R&D budget. This corporate programme is determined in conjunction with the DMTs (the Technology Platform), but is executed in the R&D department of the divisions or external institutions. In other words, the CS&T no longer possesses his 'own' corporate R&D department. His task lies in the continuous orchestrating and monitoring of the technical strategy development. Within the R&D departments of the divisions Project Managers Technology (PMTs) were appointed as liaisons with the business units. These project managers are also part of the management teams of the business units. In this set-up, the DMTs and the Technology Project Leaders play a double role: they are part of both the R&D organization and of the business. A new division for Business Development was established in 1994, which focuses on business development activities that do not fit into the existing business units.

In this transformation the vision of synergy within Gist-brocades is relevant (cf. Wijers, 1994). Thus, it is assumed that the relevance of synergy in the structure, particularly in the division structure, should be formulated. It is impossible to impose synergy top down in horizontally cooperating divisions. That just won't work. The role of the corporate organization is limited, though important. It's partly a stimulating role, for example when creating lateral linkages where internal suppliers and users of knowledge meet each other, and when monitoring the quality of management. The company management also sees it as its task to prevent the firm from locking itself into the existing technology and product/market combinations. The latter is impossible without a powerful business development department.

Learning Process

The essence of this transition lies not in the formal changes or organizational and budgetary boundaries and management responsibilities. The changes in behaviour patterns, the organizational routines, are of crucial importance. These changes do not come about just like that. Old routines must be unlearned and new must be learned. During that learning process, it appears that new solutions can bring with them new problems, and that new problems may lead to new solutions. Thus, the introduction of business units at Gist-brocades led to a lot of uncertainties in the initial phase. The units retreated, so to speak, to their own territories and focused mainly on issues they could 'score' with. As a result, the 'new', 'unknown' and 'risky' fields seemed to be quickly deserted. No man's land threatened to be created around the most interesting new areas. Furthermore, the unit management bristled up a threatening corporate intervention in order to defend its newly acquired independence. The relationship between the business units and corporate R&D in that initial phase is to be characterized as 'let's wait and see'. The researchers waited for the new ideas that were expected to come mainly from the market now, and the business units concluded that the researchers came up with few new ideas.

Gist-brocades soon recognized the potential risks of this development. One year following the introduction of the business units, the problem was unambiguously put on the table of the division and business units management. The CS&T started a discussion with his DMTs. The project portfolio which compared the risk of the projects against the potential reward was a good starting point for this discussion. In this portfolio, the dynamics of the knowledge development of the firm as a whole is made visible and compared with the development of the business. The systematic analysis, which is performed every six months, is an important tool in this process.

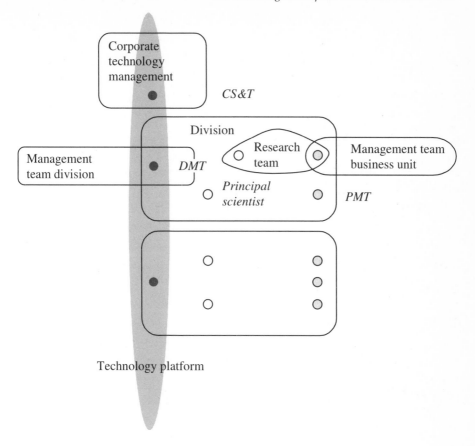

Figure 4.1. The knowledge structure at Gist-brocades.

Conditions

Such tools are not, however, the essence of knowledge management. The essence lies in the organizational basic conditions that must be fulfilled in order for a knowledge system to really work. At Gist-brocades, these are the following three conditions.

The first condition is concerned with the *steering* of the knowledge system. When today's market and technologies are the only standards for steering the innovation function, a project portfolio mainly focused on incremental innovations is the logical consequence. Gist-brocades recognizes that the steering of the divisions and business units must go beyond their financial performances. Top management will have to make the challenge of exploratory R&D visible in the firm. The project portfolios of divisions will have to be assessed on the basis of the portfolio. This reflects the challenge of 'high risk/high reward' in part of the projects. Steering is not only a matter of formal priorities and evaluations. It is also reflected by the active and observable interest and attention of corporate managers for long-term R&D.

The second condition is that a great deal of energy must be put in to make 'real teams' of such groups as the Technology Platform. Within the platform, mutual communication has evolved into an open *dialogue* throughout the past two years. Contrasts (Box 4.5) are not eliminated, but accepted as a reality.

Box 4.5. No mono-culture.

'One shouldn't try to create a mono-culture in the firm. Until recently we thought, just like many other firms, that all noses should point in the same direction. That doesn't make sense, in a management team one should keep in mind that all functions involved are equal. Members should respect the field and quality of other team members. This means that one must not make concessions to the quality of team members. But it's not to say that all members of a management team should think in the same way. The R&D managers must have the guts to put the arguments of his department forward. He may and must be a nuisance. It's imperative that the team as a whole is able to hold dialogues in which arguments are assessed on the basis of their merits.' **(Ir. J. Roels, CS&T)**

Consensus in the dialogue is created on the basis of weighing arguments. The strength of the team (both in terms of individual qualities and mutual cooperation) appears to be more relevant than the formal analytical formats used. It is indicative that the DMTs themselves give the impulse to reserve an entire day for an open discussion frequently despite busy agendas.

The third condition lies in the *direct throughputs* between the various levels in the organization. The Technology Platform is not an island. The same is true of the group of Project Managers Technology and the business unit managers. Discussions are transferred to the local team one belongs to as quickly as possible, preferably on the same or the following day.

The Future Agenda

Gist-brocades has clearly set in a new organizational course in terms of innovation throughout recent years. This does not mean that all relevant action patterns have been shifted immediately. For the time being, a number of important agenda topics will continue to be given priority. First, the R&D portfolio must devote more attention to projects having a *high reward profile*. This requires both a high proposal quality and increased acceptance of the inherent risks.

Second, Gist-brocades aims at improved *anchoring* of the corporate R&D programme. The programme must be carried by the firm's key scientists. The corporate programme is central to internal work conferences in which the managers and key scientists involved participate.

Human resource management is the third field in which innovations are necessary. The Technology Platform has an important part to play here. The portfolio round held every six months not only discuss the projects but the employees as well. The firm will also steer more on both the portfolio of knowledge and experience the researchers are expected to possess, and the knowledge and experience they will have to gain in the coming years in order to maintain and reinforce Gist-brocades' competencies. Initial steps for this have been taken, but the approach will have to be more systematic and structural.

Fourth, more attention must be given to the development of *functional discipline-centred knowledge*. Gist-brocades is currently given further shape to the function of principal scientists, i.e. the researchers that give direction to the development of functional knowledge areas within Gist-brocades in its entirety. Inherent in this is a portfolio of functional knowledge, which indicates where the firm stands and where it wants to go to.

Finally, Gist-brocades must make more use of the technological and scientific *potential outside of* Gist-brocades. The firm must learn to look more to the outside in the knowledge development: the universities, TNO, and other firms. Gist-brocades will continue to depart from its own core competencies. The build-up of new competencies is going beyond the firm's basis. The links with other competencies, mainly based on cooperation with other firms, can certainly provide some important new perspectives.

Moret, Ernst & Young: New Ideas are Generated in the Market

Innovation is not likely to be associated by outsiders with the service sector, and this probably holds true even more for the offices of accountants, tax advisors and management consultants within that sector. Yet this image of conservatism has been superseded by reality in many accountancy firms. In recent years, the accountancy sector has been forced to set a new course in a radical manner. First, because a lot of accountancy firms have internationally operating clients, and are thus expected to operate on an international scale themselves. Second, because the clients of accountancy firms demand a full range of services, from internal control, financial accounting, designing the administrative organization, to automation, tax and organization consultancy. The role of the accountancy firm has thus become much more varied than it used to be. The application of information technology (IT) is a third factor. IT has made it possible to directly tap the necessary accountancy information from the client's administrative organization. This provides new opportunities as well as new competition with software companies. It is therefore of existential importance to constantly innovate one's own package of services and add more value to the client's value chain. Moving away from classical verification, services increasingly shift into the direction of advice, for example, forensic accountancy, advising firms when they invest or settle abroad, establishing ecologically-sound systems, advising about and monitoring mergers and take-overs, advising about property taxes and actuarial matters. As a result, the modern accountancy firm has evolved into a multinational enterprise that continuously converts new experiences into new services, innovates internal processes, and transfers and supplies knowledge to its clients. No wonder then that communication, the management of knowledge, training and education are the basic elements in the business strategy of many large accountancy firms.

Box 4.6. Moret Ernst & Young.

Moret, Ernst & Young (MEY) is one of the biggest Dutch service firms in the area of accountancy, tax advice and 'management consulting'. As a partnership, MEY is a federative member of Ernst & Young International, resulting from a merger of a number of Dutch accountancy firms. In 1995, MEY employed about 4,200 people, while its turnover was approximately Hfl. 750 million. MEY's organization is built up as a matrix of regional units and sectors. Turnover is realized in the offices, while the sector's primary responsibility lies in the development and transfer of sectoral (i.e. client group-specific) knowledge.

About 7–8% of turnover is spent on training programmes, in which two streams can be distinguished. The first and most dominant stream focuses on the regular professional development of its employees. The emphasis in MEY's personnel policy is on personnel development. This dynamic perspective is also central to the recruitment of personnel. New employees know that they arrive in a firm which expects them to continue to study and be retrained constantly. This process keeps going on until the end of their careers, and applies to all organizational echelons. For example, the partners and certified accountants are obligated to spend at least 40 hours per year on permanent education. The second main stream is concerned with the innovations in the firm's most important products and processes, where the MEY sectors take the lead.

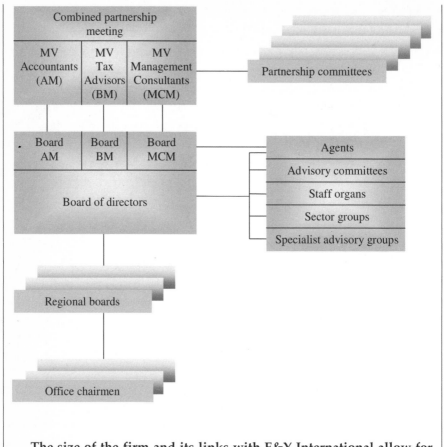

The size of the firm and its links with E&Y International allow for the use of a wealth of common know-how, for example, the 'audit innovation project'. MEY pursues a clear innovation policy, which has the following features.

New Ideas Usually Originate from the Market '

Like firms in the same sector, MEY is strongly and regionally organized and maintains long-term contacts with its clients. As a result of this interaction, ideas for new services frequently arise. New ideas mostly start as a problem a client is facing. The initial phase of the development is translation of such a problem into a rough sketch of a product. In discussions between MEY consultants and a client, the idea is brought forward to develop a new product which enables the client to make better policy decisions and to better control expenses. The regional consultants then make a rough product outline, resulting in what might be referred to as a manual. The product is actually developed after consultation with the central MEY organization and, at the local level, with colleagues from other regions. The product is brought onto the market once it has proven its use in actual practice.

New Ideas Must be Successful within the Firm

The regional offices and the people employed there are the ones that are eventually charged with the introduction of the new services. In that sense, an accounting partnership operates just like a medical partnership: in the end, the doctors are the ones who decide what medication to prescribe. Before MEY starts investing in the development of a product, it must first be 'sold' internally. Each new product requires intensive communication both in the pre-trajectory where specifications are described and in the post-trajectory where the new expert knowledge must be transferred. MEY has a system of specialist meetings in which constant discussions are held at different levels of the organization about the new needs for services from the market, proposals for product development, and the implementation of new products and services. In this sense, innovating means 'continuous communication' to MEY.

Innovation in a Decentralized Firm Requires 'Orchestration'

MEY is a highly decentralized organization. The development of a new service takes place in close conjunction with clients. This is another example of 'lead users' (von Hippel, 1986): clients that are interested in the new products to the extent that they are also willing to make extra efforts by serving as test fields. However, the knowledge thus acquired must subsequently be made available to the rest of the firm. This interaction between local practice and general usage within the partnerships calls for a central 'linking function', which is fulfilled at MEY along two lines. The first one takes place through the sectors of the firm. These groups have been established for the 17 major customers categories, such as banks, the authorities, and health care sector. The principal task of the sectors is to jointly develop, bundle, and transfer sector-specific knowledge. This is especially concerned with contextual and operational knowledge (Chapter 2).

Most sector members come from the regional organizations. The sectors are involved in personnel development to a large extent: assigning and training employees. Thus, the health care sector is responsible for its own 'home-grown' health care specialists. MEY strives to have its employees work outside a sector part of their time, as a result of which they transfer knowledge gained in one sector to another. The introduction of sectors has given the regions a more facilitative character, which is the reason why MEY speaks of a 'rotation of the organization'. A rotation which is based mainly on the opportunities for knowledge synergy.

The second line is mainly concerned with the development and transfer of expert knowledge (or 'functional knowledge'). For this purpose MEY has set up a small central 'professional skills development' unit. One of the tasks of this unit is to make available funds to support the local development. In practice the unit functions as a sort of 'drive wheel', which underpins local developments. In addition, a kind of quality control is needed. Most important, however, is the orchestration of the communication between the product designers and the other product users within MEY. MEY has chosen to integrate both the development of professional skills and transfer and training in this orchestrating central function.

Innovation Means Training, Training, Training

It is vitally important that the new products are made operational as quickly as possible in the regional organization. This is possible only by directly connecting development with training. One might say that the training of MEY employees and clients is an integrated part of product development. When a product cannot be transferred effectively, it is not a full-fledged and mature product.

The MEY approach shows that innovation of products and services, the acquisition of local practical experience, the transfer of experience, and personnel policy are all part of one single fundamental process in the organization.

Nationale Nederlanden: Knowledge Assurance

Knowledge of and experience with insurance products, risks and markets are invaluable to the large insurance companies. In many companies, this knowledge and experience used to be cherished in the formal structure of 'functional' or 'product-centred' departments. Yet a number of large insurers have recently abandoned this functional structure in exchange for a market-centred organization. The change in the insurance market has made a significant contribution to this development. The market is transforming from a stable complacent market into a turbulent market where firms have to fight to survive, and quality and costs have become decisive factors. A well-established name that inspires confidence and sound investment strategies are no longer sufficient to retain and gain competitive advantage. As in many other areas, the suppliers market has transformed into a demand market. Other developments faced by insurance companies originate from changes in the social environment in which they are operating, as a result of which insurers are challenged to reduce their cost while offering equal service at the same time. There is a strong societal necessity to reduce the cost of health care. The changes in the social security system is yet another main trend the insurance firms must anticipate, as well as the increasing damages burden caused by reduced social control in present-day society. In the general insurance sector these developments put the margins under strong pressure, and a fierce battle is fought for the market share.

The general insurance division of Nationale Nederlanden has made an important step in this development to be able to cooperate more effectively with the intermediaries. The functional organization of product groups (fire, car, income, travel insurance, and so on) has been replaced by a system of result-responsible regional units offering complete services packages. Within these units, insurance teams are operative which have been established in such a way that the intermediaries can always turn to a fixed team (Den Hertog, 1995b). The product specialists from the old organization have been categorized under market-centred groups. In an early stage of the redesign process, the company was well aware that this organizational turnaround might cause the product-centred insurance know-how to leak away. The question was where in the new organization it could allocate responsibility for the development, storage and safeguarding of the essential know-how. How could this knowledge

Box 4.7. NN General Insurance Company.

> Nationale Nederlanden (NN) is the largest insurance company in the Netherlands employing about 4,000 staff and with a turnover (1994) of more than Dfl. 8 billion. In 1993, NN merged with the Postbank/NMB to form the International Netherlands Group (ING). NN consists of two operating companies: life insurance and general (property/casualty) insurance. Recently it was decided to merge these two. The firm works with a network of 9,600 independent intermediaries.
>
> During the past years NN has extended its international interests, not only in Europe (Belgium, Spain, Italy, Greece), but also in the United States, Canada, Australia, Indonesia, Japan and Hong Kong. The general insurance company employs 1,950 staff and has a turnover

of Dfl. 1.8 billion (both 1994 figures). (Meanwhile the company is working on further integration of the operating companies Life Insurance and General Insurance.)

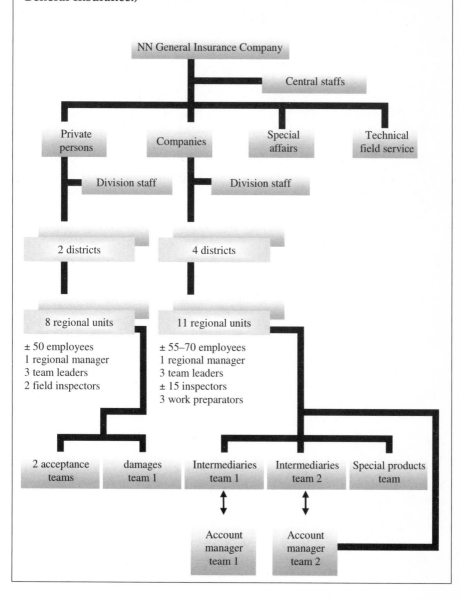

be effectively put at the disposal of the regional team members? A separate design group composed of representatives of the functions involved was appointed to design a structure for safeguarding know-how. After numerous discussions with those involved the company chose the design option represented in Figure 4.2.

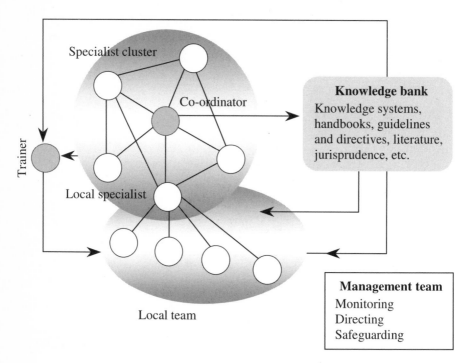

Figure 4.2. Management of knowledge cycles.

The design distinguishes three main functions:

1. The Specialist

Each regional unit has a number of specialists with their own field competence, whether this be a specific product or cluster of products, the acceptance of claims, or the assessment of damage claims. These specialists act as 'information points' in their unit. They collect questions, problems and new ideas and discuss these with their colleagues from other units on a regular basis.

2. The Coordinator

The coordinator is a member of the division staff and chairs the specialist clusters. The coordinator is responsible for adjustment of the directives and guidelines for risk acceptance (the 'policy') and assessment of damage claims. These adjustments are stored in a knowledge bank, a systematic collection of knowledge carriers: manuals, knowledge systems, directives and learning material. New knowledge is transferred to the members of the regional teams. The coordinator is furthermore responsible for updating the insurance knowledge in his/her own area as well as for the development of new knowledge. This means that (s)he is expected to provide an important input in the development of new products. In addition, it is also his or her task to invent training needs in the regions and develop new course programmes in conjunction with the training department.

3. The Trainer

The trainer also has a new role to play in this new set-up. The trainer works closely with the regional specialists and the coordinators in an effort to set up and coach course programmes. The training function has changed from a fairly distant training department into a direct professional support group for the specialist clusters and regional teams. The trainer has become one of the links in the knowledge cycle.

The management teams of the divisions have the explicit task to direct and monitor the development of new cycles and to safeguard knowledge. The introduction of this new method of developing and safeguarding knowledge can be viewed in the first place as a direct consequence of the new more decisive form of organization selected.

Box 4.8. The knowledge bank of NN General Insurance.

An impressive knowledge bank was set up at Nationale Nederlanden in just a few years' time which is accessible from virtually every workstation through the intranet (Chapter 8). Not only does the knowledge bank contain the regular procedures, rates and conditions, it is also context-oriented. Thus, the knowledge bank provides information about specific types of policyholders, such as administrators of a pharmacy, sports centres and schools. In this way, preventative advice can be rapidly and adequately supplied and the most fitting policy type can be proposed. Clients are moreover directly helped from behind the screen. Quick search procedures ensure that the client does not have to wait on the phone. The knowledge bank is used very intensively, which is a stimulus to continue to add to, update and improve the information stored.

Knowledge and experience cannot be allowed to leak away and must be made available to the regional units in an effective manner. Yet this working method also introduces a new element in the management of Nationale Nederlanden. The relevance of managing knowledge flows is explicitly regarded as a new function in the company. In this vision, knowledge development and transfer are not considered as being a sum of specialist capacity and adequate training courses. Instead, knowledge management is viewed as a continuous flow of meaningful information throughout the organization — a flow which links people together in their efforts to better serve the customers.

Pink Elephant: Systems Management as a Core Competence

"We are marketing human knowledge. That has been our line of business from the start. We want to be the quality market leader in IT management services for information intensive organizations and the best firm to work for". This slogan is used by Pink Elephant to describe its own ambition; quite an ambition for a firm that was founded in 1980 by three students of Delft University to earn some extra money. The three founders discovered an interesting market niche while they were going along. Whereas other IT firms focused on hardware and the development of software and systems, these young entrepreneurs decided to take a chance and dive into the niche for IT management services. Meanwhile, this niche has evolved

Box 4.9. Pink Elephant.

Pink Elephant is part of Pink Roccade Informatica Group NV. The firm was founded in 1980 by three students of the then Polytechnic University Delft. In search of a lucrative way of earning some extra money, the founders discovered an attractive market niche: supporting the daily production and management activities in computer centres. The firm started with highly qualified part-timers (mostly students like themselves) with high development potential. Currently (1997), Pink Elephant employs 1,400 people, the majority of them full-time. The recruitment principle has not changed, however, compared to the pioneering time: getting highly qualified young people with a potential for growth. The average age of the employees is 29. Numerous large multinational and medium-sized firms and public institutions are Pink Elephant clients.

In terms of services, the firm bears little resemblance to the "job agency" for computer operators and custodians from its romantic pioneering period. It has developed into a firm that has set the professional norm for the management and exploitation of computer and information centres in the Netherlands and holds an international ambition. The firm offers a broad range of services, varying from the management of computer systems, consultancy, audits, training and interim management, to the full responsibility of the automation infrastructure. The firm has strongly grown during the past five years: it counted 385 employees in 1988 and 1,100 in 1996. During that period, turnover increased from 15.8 million to 120 million guilders.

(This case report is based on the authors' study (Den Hertog & Huizenga 1997) and updated as to details on the basis of the publication by Massier & Boersma (1996).

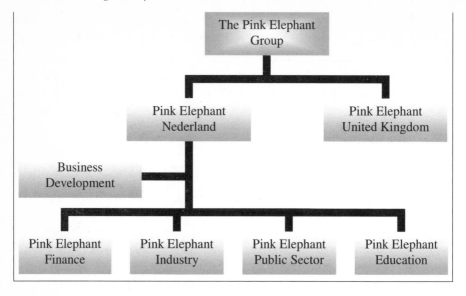

into a market segment offering a broad range of services. The work itself has also developed from simple mechanical operations to advanced knowledge work.

The enormous growth experienced by the company during the past three years in particular is based on the shift from simple to complex jobs. In this process, Pink Elephant has evolved into a partner for the integral management of IC facilities, which means that the services offered evolve with the life cycle of the clients' systems. Rather than the management of a stable system, this is a complex of systems that are continuously moving due to technological advancement and company development of clients. "Facilities management", which implies that the firm assumes responsibility both for hardware and software and for personnel, is a new challenge for Pink Elephant. The huge inherent investments forced the firm to look for a partner with a considerable capital at its back. Pink Roccade became that partner in 1992.

Knowledge management and personnel management are considered by managers of Pink Elephant as the most important factors for success. Employees have to continuously prove their added value at the clients' houses in relation to the employees of that client. This is possible only when the "Pink knowledge" of the "Pink knowledge carriers" are constantly maintained, elaborated and transferred.

A Changing Technology and a Changing Market

The growth of the firm fits in a development in which companies strive to outsource the activities that do not belong to their core activities to specialized firms which are able to perform these activities more efficiently and professionally. These companies have become aware that 70% of the automation costs are spent on management and maintenance. It is through Pink Elephant that they have chosen for a more process-like approach of management and systems maintenance. At the time Pink Elephant was founded, this development was still in its infancy. The computer centre service companies operating in this market mainly delivered capacity to answer the urgent need for qualified personnel felt by the constantly operating computer centres. First, they offered their clients flexibility to be called upon at unexpected moments. Second, they offered efficiency, because they were able to provide the services at costs that were lower than those charged internally. This opportunistic approach proved successful at a time when the operation of computer centres was predominantly a routine matter. Until the mid-1980, it looked as if the technical development of computer systems would only simplify the operation. This development has distinctly changed again in recent years. The management of computer centres has become a professional matter, placing high demands upon the operators, custodians and their management. This can be compared with the processing industry, where the systems are highly complex and costly. In such systems, a minor disturbance may have very serious consequences. Although it is not very likely that such disturbances occur, they do call for immediate and adequate action.

Systems Management as a Core Competence

Pink Elephant was the first company in the Netherlands to recognize these developments: a market that was growing due to the strive for outsourcing and the necessity to professionalize system management. It was evident at a very early stage that the rapidly growing firm was not be able to continue to exist on the basis of price and flexibility alone, because such a policy can be easily copied by other firms. This holds true especially for an undisciplined market without norms and standards, in which the competitors behave like "cowboys", so to speak. The market in which Pink Elephant operated lacked a professional norm. There was no leading vision of the profession that was accepted inside the sector, nor did there exist tailored training. The moment the market offered a new perspective and the technological development asked for that, there was a gap that Pink Elephant leaped into without a moment's hesitation. Pink's management realized that in the long run, the firm was to be viable only when it set the norm for the development of the profession of systems management. The firm introduced a method that systematically describes all processes of control: ITIL — The Information Technology Infrastructure Library. ITIL was developed by the organization that advises the British government in the area of information technology. This development has not come to a standstill. ITIL is given further shape by implementing experiences that Pink gathered with its clients in recent years. One might speak of "lead users" (cf. Von Hippel, 1986) here.

Its current company strategy draws this line even further. The cooperation with the lead users in the development and implementation of new products proved to be a good experience basis for setting the next step in Pink's business development. To date, the firm has positioned itself as "transformation partner". In other words, Pink Elephant takes the continuous business transformations of the client firms as the point of departure for its own services. It offers the customer a partnership in supporting the transformations of the customer by introducing, implementing and managing state-of-art IT solutions. This strategic change has far-reaching consequences for Pink's own organization. For the operation, it means an even stronger focus on the customer as an organizing principle. But this is just half of the story. Such effort is due to fail when at the same time Pink's employees are not empowered to deal with the new tasks. This may sound as a paradox: the choice for the customer as the leading organizational principle means at the same time a choice for an organization which steers on knowledge. Pink employees are expected to have insight into the company processes of clients ("contextual knowledge"). They must possess advanced professional know-how ("functional knowledge"), as well as organizational talents ("operational knowledge"). In other words, the firm that started in response to the lack of qualified personnel rapidly changed into an innovative enterprise, a forerunner in its area. This case shows the strive for core competencies (Prahalad & Hamel, 1991), competencies put to creative use in order to deliver products and services that other firms cannot offer, and to explore new markets.

Steering on Knowledge Development

Pink Elephant's success is not to be attributed only to the way in which it seizes the moment. Crucially important was the way in which Pink linked its innovation strategy to an integral vision of the management of the knowledge flow. Three basic instruments of the knowledge enterprise play an important role here: the (lateral) knowledge organization, personnel management, and IT.

The knowledge organization. The (virtual) knowledge organization stretches out over the entire firm and focuses on the collection, development, control, use, and diffusion of knowledge. This knowledge organization is formed by the individual employees, knowledge-related organization units and knowledge-supporting resources. Coordination of the knowledge organization is carried out by Pink's business development department, which evolved from the R&D function at Pink. Within that department, the sections are responsible for updating the knowledge and stimulating the knowledge exchange in clearly outlined sub-areas of Pink Elephant. The sections are composed of employees of the subsidiaries, which work for business development for a fixed period of time and are subsequently replaced. The sections diffuse the new knowledge using a variety of possible resources: papers, meetings and the intranet. Knowledge transfer is an important facilitative service in this process. It might be viewed as the paper and electronic library of Pink Elephant, where its employees can pick up and add new knowledge. Knowledge transfer is seen as the internal broker of knowledge.

Business development also coordinates and supports innovative projects. Every Pink employee is encouraged to come forward with ideas for a new service, course, or working method using a "start document". The proposal is eventually assessed by a steering group presided by the board of managers and further composed of the business development manager and all directors of the Dutch subsidiaries.

Personnel management. From the outset, Pink Elephant has recognized that the management of the Human Resources is at the basis of its company policy. This is reflected, among other things, in its current mission: Pink Elephant seeks to be "quality market leader in facilitative IT servicing to knowledge-intensive organizations, and the best firm to work for". This mission has not appeared to be an empty slogan throughout Pink's development. Looking at the ambition of the firm, it is an absolute priority. Ninety percent of the work is performed at the clients' premises, which means that it must constantly invest in the relation with its own staff. In addition, Pink Elephant has chosen to train its own staff. Around 10% of the gross income is spent on the development and maintenance of the knowledge organization.

Good training. Pink Elephant's philosophy is not to keep the knowledge gathered for themselves, but to set a standard in the field. In other words, it is creating a market by transferring its own knowledge as effectively as possible. In order to make a profession of systems management, Pink Elephant has set up a training programme in conjunction with the Rijkshogeschool IJsselland (a college of higher education), offering courses specifically focused on systems management. The programme's application-oriented component is offered by Pink Elephant staff. The training programme is also used for the professionalization of the firm's own (young) work force. As mentioned previously, Pink Elephant invests large amounts of money in its staff's training: 10% of its gross income. A large part of the training programme developed in-house is sold off again by bringing them into the market by the Education subsidiary. Meanwhile, Education has turned into a full business. In the past, the development and training functions were integrated into "Education and Development". This structure allowed for a fast and adequate transfer of knowledge when shaping new services and processes. Recently, these two functions were split up. The commercial objectives of the training programmes and the creative objectives of development appeared to be incompatible. In the present organization, the strong linkage between training and development is safeguarded by a product manager responsible for the development of training services.

The 'pilot' system. Pink Elephant has developed its own clear standard for its services, which must be occupied by the relevant staff. It is here that Pink employees must prove their added value to the clients' personnel. This is the reason for Pink Elephant to plot clear career development paths of individual staff members. A "pilot" (or "career-counsellor") from the personnel department is appointed to each employee. Twice a year, career interviews are held with this pilot on the basis of a career development plan. This plan keeps track of the knowledge and skills each employee possesses and those he (or she) is yet to develop. The latter is partly a matter of training. More importantly, on the basis of career development information, a desired experience path is plotted, which serves as the basis for the employee participation in projects. This means that the allocation of staff to projects is used as an important steering device in order to stimulate employees' personal development and, thus, to anchor the firm's core competencies in the Human Resources. This approach gives clarity to the employees, their pilots and to the organization as a whole. In that sense, the employee is responsible for his or her own future.

Looking back and looking forward again. The case of Pink Elephant is a success story. The growth accomplished, the rise in stockholder value and the respect among client firms are undeniable proof for that. However, at the same time there are signs which urge Pink's management to continue to be alert. Pink has a young and critical workforce which has many alternatives on the labour market. The basic problem Pink Elephant is facing is in fact a consequence of its success. Pink Elephant is no longer a small and informal company. However, the firm still has the same innovative ambition as in its pioneering days. The inevitable consequence of rapid growth is that the distance between strategy making and concrete strategies has become larger. Large meetings still serve to "broadcast" the new images of the firm throughout the organization. The intranet can also be regarded as an effective instrument to *reach* all employees. However, to date the *reciprocity* (cf. Brown & Duguid 1997) of the communication has become far more difficult to accomplish. The basic lesson that Pink's management has learned in the past years is, that the one-to-one communication between individuals, team and management must be strengthened once again. This means both the dialogues between the board and middle management and between the latter and the field workers have to be intensified. Pink's training system and its intranet are useful tools to support this process.

Stork N.V.: Advanced Knowledge in an Advanced Organization

Stork is a technologically advanced company with a rich past. The firm was founded in 1827. It has encountered and survived all industrial revolutions as a machine-centred corporation. The history of the firm reflects all important and far-reaching developments of modern industry. Originally a producer of heavy industrial capital goods for local markets (particularly for the textiles and paper industries and railway construction), Stork has transformed into an internationally operating corporation. The firm has applied itself to the manufacturing of advanced industrial systems for a broad range of markets as well as to industrial services (Box 4.10). This combination makes Stork into a full-fledged engineering firm. The combination of technological disciplines in products and services in an integral knowledge structure provides the decisive advantage in the market place.

Box 4.10. Stork as a world-wide operating producer and service provider.

> Stork employs more than 18,000 staff, has a turnover of Dfl. 4.1 billion, and achieved a net result in 1995 of Dfl. 108 million. The strategic intention is described by Stork as 'a world-wide operating technology corporation, which derives its continuity from the quality and motivation of its employees, directed towards the sustainable success of its relations' (Annual Report, 1995).
>
> Stork (1995) is composed of over 60 operating companies, all of them operating in the market with a large degree of autonomy. This form of organization has been chosen to give meaning to entrepreneurship, customer responsiveness and flexibility. On the basis of marketing or technical expertise in the implementation process, its activities have been classified in five strategic business units. In this unit organization, related activities are closely linked together in organizational terms, as a result of which Stork can concentrate on specialist activities and key skills and provide the customers with broad support. The strategic mission of the firm states yet another priority: knowledge synergy. Stork has made major efforts in recent years to retain that knowledge synergy within a far-reaching decentralized structure.

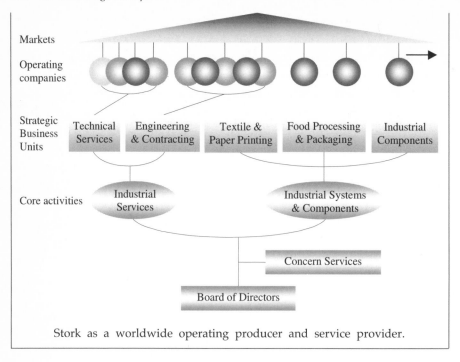

Stork as a worldwide operating producer and service provider.

Knowledge Synergy in a Decentralized Corporation

Pumping systems, filling and packaging systems and textile pressure systems were the major heavy capital goods at the heart of Stork's product package until the 1960s. Know-how was initially anchored in the production of machinery to a large extent. Knowledge development was assured through a robust central department: Physical Dynamic Research (FDO). The markets served by Stork up until that time differed strongly. The firm itself was heavily dependent on government decision making. These were demanding times for the firm.

In the 1970s, the firm made the strategic decision to spread the risk through diversification, thus making it less dependent on the central government's expenditure policy. The firm moreover chose for a higher knowledge intensity of products and for the development of technical services ('engineering consulting') as a separate business. This change in course led to a change in the firm's structure. The firm came to be composed of self-managing entities (business units) which served specific groups of customers, and which were, at this time, strongly mono-disciplinary in orientation. In that sense, Stork was one of the first industrial companies in the Netherlands to make a fundamental choice for the unit organization. This organizational reversal was not realized from one day to the next. First, decentralized customer-centred patterns of behaviour had to be learned, and 'centralistic' patterns had to be unlearned. This implied a major change for the central knowledge development department FDO, which no longer had feeling with the market and was forced to assume a new role: the role of consultant. Apart from the continued need for support by existing organizational processes of conventional products and services, this required the development of new organizational routines.

This strategic change process was difficult and costly. It was not until the mid-1980s that Stork was back on track. This became manifest in the strongly improved business results of the firm in 1984 after suffering losses for years. However, the limits of the unit organization also became manifest in that same period. The business units had so far been heavily dominated by single disciplines such as mechanical and electrical engineering. In other words, the boundaries of the functional disciplines and the marketing by the business units coincided and reinforced each other. In the late-1980s, the development of the business and technology placed new demands upon the unit organization. Assignments became more complex and the coupling of different technologies offered new perspectives for the company. Stork evolved primarily into a *system developer* and *system consultant*. In the market, the accent increasingly shifted to integral solutions and acceleration of the development and production trajectory (time-to-market). The answer was sought in streamlining the primary process. Integral product innovation and production innovation became policy priorities for the business units. This required an increased appeal to highly qualified personnel from different disciplines. Multidisciplinary cooperation became crucially important, which was not to stop, however, at the boundaries of the business units.

The company became aware of the importance of integrating different technical disciplines in order to serve common markets. Harmonization of various technological flows was expected to form the basis for Stork to distinguish from other companies. The development of core competencies could go beyond the market orientation of the business units. The synergy between technological competencies was expected to provide the company with new products and services with more added value. However, the strong demarcation of these knowledge areas within the boundaries of the business units was a handicap. It was recognized that the unit organization threatened to fall short in assuring, developing and exploiting knowledge synergy across the functional (= disciplinary) boundaries and business demarcations. Yet the relevance of the unit organization was indisputable. It had proved to be a splendid instrument to convert the firm's technical competencies into good currency in the market place. Stork's top management could no longer escape from the question how it was to safeguard the knowledge synergy in a strongly decentralized company. The answer to this question was sought in knowledge management: a multidisciplinary approach going beyond units.

The Knowledge Structure

Stork's current knowledge structure focuses on the development and safeguarding of knowledge. Its main objectives are:

Exchange of knowledge: stimulating the knowledge flows among units and between units and the central R&D function;

Exploration: spotting new promising technological developments and applications in the market place.

Coordination: defining common priorities in the development or acquisition of leading-edge technologies.

Four control levels are to be distinguished in this knowledge structure. The point of departure for the structure is the division of the business (Box 4.10). At the basis are the *operating companies* (business units or entities), where most knowledge is flowing, and stored in routines. The operating companies are the firm's decentralized knowledge centres, which possess information about the market, obtain new impulses from the market for new applications, and have insight into the system performance and client-specific demands imposed upon these systems.

The knowledge centres are connected in four *knowledge networks*, which form the strategic control level in the knowledge structure. They focus on the most important themes that go beyond groups and units. At this level, the group managers and the Technology and Innovation department are in continuous dialogue about the priorities in the development of leading-edge technologies and enabling technologies. A major part of the resulting research programme is subcontracted to the technical universities and institutions such as TNO. Due to this cooperation, Stork has ensured the acquisition of new know-how and routines related to the fundamental technological developments.

Within the four networks, a total of 18 *knowledge clusters* have been established. These clusters are composed of specialists from the business units, and are connected with the Technology and Innovation department. The discipline-centred clusters focus on the common sub-areas within the four key themes.

The knowledge cluster may be viewed as an internal market and meeting place, where new developments are spotted, experiences exchanged and plans made. This is where cross-fertilization takes place between the business units. Informal communication is vitally important here, which is put forward during the 'theme days' generally organized 'on location'. But the clusters also function on a formal basis: they report both to the business units and to the management at group level.

Communication is this knowledge structure is both top down and bottom up. The top-down flow is mainly concerned with the mission, vision and strategy of the company. The bottom-up flow essentially transports accumulated knowledge. Both flows interact: policy is fed by signals from development, and development is given shape by policy. The utilization of technological opportunities is thus incorporated in the internal knowledge network and in relation with external sources of knowledge.

The Dynamics of Knowledge

Knowledge is not a static given. Knowledge management should focus on the dynamics of knowledge. Stork distinguishes three basic elements (Figure 4.3):

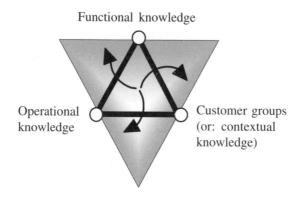

Figure 4.4. Stork's knowledge structure.

Functional knowledge: discipline-centred knowledge;

Expertise: the experience gained in previous projects with applications and the capacity anchored in routines to solve problems;

Knowledge of the customer: knowledge about client needs, and insight into the production processes and associated problems of clients.

The interaction between these three elements provides the dynamics of the firm's competence. When developing new areas of competence, two existing knowledge fields are the point of departure. Thus, it is possible to develop products and services on the basis of existing functional and operational knowledge derived from a known market. Or it is possible to build new operational knowledge on the basis of existing functional knowledge in cooperation with known customers. Figure 4.3 is a graphic representation of the interaction between the three key elements. The triangle can be folded out to three sides, thus symbolizing the three directions of development: acquiring new functional knowledge, customer knowledge and application knowledge.

The instruments for knowledge management used at Stork focus on the development of lateral groups. These groups are not isolated, but are both part of networks in which knowledge is diffused and of processes in which policy is defined. The knowledge structure is built up step by step, without a blueprint at its basis. The knowledge structure was further developed and later formalized. The instruments themselves are always open to improvement. A large number of clusters are still mainly functional and mono-disciplinary in character. It is recognized not only that synergy should be achieved across business boundaries, but also that more synergy should be achieved right across functions. Additionally, other instruments, such as information technology and personnel policy, are being utilized to underpin the knowledge structure, where management development is one of the areas deserving special attention.

Chapter 5

Regimes for the Knowledge Enterprise

Firms, and market share leaders in particular, are constantly evolving. In order to safeguard, defend and develop a leading position, boundaries, including organizational boundaries, must be stretched continuously. For the knowledge enterprise, the control of innovation processes is of special relevance. This chapter compares the seven market share leaders presented in the previous chapter from that perspective. A typology of innovation regimes will provide the points of reference over time. Hedging, programming and streamlining are viewed in this approach as developmental stages of the innovation function. The analysis has led to four conclusions:

- Streamlining is a dominant trend, and nobody is willing to go back into time.
- Streamlining causes synergy problems in the knowledge enterprise.
- Firms are once again investing effectively in knowledge synergy.
- Knowledge synergy is effected by making choices in a learning organization.

This development forces companies to deal with paradoxes.

Three Innovation Regimes as Points of Identification

When comparing organizations we often tend to take random moments in time — 'snapshots' — as the point of departure. We try to read a successful formula from the differences we observe at moment X. In fact, this is the principle of benchmarking. The risk of this approach has been documented in detail (Stacey, 1996, p. 207) by Peters and Waterman (1982), *In Search of Excellence*. Five years after the study had been carried out, two-thirds of the excellent firms disappeared from the top five of most successful companies. While some of the firms returned to the top later, others became stuck in the calm. Snapshots don't show movement. Frontrunners that fall back, or average firms that are coming on, cannot be distinguished by just looking at moments. More important than the snapshot is the story the firms have to tell. The story which shows where they come from; which tells what problems and challenges they faced and; what steps were taken and the consequences of these steps. That is how we will look at the case studies of the companies in this chapter, and we will try to recognize contrasts and parallels. Beacons are a familiar means to determine one's position at sea. Similar points of identification or recognition are also relevant to the analysis of business development. For the knowledge enterprise, it is particularly relevant how the firms have given shape to the management of their knowledge development and innovation processes. At the basis of each form of process management is a specific explicit or implicit organizational logic. Organizational studies have revealed (Cooper, 1994; Roussel *et al.*, 1991, Den Hertog *et al.*, 1996) that fixed patterns can be identified in the way in which these forms (or 'regimes') of process management follow one another. Insight into that change in organization regimes provides reference points to determine a firm's current position and chart the future course. This insight offers a framework for interpretation of one's actions. The analysis of the case studies presented in Chapter 4 will make use of the typology based on a MERIT study (Den Hertog *et al.*, 1996) into innovation processes in the processing industry.

Three phases can be identified in the development of the organization of the innovation in the leading companies. Each phase is characterized by a specific regime, which determines the way in which priorities are identified, funding is settled, the work is divided, and progress is planned and controlled. The three phases are preceded in a historical sense by a pioneering phase in the older firms, in which the lab, close to the factory, had a kind of 'service function'. The large diversified companies still show elements of the three innovation regimes in various combinations today.

Hedging

'Bring a number of brilliant scientists and engineers together, provide them with the time and the resources, and results will follow automatically'. The ADL advisors (Roussel *et al.*, 1991) refer to this as the 'philosophy of hope'. This philosophy has long been the legitimization for firms to isolate the R&D function from the daily hubbub of sales and production. An impressive building was constructed in a green meadow or on a green hill: the central lab, which was to become the heart of corporate R&D. The manager reported directly to the Board of Directors. The budget was determined by the confidence in science and technology and the firm's financial scope. Thus, the R&D budget of many oil companies has accurately followed the fluctuation of the oil prices. Under this regime, the cost of R&D is apportioned among the divisions without discussion. Within the hedge of the laboratory, the organization unmistakably shows features of the professional bureaucracy (Mintzberg, 1979). The work is left in the care of functional departments each focusing on their own field of expertise. Day-to-day management is primarily led by professional norms. Looking at it this way, the organization bears much resemblance with a university. The name 'Physics Laboratory' which was selected by Philips in the 1920s seems to be indicative in this context.

Programming

As the division management became more powerful, opposition arose in the company. The division management wanted value for 'its' money. In a number of branches of industry, specifically in the American defence, aircraft and spacecraft industries, customers exerted a lot of pressure to better steer development processes both in terms of time and cost. This has led to the development and introduction of formal control systems such as PERT and CPM. With the exception of a new control system, the internal organization of the R&D department retained the same structure. The development process was still regarded as a sequential process, as a relay race where the baton was passed on from one department to another on critical moments. A complex flow of documents had to ensure that adequate agreements were being made between the functions. In addition, the decision moments for 'Go' and 'No Go' were clearly indicated. Florida and Kenney (1990) refer to this regime as the 'factory model' for innovation. Cooper (1994) uses the phrase 'stage-gate model'. Division of tasks, standardization and formalization are viewed as keys to innovation effectiveness. Under this regime, part of the corporate R&D funds are earmarked for projects formulated in conjunction with the divisions. There exist big differences between sectors. In the chemical sector, R&D continues to be strongly concentrated in the corporate lab, while in the electronics industry the divisions build up their own development functions. Within these divisional innovation departments, however, we find the same compartmentalized functional structure and the same emphasis on formal control mechanisms.

Streamlining

During the 1980s, optimism about the programming approach diminished greatly. A large number of leading American and European firms fell behind their Japanese competitors both technologically and commercially. The innovation function had become too isolated from the market. Additionally, the innovation chain itself appeared to be clogged up by bureaucracy. Using the words of Dennis McKeever, vice-president of Dow, this called for '(the) elimination of functional silos that insulate a competence in one part of the organization' (Kiesche, 1993, p. 16) The formal control systems seem to act as a brake rather than an accelerator.

For the first time, the location, design and responsibilities of the innovation functions are fundamentally put up for discussion. The innovation function must be more closely linked to the business. The functional model of the professional bureaucracy must be released, and the division and business units should be given the responsibility to decide what happens with the largest part of the funds. It is imperative that innovation be viewed as a process that runs upstream from the conception of a product to the distribution downstream. It is not a sequential, but an iterative process, in which development phases purposefully overlap and functions cooperate with one another intensively. This leads to a complex set of measures in many firms which aims to streamline the innovation function. Bureaucratic obstacles are removed, dead weight is rejected, and vigorous management must ensure that 'good ideas' are piloted to the market as quickly as possible. This requires the following steps:

1. Shifting responsibilities to the business unit

The introduction of business units runs more or less parallel with the streamlining of the innovation function (cf. Wissema, 1994). In a large number of firms the formation of business units has 'evoked' the decentralization of responsibility for innovation. A distinction should be made here between the actual allocation of innovation activities in the business unit (at Stork) and the shift of responsibility for corporate R&D to business units (at DSM Andeno). For example, the chemical giant Hoechst (Rotman, 1993) has reduced the share of 'free' R&D in the corporate budget from 75 to 25%, the remaining part being steered from the business. In most diversified companies, this percentage is currently between 10 and 25%. Most large corporations

[62% according to an American study (Wolff, 1995)] have preserved a hybrid structure.

When discussing the allocation of funds the argumentation is reversed increasingly. It is no longer the question why innovation must take place in the business units. Rather, the legitimization for corporate R&D programmes is disputed. Lewis and Linden (1990) point out that there exist only two essential grounds for that legitimization: (1) the company follows the strategy of technological leadership, and (2) a high degree of technological synergy must be achieved across business units. In this vision, corporate programmes have no reason for existence unless these two preconditions are fulfilled.

2. Entrepreneurship of the R&D function

The attitude of corporate R&D itself also changes. An active attitude is expected from this function (Rubenstein, 1994) in its dealings with the business and external institutions. R&D managers should behave more like 'entrepreneurs': they should clear the way for market relations within the company. Business units are to be viewed as 'partners' or 'customers', and a critical inventory should identify activities that can be subcontracted. Additionally, promising ideas and technologies must be sought outside the company. After all, entrepreneurship also implies that risks be taken and choices made. When making choices, one is led by the relevance of specific knowledge areas to the business, resulting in a clear focus for which the portfolio of R&D projects and programmes is tested.

3. Horizontal organization

At the organizational crossroads of functions and projects, the latter are given priority more and more often. The organization is oriented towards the horizontal flow of knowledge which eventually produces the new product, service or process. The functional departments supply capacity to project managers whose influence on the entire development trajectory is large. The project managers ('heavy-weight project leaders',

Clark *et al.*, 1988) are running the show. The work is increasingly performed in self-managing multidisciplinary teams. Research has revealed (Cobbenhagen *et al.*, 1994) that the frontrunners in the area of innovation have made more progress in strengthening the horizontal axis of the organization than pack members. The majority of them choose (Table 6.1) for the project matrix and the project team.

4. Cooperation in the chain

The relationship between supplier and customer plays an important role in the streamlining regime. The supplier views the customer more and more often as a source of new ideas (Von Hippel, 1986). The suppliers are becoming problem solvers, who get under the skin of their customers in order to be able to provide a complete package of products and services. They try to get a clearer picture of the 'customer's customer'. There are several ways to do so:

- Improving communication with the customer;
- Being present in the end-market;
- Sharing development programmes;
- Participating in customer firms.

In most cases, this development implies a gradual change in the economic exchange relationship between customer and supplier: from a market relationship towards an organizational relationship (cf. Williamson, 1975). The line of horizontal organization is continued, so to speak, beyond the boundary of the corporation. Mutual trust is vital. Sometimes it will be the supplier who faces major uncertainties, sometimes it's the customer. For example, a supplier specialized in chemistry or engineering is expected to attach great importance to the reliability of its customers, while for bulk producers the reliability of suppliers is far more relevant.

This regime implicates that the innovation function is streamlined in organizational terms, not only because the knowledge flow is chosen as a point of departure. The aim is to reduce the management burden by drastically reducing the organization's complexity. At the same time, the flexibility needed to respond to and anticipate changes in the market increases. The above-mentioned components contribute to this. The focus on 'core business units' cuts off side-roads. Cutting back long-term R&D diminishes the incessant tension between what should be finished today and what the future promises. Giving priority to the project flow above the functional flows creates clarity. Finally, decentralization to the business unit ties research, product development and production closer to the customer. Consequences of interventions will become visible more rapidly and hence it will become easier to steer the process.

Conclusions

The four following conclusions will attempt to reflect the thread of the company case studies.

Streamlining is a Dominant Trend

All of the participating firms have experienced an intensive organizational innovation process throughout the past years. Safeguarding, consolidating and underpinning the position as market share leader was the driving force behind this renewal in all the firms. There was no doubt about the need to stay firmly in the saddle of market share leader. The sense of urgency was fed by a clear signal or combination of signals, in particular the loss of market share, declining profits, and the need to shorten the time-to-market. Companies such as Nationale Nederlanden and DSM Andeno made a fresh start from a relatively comfortable position with positive returns. The annual reports of AVEBE and Gist-brocades reveal that their starting position was far less favourable, and that improvement of results was their immediate concern. For Pink Elephant, the youngest firm, market leadership was a challenge early in its development.

Yet the difference in starting position cannot be traced in the efforts and commitment built up in the firms to initiate the change process. In addition, all of the participating firms have set out a comparable course, regardless of the business in which they operate. The common denominators were:

- A distinct market-centred organization;
- Decentralization of tasks and responsibilities to division, business units, and within these, business teams;
- Reinforcement of horizontal lines and reduction of functional (vertical) connections.

To use the terminology of Nationale Nederlanden, one might speak of a 'rotation' of the organization. This process has been referred to as 'streamlining' in this study. The change process has been prompted in all of the firms by changes in the business environment. This process can be partly understood as a way to better adapt to customer demands, more specifically in terms of time-to-market and service and product quality. However, the change process was concerned not only with a process of adaptation. The firms have also initiated the changes to secure a better position in the market in terms of products and services with a higher added value: special products and services and integration of (products and) services. This required a heavier role of development and application of knowledge, not only within R&D but in the entire chain from product conception to production and distribution.

Streamlining of the organization has been a time- and energy-consuming effort in most of the firms. It was impossible to carry through the changes with one stroke of the pen. Obsolete management routines and behaviour patterns had to be unlearned first. The unwritten rules of the organization (Scott-Morgan, 1994) had to be uncovered. Apart from the change of structures, it is not surprising that huge investments have been made to change the organization culture and management development. A number of clear differences in phase can be observed. Pink Elephant chose to streamline the organization soon after its foundation, and MEY had been familiar with a heavily decentralized regional structure for a long time. Stork and DSM Andeno also had previous experience with the introduction of unit management. For example, the Stork operating companies had a fairly independent position for a longer period of time, and DSM Andeno has been taken over from Oce van der Grinten as a more or less 'complete' firm. Finally, AVEBE, Gist-brocades and Nationale Nederlanden have only just dealt with the formal restructuring of the organization.

Streamlining Generates Synergy Problems in the Knowledge Enterprise

New solutions bring with them new problems. That seems to hold true for each of the firms. Business units, decentralization, customer responsiveness, and a powerful project management are not the final solution to 'all' organizational problems. *Organizational boundaries* are shifted, thus leading to new interface problems. An old law applies here (Lawrence and Lorsch, 1969, see Chapter 6): each differentiation in the organization requires integration. In the unit organization, the maintenance, development and transfer of *functional knowledge* threatens to get in a tight corner. Specialists are spread over the firm, quickly adding more value within the units and project groups they are part of. They are more closely tied to the process and cooperate with other disciplines more than they used to previously. Yet the supply of new functional knowledge threatens to suffer in most companies. The exchange of knowledge among units is difficult and the motor for the development of new functional knowledge does not run as smoothly as it used to. Business units and project teams have been given a sharper focus; they know better what does and what does not belong to their core. The effect of this is that the seeds for new business and new projects within these units do not thrive well. *Business development* threatens to become a 'business-foreign' activity because today's customer always come first before tomorrow's customer.

However, it's not only new organizational boundaries that generate problems. *Time boundaries* equally do so. All of the firms unambiguously give priority to short-lived activities. New initiatives are expected to lead to results rapidly, and preferably with the least possible risk. Long-term objectives get trapped. Not only have some firms cut the budget for long-term developments, they have also allocated less time to activities within that budget. Finally, *geographical boundaries* also play an important role. Business units have become the heart of firms that are strongly spread in geographical terms. Thus, we observe in all of the firms from the processing industry discussed here that the direct link between the 'site' (the factory') and development (and sometimes sales as well) is loosened, and replaced by steering 'from a distance'. The question whether it's the business units that cause these longer geographical lines or increasing globalization is not an interesting one. It is given that larger distances must be bridged both in terms of steering and in terms of knowledge exchange. The conclusion to be drawn from this analysis is that synergy in the streamlined organization, that is to say synergy of knowledge to an important extent, is becoming a fundamental problem in firms that are increasingly dependent on the efficient use of knowledge in terms of competitive capacity.

Firms are Once Again Investing in Knowledge Synergy Efficiently

The period now lying behind us can be characterized by terms as 'slimming down', 'downscaling', 'lean corporation', 'head count', and the 'primate of the market'. Throughout that period, the word 'synergy' was taboo. Synergy was regarded (Wijers, 1994) as a trick to maintain old centralized structures. Today, with a large number of firms having made much progress in streamlining their organization, the word starts to regain a new and positive meaning. The concern for coherence is openly expressed once again.

Perhaps, in heavily decentralized firms it is even easier to see what parts can, or should be, connected to form an entity. In this process, 'knowledge' appears to be a highly important linking agent (Figure 5.1). This is illustrated by the innovation of the Nationale Nederlanden organization. The introduction of a new structure to safeguard functional knowledge took place almost simultaneously with the introduction of regional business groups. This firm was strongly aware that it was reversing the switch in one movement. It recognized that its market position was heavily relying on exclusive knowledge of the insurance business. If such know-how cannot be assured within the business groups, separate organizational measures will have to be taken to achieve this.

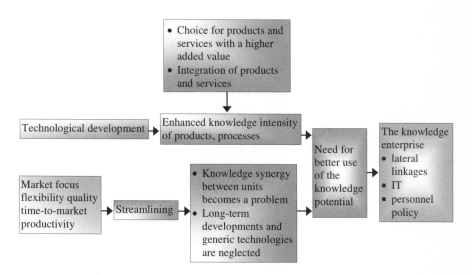

Figure 5.1. Improved utilization of the knowledge potential.

The other firms have reached a comparable conclusion after introducing business units. It is important that each of the participating firms has put much energy into formulating the knowledge ambition. Identification of the core competencies has triggered off the knowledge enterprise. The annual reports of the majority of the firms explicitly point out the relevance of knowledge management, which is expressed particularly in coupling the firm's strategic objectives. This might lead, as we have seen in the case of Gist-brocades, to a far-reaching reshuffling of the business portfolio.

The formulation of the knowledge ambition raises the question of how the knowledge potential can be applied better. It is for that purpose that the participating firms have invested in new instruments that go beyond the organizational boundaries that had just been erected. Lateral organizational linkages (knowledge cluster, sections, sectors and technology platforms), IT and boundary-crossing personnel management (see Part 3) all play an important role here. Some firms have made more progress than others. The industrial firms emphasize the organization and decision making in terms of the utilization and allocation of R&D. Stork and DSM have put a great deal of effort into the development of lateral linkages. AVEBE and Gist-brocades initiated investment in the knowledge enterprise at the time of study. It is obvious that the service-providing firms should regard personnel management as a vital instrument for the knowledge enterprise. Nationale Nederlanden and Pink Elephant have followed a similar course from the three different points of perspectives. Stork, DSM Andeno, Pink Elephant and Nationale Nederlanden aim to bundle the three instruments into a coherent configuration for the knowledge enterprise, in which the central group or (technology) manager plays an *orchestrating* role. Remarkably, 'new business development' has been cast into a separate organizational entity in most of the firms, usually operating *next to* the other business units or divisions. The business development group is given a separate status in most firms with short lines to the strategic management, for example in the form of double roles: technology managers who are also responsible for business development. The relations with the other business units, however, are no less relevant in the firms studied. In that sense, business development can also fulfil a synergetic role.

Knowledge Synergy is Generated by Making Choices in a Learning Organization

Some managers and organization consultants come up with a toolkit filled with instruments when confronted with terms as 'knowledge synergy' and 'knowledge management': group-ware systems, expert systems, technology councils, tech expos, skills maps, and knowledge clusters. We have not come across such managers and consultants in the participating firms, although the use of these instruments is recognized by their managers. For example, some of them observed that too little use has been made of instruments such as personnel management and IT so far: 'We're heading there, but we've only just started'. More important is the insight that the introduction of the business units is followed by a new organizational challenge, which goes beyond the implementation of new techniques and systems. Thus, Stork (Annual Report, 1995) views knowledge management as one of the corner stones of its innovation and technology policy. The utilization of the synergy potential within and among units has become a policy priority in the firm. One might describe this challenge as the development of the 'learning organization across existing organizational boundaries'. This development process should fulfill the following vital preconditions.

1. 'Doing the right things'

What know-how and skills (or core competencies) are crucially important to our firm and what do we want them to achieve? These two questions refer to the firm's knowledge ambition. When the core competencies of a firm are not clear and one is unable to tell in which direction competencies are to be developed, it will be very difficult to utilize opportunities for synergy. A focus as well as a 'sense of urgency' is needed to give knowledge synergy a strategic significance.

It is not surprising in this context that most of the participating firms have picked up the philosophy of Hamel and Prahalad (1994) about core competencies. The resulting choices may have far-reaching consequences, such as:

- New investments and des-investments in technological know-how;
- Selling company parts;
- Purchasing firms;
- Establishing strategic joint-ventures;
- Increased cooperation with universities and other suppliers of knowledge.

In addition to products and market, knowledge has thus become a decisive factor in composing the business portfolio.

This vision has significant consequences for the decision-making and communication processes within the firm. The question is 'Are we doing the right things right?'. In order to answer this question, the following preconditions emerge.

2. Orchestrating thinking capacity

Synergy only provides new energy when energy is added to get the system going. A threshold must be overcome. To put it differently: as the independence of project groups, unit and divisions increase, it will be more difficult to keep the whole together. A small but advanced orchestration function can fulfil a vital role to evoke and maintain synergy. Such a team must be capable of assessing the plans of business units, recognizing opportunities for synergy, following external developments, and proposing ideas to the firm's management and unit managers. In approaches such as these, one must prevent an old centralized structure from being built up again through a back door. Orchestrating calls for the skills of a tightrope walker. If the balance tips to one side, the orchestrator will lose his position, and the balance will continue to be unstable. Firms that have developed these skills (such as Gist-brocades and Stork) seem to be able to chart a forceful technological course at concern level in the case of extensive decentralization.

3. The quality of management

These choices are not made in the participating firms in isolation from corporate headquarters, but come about in the dialogue with the most relevant central and decentral actors. Strategic choices are the result of a continuous process rather than of a once-only strategic analysis like they used to. This places high demands upon the quality of the management, both at the corporate and at the unit level. Managers are expected to:

- look beyond the boundaries of their own organizational domain or knowledge area;
- be able to 'really' cooperate in teams, in which conflicts of interests, differences in visions and conflicts are no exceptions;
- be able to make the connections (as 'linking pins') in the communication and decision making between various organizational levels;
- continue to think.

All of the firms fully underline the significance of an advanced management favourably disposed towards change. All the same, they have all encountered obstacles in the change process. Sometimes comprehensive changes were not possible until the composition of management had changed. In other cases, the changing of the guard took place while the process was on-going, or fresh blood from outside was taken on. This has led in most firms to more focused attention to the in-house training of managers that are able to think in integral terms and keep moving.

The creation of teams in heterogeneous groups in which the members look after different interests has not been an easy task for many managers. This is far more difficult than creating teams within units that are assessed on the basis of one collection of performance standards. Managers have told us what it takes to achieve a standard in one's behaviour. They have told us about the temptation to revert to authoritative behaviour or hidden agendas. The majority of managers are far from satisfied about the realization of the new communication norms. For example, the fresh business unit managers are not eager, to put it mildly, to give up their recently acquired autonomy, although those involved do observe that there is a breakthrough and point to the efforts they make to break old (non) communication patterns.

4. Another way of working at the basis

Knowledge synergy cannot be prescribed by decree. Synergy is generated because people on the shop floor 'visit' each other and 'shop' with each other; because they look outside more often and show others in, and have freed themselves from the not-invented-here syndrome. Another way of working is a true reversal in culture in many organizations, which calls not only for leadership, but also for support throughout the organization. The opportunities to directly involve the knowledge workers at all levels or the organization in this undertaking should be exploited again and again. Often, these opportunities naturally follow from daily practice, for example when:

- personnel is temporarily exchanged in the case of an acquisition;
- internal course programmes are prepared;
- project teams and work and study groups are composed;
- information systems are set up;
- salespersons and engineers approach the customer together;
- other companies and knowledge centres, trade fairs and conferences are visited;
- new employees are trained.

These are occasions where employees temporarily leave their 'fixed workplace' and are given the opportunity to look beyond their own boundaries and make their capabilities available to others. To use a metaphor from biology: the walls that separate organizational entities become permeable.

The instruments (lateral linkages, IT and personnel management) provide opportunities to make the new working method effective and efficient. They provide improved insight into the internal demand for and supply of knowledge and lower the threshold to have a look in each other's 'shop', particularly when they are used in a mutual connection. These lessons can also be learned from Nationale Nederlanden, where training programmes, knowledge clusters, and the knowledge bank are the components of one single knowledge system assured by the management. Synergy assurance is vitally important. Organizations with self-managing units need a continuous stimulus or incentive to look beyond one's own boundaries.

Orchestration

The case studies prove that the streamlining of the innovation function is not the final answer to the organizational problems surrounding innovation. Companies view streamlining as an unmistakable step forward. Particularly during the past five years, it has become clear that this new solution is accompanied by new (or perhaps even very old) problems. These problems manifest themselves at the very moment companies are implementing the new regime with plentiful energy. Prahalad and Hamel (1990, 1994) have confronted a lot of managers with the other side of the 'streamlining coin'. Customer responsiveness, price and quality are not sufficient in their view to survive as a large corporation in the longer term. In order to maintain one's position in the market of tomorrow and the day after tomorrow, the knowledge and resources from the entire corporation must be bundled to develop core competencies, which the firm can use to distinguish itself. This bundling seems to be in sharp contrast with the decentralization characterizing the streamlining regime. This field of tension has clearly come to the fore in the innovation literature of the past five years (Arnold, 1992; Rubenstein, 1994; Szakonyi, 1992). Central to the literature is the question (Rubenstein, 1994) on whether the sharply focused business units are able or inclined '(to support) the kind of research that generates or develops more radical ideas for new products, processes, and services'. The R&D manager (Arnold, 1992) is kept under the thumbs of the business unit managers, who are under pressure to book results quickly: 'Being close to the customer encourages incremental development, and rarely inspires breakthroughs, simply because customers tend to have an evolutionary view of their need and rarely support a visionary spark'. Yet a better understanding of the market demand is considered to be important. We underline, however, that this does not replace 'an independent, self-confident R&D function of critical mass to provide required technological possibilities'. Additionally, it is pointed out in the literature (Roberts, 1995) that a large number of Japanese firms have set in motion a movement in the opposite direction. Far more than their American colleagues, Japanese CEOs are involved in the integration of technology in the corporate strategy. The influence of the CTO (Chief Technology Officers) at the level of the Board of Directors is moreover much more powerful.

Another field of tension in the unit organization ensues from the new role and position of functional departments. Functional departments have been forced to make a (substantial) step back. Sometimes they were even swallowed up in product or market-centred units. Yet the supply and maintenance of *functional knowledge* continues to be vitally important in most organizations. The priority given to the market and the product at the matrix crossroads introduces the risk that the steering of functional knowledge is neglected. The functional knowledge workers are divided over the firm and have lost their home base as well as their power base. The problems that might result from this do not become visible at once. They do not become visible until major or intermittent changes emerge within functional knowledge areas. Changes that the firm must absorb and transfer internally. This does not mean to say that the clock must be turned back. However, it does mean that new organizational measures should be taken to safeguard the supply of essential functional knowledge.

This observation has significant implications for the *logic* on which knowledge regimes are based. This logic is univocal in the streamlining regime, in which consistent choices are made. A great deal of firms understand these choices as being choices between options that exclude each other:

- More incremental research *or* more long-term research;
- More influence for the business units *or* more influence for corporate R&D;
- Market pull *or* technology push;
- Serving markets *or* creating markets;
- Product and market-centred organization *or* functional organization;
- Being the boss in one's own business *or* synergy among businesses;
- Formal control *or* informal cooperation.

One might speak of an or/or approach here. Two contrasting arguments are presented and the decision maker is expected to choose either the first or the second argument. It's the logic of Aristotle: if one argument is 'true', the other must be rejected. Paradoxes are not accepted, but must be resolved. Western management thinking is apparently based (Pascale, 1990; Stacey, 1996) on a paradigm that prescribes unambiguity, consonance and coherence. If one argument does not work, we will have to look for another. And if that does not work either, perhaps we should revert to the initial argument.

Pascale (1990) uses the word 'orchestration' in this connection. It refers to a dialectic style of organization development in which opposites produce a new synthesis through learning. In our view this is the essence of the regime of the knowledge enterprise.

The key question is whether harmonious consistent organizations can effectively respond to the inconsistent, conflicting and paradoxical demands imposed by the environment. It is increasingly argued (Cameron, 1980; Pascale, 1990; Stacey, 1996) that such environments call for a continuous state of creative tension. A tension which keeps the firm alert, puts deep-rooted routines up for discussion, and continues to test accepted points of departure. In other words, replacing the or/or approach by and/and thinking. This will not clear the path for chaos and anarchy, but implies that within one single organization one will at the same time (Hamel and Prahalad, 1994):

- want to stretch goals and look further into the future ('expeditionary marketing' and 'corporate imagination'),

- want to utilize the resources more effectively ('leverage of resources').

It is not surprising that leading firms, with an established reputation, are having most difficulty with doing so. They are often tempted (see Box 5.1) to fall back on patterns that proved to be successful in

Box 5.1. Choosing B instead of A, or let's still take A?

When firms face control problems they tend to choose coherent, stable and univocal solutions. If Solution A does not work, they choose Solution B. Of course in the past there was a reason for picking Solution A, because it fixed a problem. Today, by picking Solution B problems are not always solved the way they used to, but somehow firms are prepared to put up with that. If the old control problems start to be dominant again, however, they tend to revert to the old situation. Let's look at two examples.

Firm P has dissolved a division and restructured it into six business units to be able to carry out processes more closely to the market. Within two years' time, the new solution appears to lead to major problems: synergy is lost in purchase and long-term R&D, and the customer is fed up with doing business with six different sales departments in one firm. A new solution is sought: four business units are merged into a unit that is suspiciously similar to the old division.

Mass producer Firm Q is highly sensitive to economic fluctuation. The firm has decided to focus on specialties, which are less vulnerable to the economic climate. A special business unit is established. The firm is well aware that the fairly formal and hierarchical management style from mass production does not fit in this environment. It will have to provide more space for creativity and flexibility. Yet the new unit dips to the other extreme, resulting in a laissez-faire climate. After three years, the firm is forced to conclude that it lacks focus and coherence. A clear perspective of profitable business fails to materialize. The impatient Board of Directors intervenes by substituting the business unit manager by a marketing manager who has won his spurs in the mass industry. The latter views 're-establishing order' as his first task. All of the well-known cost control techniques are once again dug up.

the past. Yet market leaders don't have a choice: if they want to continue to lead the market, they are forced to broaden their horizon.

The consequence for the knowledge enterprise is that it will have to deal increasingly with different organizational logics at the same time. The streamlining regime will tend to be more programmed in future years. For example, at DSM Andeno streamlining has accelerated the introduction of formal control systems. The systems are no longer the formal corset used to force groups with conflicting interests to cooperate. Instead, they are the tools for organizational units to steer themselves. Pink Elephant has recently chosen to integrate the development function in a separate unit, which might be regarded as a form of hedging. Additionally, most firms feel the increased need for binding control in a streamlined decentralized organization. Not to steer activities bureaucratically from one point, but rather to challenge the business to shift its boundaries. Orchestration might be regarded in this respect as a new combination of the earlier three regimes. This does not mean falling back on old habits, but a consciously chosen strategy aimed at synthesis.

PART III
THE TOOLS

Chapter 6

Lateral Organization

Every organization possesses interior and exterior boundaries. Exterior boundaries show where the organization stops and the market place (the 'environment') starts. Interior boundaries demarcate the internal ordering. Organizational boundaries can be an obstacle in the knowledge traffic. Sometimes a toll needs to be paid, and mostly stopovers are inevitable because the hierarchy is in charge of the boundary traffic. Moving boundaries, for example by forming self-managing units, may be a remedy for part of the knowledge traffic. However, new boundaries are bound to emerge between the new units. The following boundaries can be distinguished: inter-functional, inter-unit, hierarchical, geographical and exterior boundaries. The knowledge enterprise must develop the ability to give way to the boundary-crossing knowledge traffic without burdening the hierarchy. Galbraith (1994) refers to this ability as 'lateral organizational competence'. The formation of lateral linkages is an instrument used to develop this competence. After addressing the various types of lateral linkages, this chapter focuses on their design and implementation.

Organizational Boundaries

Boundaries are established in each firm or institution. Their aim is to draw a line around a group of activities and the people that perform them. Exterior boundaries demarcate where the organization begins and where it stops. Interior boundaries show how an organization is ordered internally. The result is a division, business unit, factory, subsidiary office, department, project group, or a team. They are the entities of the organization. An organization can be ordered by classifying activities of the same type (planners with planners, chemical analysts with chemical analysts, welders with welders). In this case, one speaks of a *functional organization* based on the principle of functional concentration (De Sitter, 1994). Organizational boundaries can also be drawn around activities that are related to the same product, service or customers, resulting in the *product-centred* or *market-centred organization*. The basic argument behind drawing boundaries lies primarily in the steering of the organization. It is assumed that grouping certain activities ('division of labour') leads to more effective steering of these activities. Two typical rudimentary steering elements can be recognized, regardless of the ordering principle applied, when drawing the boundaries:

- A hierarchy that tells the employee who his colleagues are, who the boss is, and who is the boss's boss;
- A bookkeeping that shows the costs and profits of the entity.

Organizational boundaries moreover reveal the *identity* of the entity: the basis for the entity's culture. The members of the organization identify with their entity strongly or less strongly. As time goes by, collective behaviour patterns arise which are based on the norms and standards characteristic of the entity (see Chapter 2). The culture is the result of a largely autonomous process which is hard to influence. However, the boundaries may be shifted from one day to the next due to a formal decision, which organizations do constantly because circumstances keep changing. Activities and employees are regrouped to enlarge the effectiveness of the organization. The arguments for shifting boundaries are diverse, reinforce each other and are sometimes contradictory:

- *Upscaling*: production can be cheaper by integrating factories;

- *Bundling*: flexibility and decisiveness can be enhanced by bringing the basic functions closer to the market in a business unit or multifunctional team;
- *Unbundling*: the complexity of the organization is reduced by introducing parallel product flows or by hiving off activities;
- *Hedging*: new activities can be tackled without external interruption;
- *Redistribution*: the organization is rearranged to find a new balance of power.

Shifts in boundaries do not always lead to the intended effect, for example when they are based on political arguments, and functional arguments are used to legitimize the political decision. This phenomenon is most visible when ministries are reshuffled to make room for a politician. Thus, in 1996, a ministry for infrastructure was created in Israel to create a government seat for Sharon. Additionally, cultural differences may put a spoke in the organization's wheels. It appears to be very difficult to integrate firms or units each having their own identity (Olie, 1996).

There exists another limitation to demarcating new organizational boundaries: when activities and people within separate units are brought together the need to coordinate a number of these activities across units will arise automatically. Differentiation has its price: the price for integrating the entities into a larger whole. Lawrence and Lorsch (1967) show that this development is strongly linked with the growth of the organization. In this growth, the organization first differentiates in internal functions, followed by differentiation in the relevant groups in its environment, for example regional sales and service subsidiaries, a group for business customers, or a polyclinic. Reintegration into self-managing units (such as business units) is a subsequent new ordering with the aim to reduce the enormous administrative burden resulting from differentiation. Yet integration into self-managing units itself may also be viewed as a form of differentiation: differentiation according to product/market combinations. Thus, most of the examples presented in Chapter 4 make clear that the transition of a functional to a product- or

Box 6.1. Persistent boundary conflicts.

Twenty years ago, two medium-sized hospitals in a Dutch city were amalgamated as part of a large-scale merger wave in the health care sector. Advantages of scale were the dominant arguments for the merger. The resulting hospital was given a new name, a new board of management, and a new administrative organization. The two buildings were to be replaced by one brand-new building. However, the relatively sound external cooperation was changed into a poor internal cooperation. The old names of both hospitals continued to be used in internal communication for twenty years. Integration of the polyclinic outpatients' departments was an agony. Fierce conflicts were fought about the occupancy of the operating theatres. Mobility of the nursing staff among the two hospitals was hardly effected.

Management was almost fully absorbed by the new-construction project. Fifteen years went by until they finally agreed on the plans. The external pressure to really deal with the integration increased. It was not until an entirely new generation of health care managers, specialists and board members had succeeded the old generation that the old conflicts about boundaries ceased and the boundary markers were cleared away.

market-centred organization usually evokes the need to secure the integration of functional activities. This raises the question of synergy between the subparts. What binds the subparts of the organization and how should this binding be brought about? In this sense, organizational design is always a combination of differentiation and integration (Thompson, 1967; Lawrence and Lorsch, 1967), whose pros and cons must be constantly weighed. These pros and cons may change over time (Box 6.2). The advantages of differentiation may turn into a drawback and vice versa.

Basically this holds true of the knowledge enterprise as well. Differentiation into business units binds marketing, development and production (or implementation) closer to each other. The same goes for the build-up of a powerful project organization. The knowledge flow along the innovation trajectory is thus strengthened. The examples

Box 6.2. Shifting Boundaries.

Firm A is setting up a new group for research into applications of new materials in its products. Know-how and experience must be developed in the firm from scratch. The meagre expertise was previously fragmented over the firm's divisions. It is quite common in such a situation to protect the group from the rest of the firm for some time ('hedging'). Integration within the business units yields little in that stage and takes time and energy. Close cooperation in the team is required to establish the foundation for a new knowledge domain. Yet hedging the group becomes increasingly dangerous because the group tends to live its own life. In Firm A, it was usually the vice-president in person who defended the project at the annual critical evaluation. Therefore, it took five years for a real discussion to set in motion about the way in which the knowledge of the group was to be concretely applied in the divisions.

IT Firm B started as a developer of an administrative software package. It gradually added a second branch of business: outsourcing programmers and analysts. Initially both customer-focused branches were integrated, which offered great advantages. The package provided entrance to the customer, and the relationship with the customer was gradually extended by providing the additional service. Meanwhile, the latter has strongly grown and the turnover of the packages is in a downward movement. The service has become the core activity and the sales of packages a sideline. From an advantage, the integration has now turned into a drawback, because a lot of companies that hire IT personnel do not wish to be stuck to the software-packages of Firm B. The firm has decided to move the sales and maintenance of packages to a separate private limited company. It no longer invests in new developments and expects a gradual run-down altogether.

from Chapter 4 clearly illustrate this. However, they also show that the new boundaries may lead to new obstacles: the exchange of knowledge among the units becomes a problem due to a variety of causes. First, a boundary narrows one's field of perspective. As soon as boundaries are established, people tend to look less to the outside and more to the inside, leading to the 'not-invented-here syndrome,

(Katz and Allen, 1982). Additionally, they look less far beyond the horizon; today's business is what counts, tomorrow's business is far away. Second, the obstacle arises due to the bureaucratic mechanisms that are strongly present even in a unit organization. In the classical bureaucracy, the boundary traffic is largely dealt with by the hierarchy. If Unit A wants to use knowledge from Unit B, the manager is called upon who is part of the management group also representing the management of Unit B. This hierarchical detour clogs up quickly, especially when the need for crossing boundaries increases. Moreover, the hierarchy protects the knowledge domain. Staff departments in particular tend to defend their domain and fight off other knowledge suppliers. They tend to keep their cards to their chest. In such an environment, data banks are accessible only to one's own unit (see Box 3.4). For operating entities (such as factories and business units) the direct financial interests prevail. Their knowledge workers are used in the unit's own processes as effectively as possible, and are seconded only when the primary task allows for that and the other party is prepared to pay the costs. In other words, organizational boundaries stimulate toll collection for the boundary traffic. Also, due to the preoccupation with the tasks of one's own unit, the Unit A workers are seldom aware of the useful knowledge available beyond the boundaries of their unit. Finally, boundaries are often an obstacle to closing the control loop. For example, the field service of an insurance company that monopolizes customers contacts (i.e. the intermediaries) will tend to forward customer complaints to the office staff untimely and incompletely.

The Lateral Organization

In contrast, the relevance of border-crossing boundary traffic is strongly on the rise. The reasons for this have been previously mentioned in this book:

• The integration of products and services;

- The concern for unit-crossing core competencies;
- The importance of cross-fertilization in the developments of new products;
- Increasing globalization;
- Increasing complexity of processes, products and services.

From this point of view, one might wonder whether an organization cannot do without boundaries or with fewer boundaries. A growing number of authors answer this question in the affirmative. Karl Weick (1993) takes a challenging stance in this debate. In his vision, the myth of the 'makeability' of an organization having univocal boundaries must be forsaken. Organizational architecture is the result of continuous improvization. Others point to the evolutionary principle of self-organization (Morgan, 1986; Stacey, 1996), or, to use another metaphor from biology (Florida and Kenney, 1990): the organization is like a micro-organism, an amoeba that constantly stretches its boundaries to food and turns away from threats. Closely related to the latter is Mintzberg's (1979) image of the 'adhocracy', in which cooperation and authoritarian relationships are not structured (*'ad hoc'*) until a new task presents itself. Finally, the literature points to the increasing importance of self-generating networks, virtual organizations, whose members communicate electronically, but which actually — or better: formally — do not exist.

The authors of this book take a pragmatic stance in the debate about this question. Organizational boundaries will continue to exist as long as there will be hierarchical relations and responsibilities for results and budget in organizations. The increasing tendency to hold firms and units accountable for their results and behaviour (for example, for polluting the environment) is a counter-force against the blurring of boundaries. Apart from this, we pointed out that the removal and blurring of boundaries will evoke or reinforce new, other boundaries. Finally, the question is raised whether the fashionable terms used to describe the future organization can be used to formulate normative organization strategies. For example, a knowledge network is not a result of reorganizations. Networks are not 'introduced', they develop on the basis of a number of organizational conditions. The latter *can* be influenced. In short: we do not advocate a futuristic model of the 'boundary-free knowledge enterprise'. Instead, we argue in favour of the reinforcement of the ability to develop, transport and apply knowledge across organizational boundaries. Galbraith (1994) refers to this ability as the firm's 'lateral organizational capability'. The use of the organizational instruments that are at our service is referred to as *lateral organization*. The next two chapters will delve into the instruments of personnel management and information technology. This chapter will focus on the instrument of lateral groups. Lateral groups are defined as follows: Groups composed of representatives from different organizational entities, focusing on the coordination of common activities, whereby the hierarchy is burdened as little as possible.

These lateral linkages are applied for coordination purposes right across five different types of organizational boundaries:

- functional boundaries;
- boundaries between business units;
- geographical boundaries;
- hierarchical boundaries;
- exterior boundaries.

Inter-Functional Lateral Linkages

The multidisciplinary project team in product development is an example of an *inter-functional* lateral linkage. An organization steering on functions as well as multifunctional projects is called a matrix organization. There are several types of matrix organizations (Klimstra and Potts, 1988). The most important differences between the variants of the matrix organization are concerned with one dimension: the degree to which the organization steers for integration between functions. In practice, six variants can be distinguished along this dimension (see Table 6.1). In the least integrated version the managers

Table 6.1. From functional organization to project organization.

Organization type	Pack members	Frontrunners
Functional organization The project is divided into segments and allocated to the functional (sub)-departments concerned. Departments often work on a project successively. The project is coordinated by the functional management and higher management echelons.	36%	3%
Functional matrix A project leader with limited responsibility is appointed to coordinate the project through the various (sub)-departments. The functional managers retain responsibility for their own specific segments of the projects.	29%	24%
Matrix organization A project leader is appointed to supervise the project, and shares responsibility with the functional managers. In general, the project manager and the functional managers make joint decisions.	14%	15%
Project matrix A project leader is appointed to supervise the project, who shares primary responsibility for completion of the project. Functional managers provide manpower and the functional expertise required.	17%	40%
Project team A project manager is appointed to supervise a project team, which is composed of a core group of people from different functional departments. These are linked or seconded to the project on a full-time basis. Functional managers have no formal involvement.	4%	28%

of the functional departments clearly call the shots. At the other end of the continuum, the project leader runs the show from the early beginning of the project right up to implementation. In this variant, the functional units are in the first place suppliers of capacity. Research (Table 6.1) has revealed that frontrunners in the field of innovation distinguish from pack members in their branch of business by strongly steering on the integration of functions. We have recognized the same trend in our case studies. Most of the firms develop from the functional to the project-centred end of the scale. When they reach this point, we speak of a 'rotation' of the organization, where the different functions are fine-tuned to each other in the projects. The lateral linkage (project group) has become a regular work unit.

Lateral Linkages Between Self-Managing Units

1. Knowledge clusters

The second application of lateral linkages focuses on self-managing units (business units) within a firm. The design of lateral linkages between business units is based on the relevance of synergy between the units. In its most concrete form, synergy is concerned with the *effective* use of knowledge sources. Business units are able to use each other's know-how and experience. For example, business units at Gist-brocades and AVEBE subcontract development activities to each other and make use of each other's equipment, raw materials and customer contacts. In firms that have clearly chosen for the unit organization and the run-down of the functional organization, lateral linkages can be applied to prevent functional knowledge divided over the units from fragmenting, eroding or leaking away. The *knowledge clusters* at Stork and Nationale Nederlanden can be viewed as lateral linkages that are expected to avoid a similar process. Based on functional knowledge areas, the clusters consist of representatives from the self-managing units. In both examples there is a cluster coordinator who is responsible for the cluster's progress and is the link with the corporate organization.

Galbraith (1994) refers to this coordinator as the *integrator*. In his vision, the integrator is a 'small general manager' without formal authority. Formal authority continues to be present within the line organization, with the integrator ensuring leadership when conflicts between self-managing units present themselves. This is what makes it a very difficult role: exerting influence without having authority in the field of tension between units each of which cherishes its own interests. The knowledge cluster (Figure 6.1) in larger organizations is the core (the inner circle) within a broader network (the outer circle). The role of the knowledge cluster might be compared with the executive committee of a professional association.

2. Strategic lateral linkages: technology council

Apart from an operational role, interfunctional lateral linkages may also have a strategic task. In that case they not only ensure the exchange and supply of knowledge, but they are also responsible for:

- Spotting knowledge needs;
- Assessing the state of the art;
- Advising about priorities for knowledge investments;
- Creating conditions for knowledge synergy;
- Formulating the *mission* for the knowledge enterprise.

The technology council fulfils a similar strategic role in large multibusiness organizations. This might be referred to as the 'knowledge council' in a service company. The council performs the strategic dialogue of the knowledge enterprise. In industrial companies, it is usually composed of R&D managers from divisions or business units and a limited number of R&D people ('key scientists') that hold a key positions within the firm. In a service firm as Pink Elephant, the knowledge council consists of managers of the operating companies, the R&D manager, and is chaired by a member of the Board of Directors. The chairman of the technology councils in industrial firms is mostly the firm's *technology manager* (also called Chief Technology Officer (CTO), or in the service sector: Chief Knowledge Officer (CKO)). Rather than steering corporate R&D his main task is to orchestrate the knowledge enterprise, using his power only in exceptional cases. The technology manager is the link with the top and ensures the technological input in the corporate strategy, giving special attention to long-term (new) business development.

3. Knowledge centres

In some firms, the integrator function develops into a true 'department'. Thus, the CTO at Gist-brocades is supported by a small high tech think-tank, and new competence or knowledge centres are set up in many service companies. This implies that in the context of a decentralized unit organization, a functional group is once again installed. The decision to do so is not an easy one, because it creates by definition a field of tension with the line organization. However, the decision may be inevitable because of various reasons:

- A change in course in the definition of core competencies that requires intensive coaching;
- Securing the core competencies;
- The need to safeguard business development;
- The need to recruit new know-how in a relatively short period of time;
- The management and maintenance of a common infrastructure.

The question is whether such departments are set up to last forever, or only as a temporary facility. For example, it may be obvious that the software sector will choose a temporary solution for the millennium problem: it is a problem that will (hopefully!) pass. Such a knowledge centre has the character of a boundary-crossing project team which must be able to rapidly anticipate market developments. Other organizations (universities, suppliers, and clients) are frequently involved in such strategic projects. A project may be important to the extent that a programme director is temporarily appointed and charged with a special task which must be carried out throughout the organization. Thus, many companies appointed a corporate manager for Total Quality in the 1980s. He was responsible for getting the various company departments of the concern to work for a common quality goal. The programme manager provided the framework, communicated the message, and played the role of knowledge broker.

In any case, it is important that when such entities are designed one clarifies their aim:

- A job with a beginning and an end that must be completed rapidly;
- A quick transfer to the line organization;
- The development into a business unit;
- A new functional group for new strategic knowledge;
- Securing common facilities;
- Permanent support from the strategic top for matters that under no circumstances are to be dealt with at unit level.

Such groups which can serve the interests of the firm in its entirety may sometimes continue to be part of a self-managing unit. In that case they are given the additional central task of a *knowledge centre*. It may be obvious that a similar group must also be given the budgetary space and according rewards for its 'central' task.

4. Knowledge networks

In larger organizations (for example Stork) the lateral linkages are often part of a *knowledge network* (Figure 6.1). The knowledge cluster (the inner circle) might be regarded as a junction in the network. To use a metaphor, they are the bolts that anchor the network in the organization. They are an essential link in upstream communication. The knowledge workers in the field in question (the outer circle) meet each other at workshops, tech expos and courses organized by the clusters. Electronic mail and internal discussion lists and newsletters are additional communication channels in the network.

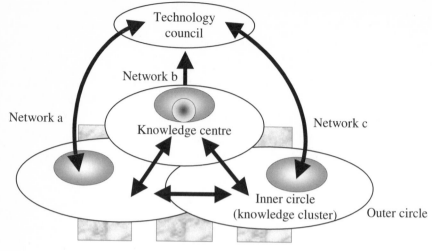

Figure 6.1. The knowledge network.

The technology council (or knowledge council) is the policy-making heart of the network where the knowledge ambition is formulated, on the basis of both strategic considerations and signals from the company. The council moreover advises the line organization to take the decisions when the lower level fails to come up with an answer. Finally, the council is also accountable for the working of the entire network. The council creates the conditions, follows the quality of boundary traffic and intervenes in conflicts when necessary ('management by exception'). The same functions are found in smaller organizations, where the different groups and networks mostly show strong overlap.

Geographical Lateral Linkages

Increasing internationalization and globalization confront the knowledge enterprise with the necessity to bridge organizational as well as geographical boundaries. It's not only the export and geographical diffusion of production facilities that require the geographical diffusion of knowledge. There are a great number of large companies in the global market place where strategic functions as marketing and R&D are geographically spread. The role of geographically spread company components in a knowledge enterprise may differ strongly per firm, but also within a firm itself. These differences become manifest when looking at the size and direction of the knowledge flow the company component belongs to. Figure 6.2 compares the size of the incoming and outgoing knowledge flows. In this way (Gupta and Govindarajan, 1991, cf. Galbraith, 1994), it is possible to distinguish four different strategic roles in the knowledge enterprise:

- global integrator
- integrated player

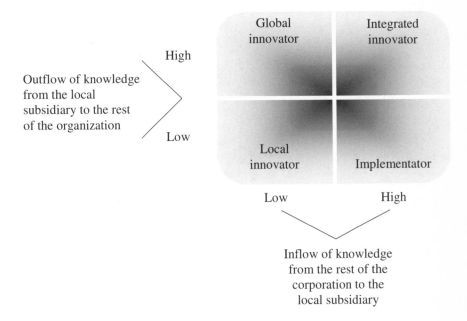

Figure 6.2. International knowledge strategies.

- implementator
- local innovator

The business unit itself, in its role of *global integrator*, is the main source of knowledge. This role used to be played previously by the business units in the corporation's home country, for example DSM Andeno. This has changed in recent years. Thus, the geographically spread business units of Ericsson fulfill a global innovative role in the Swedish concern, while production is allocated to other countries. Telecommunication is a sector in which such global diffusion is fairly frequent (Galbraith, 1994). Other examples can be found in the chemical and pharmaceutical sectors, where firms have been predominantly acquired during the past years on the basis of their knowledge. Acquisition is a way of broadening the concern's knowledge base within a short time period. The role of global innovator imposes high demands upon the boundary traffic, in which the business unit plays a stimulating and integrating role. The global role is not an easy one for smaller business units with strongly spread knowledge clients, particularly when it has to compete with other units for the attention of local sales groups. Lateral group meetings are usually expensive and differences in markets and cultures make group communications a heavy task. As with AVEBE, this seems to hold true especially when new products and services place higher demands on the local organizations.

The *integrated player* also fulfils a global strategic role, but moreover relies heavily on knowledge from the rest of the firm. This role is particularly manifest in business units which clearly serve their own markets with their own products, but which make ample use of generic knowledge. This situation is common in the sector of consumer electronics and computer hardware (for example at Philips and IBM). The role of integrated player fully depends upon the working of the knowledge enterprise. The knowledge synergy between business units and operating companies is an existential prerequisite in this type of organizations. It may be obvious that all instruments of the knowledge enterprise are applied in an integrated manner. In most firms, a central or corporate direction is indispensable. At Stork, this integrating role is played by the corporate function technology management.

The *implementator* mainly uses the knowledge of other units. The knowledge traffic is basically one-way traffic. Examples are the foreign operating companies of Gist-brocades and AVEBE. The emphasis is on sales and/or production. Most of these are firms that were taken over to be quickly brought up to a higher supply level of knowledge. The implementator is the complement of the global player. The role of implementator does not imply that the company component is allowed to neglect the build-up of its own competencies. A critical mass of own knowledge is needed (Cohen and Levinthal, 1990) to be able to absorb other knowledge.

Local innovators possess virtually all the knowledge that is needed to serve the local market. The demands imposed on the local market are specific (or 'idiosyncratic') to the extent that the knowledge of the company component has little value for other markets. Local innovators are frequently found in the food industry and insurance sector.

Shifts in the role patterns are particularly relevant to the knowledge enterprise. Within one single company, a variety of patterns stand out simultaneously. Table 6.2 shows the most important trends.

When such shifts in roles take place, a gradual and incremental improvement of the knowledge enterprise does not suffice in general. A new 'knowledge enterprise plan' must be made. We have called this plan the *knowledge ambition*. A first step is generally that a lateral linkage is formed which allows for the dialogue with the most important partners in the knowledge enterprise.

Hierarchical Lateral Linkages

Hierarchical boundaries, too, may be an obstacle to the knowledge flow. This becomes manifest mainly in firms which require a fundamental restructuring of the organization. Examples are the introduction of a TQC programme, the integration of a firm following an acquisition, or the build-up of a new business. At that moment,

Table 6.2. Shifts in roles.

Shift	Cause	Consequence
Global → Integrated	The introduction of business units or the integration of a new acquisition	Build-up of a knowledge network on the basis of a partnership of business units and a stimulating role of the corporate organization
Integrated → global	The creation of business units from parts of existing company components	Strong integration of knowledge domains, stimulating and initiating role of the business unit
Implementator → global	Decentralization of R&D to operating companies	Build-up of new knowledge centres or transfer of knowledge capacity, shift from knowledge utilization to knowledge transfer
Local → implementator	An acquisition	The unit is connected to the corporation's knowledge domain as quickly as possible. Investment projects, personnel exchange
Local → global	An acquisition or the opening of new markets outside of the home country	Development of knowledge about other markets. Development of a stimulating and initiating role for knowledge development and knowledge transfer

the administrative knowledge of various hierarchical levels must be applied at the same time. The regular hierarchical channels may clog up quickly especially when things are urgent. The hierarchical layers threaten to act as filters in the communication. A strategy that may offer a solution in such a situation is the temporary establishment of a group representing both the various levels and the various entities or functions. Such a group is referred to as a diagonal connection or 'deep slice' (Gustavsen, 1992).

External Lateral Linkages

Most of the firms in this study have strengthened the ties with suppliers and users of knowledge based on various arguments, one of them being the focus on core activities and core competencies. This is because the firm must mainly focus on the knowledge areas that really differentiate in terms of competition. This is possible only by reserving attention and hiving off or subcontracting activities that do not belong to the core. In other words (cf. Williamson, 1975), an organizational relation is exchanged for a market relation. Despite, or perhaps even thanks to these developments, the external knowledge relations of firms and institutions seem to be increasing rather than decreasing. Thus, 'outsourcing' of exchangeable knowledge always requires a certain degree of coordination and knowledge of purchase. At the same time, the position of the firm in the total value chain becomes increasingly important. Specifically for knowledge-intensive firms it holds that the supply of knowledge is not generally a pure market transaction. It has to be possible to look into each other's kitchen. The knowledge network with the new knowledge suppliers should at any rate be designed in an effective way, for example by involving the suppliers in project groups. In most cases the lateral linkage (see for example DSM Andeno) is based on a one-to-one relationship because both suppliers and clients do not want to throw their competition-sensitive knowledge out on the street. Yet the importance of knowledge integration in the entire development chain is increasingly recognized. Thus, AVEBE focuses on innovation in the beginning of the value chain (the potato growers) right up to the end of the chain (the customers).

A second argument for establishing lateral linkages is that the firm must make *more effective use* of the knowledge developed in its environment. A substantial number of large firms have started co-operation with universities and other (public) research institutions, mainly for fundamental and exploratory research. The importance of gatekeepers was clearly recognized in the 1970s (Allen and Cohen, 1969). Large corporations mostly organize the lateral linkages directly with the institutions involved. They invest in research positions at universities and actively participate in discussion groups set up in conjunction with these institutions. Together with the intensification of R&D programmes of the European Union an additional complex of cooperation has arisen between firms and universities. For smaller and medium-sized firms, this integrating role is mostly played by trade associations, industry-specific institutes and innovation centres.

Separate forms of cooperation are the strategic alliance and the *joint venture*. These can be based on two motives. First, to bundle efforts for new developments that go beyond the power of separate companies. An example is the joint development of a new generation chips by IBM, Philips and Apple. The second motive is the possibility to develop new products and services or to penetrate new markets on the basis of new combinations of core competencies of the separate firms. The firms keep their own styles and create new unique combinations by linking their core competencies in a new firm. Chemferm and Holland Sweetener are examples from our study. Such lateral linkages generally have a high risk/high reward profile. It's

Box 6.3. A small firm playing an integrating role.

A small Dutch coating firm employing 45 people was the motor in an audacious cooperation effort. The firm supplied coating for wooden window frames for house construction. The developer of the firm picked up a new development in the United States, just by reading about it in a professional journal and grabbing the phone. The technique was used for an entirely different process, but might well be applied for the firm's products. The use of 'powder paint' on wooden surfaces was a new and unique application required the necessary development work. The firm went looking for cooperation partners for a development project, and found them in the total value chain: a semi-public institute for chemical research, the supplier of coating equipment, the producer of construction components, a building contractor, and a municipality. The project was moreover supported by the central authorities on the basis of environmental considerations.

not only bigger firms that initiate such cooperation efforts. Smaller firms may also fulfill an integrating role (Box 6.3).

Generally speaking it is not easy to bring about good communication between representatives from various disciplines who, moreover, worked on totally different products and in different cultures previously. The risk of failure is too high.

The Design of Lateral Linkages

The organizational lateral linkage is no panacea for all irregularities that may result from organizational differentiation. Thus, words like 'committee' and 'advisory council' in common parlance often have a negative overtone. 'Commission management' is certainly no honorary title. Both governments and firms are repeatedly forced to dissolve time-consuming and little productive commissions and work groups. Lateral linkages must be designed intelligently. Their added value must be assessed on a regular basis. A number of important lessons can be derived from practice.

1. Informal and Formal Lateral Linkages

The question that rises again and again is to what extent lateral linkages should be given a formal status. Fortunately (Galbraith, 1994) a major part of knowledge integration in the organization takes place spontaneously and on a voluntary basis. Several people start talking about a specific subject and discover the advantages of a more intensive contact. They involve a few more colleagues and suggest to meet on a more regular basis. In most cases it's not these meetings themselves that produce most of the results, but rather the informal contacts in between. Informal networks grow and cannot be 'introduced' by decree. It is possible to create conditions under which such informal cooperation is reinforced. The most important conditions lie in the possibilities to get in touch with others, during meetings, through email, job rotation, and in courses. Managers can stimulate such contacts by having their staff look into each other's kitchen and opening the doors to their own kitchen. Crucial here is the geographical vicinity. It is extremely dangerous to geographically spread a knowledge centre following an administrative decentralization. This is the reason why firms like AVEBE and Gist-brocades have kept the R&D groups in one central location in the streamlining process. The value of a common lunch area should therefore not be underestimated, even in the age of internet and intranet.

Formalization of a lateral linkage may be necessary when:

- there is a need to make the lateral linkage responsible and accountable for a specific task;
- the lateral linkage is receiving substantial resources;
- decisions are delegated to the lateral linkage.

In the case of *formal* lateral linkages, like those we find in the project organization, there exists, as we have seen previously, a sliding scale, ranging from the representative discussion group of different functions to a close work organization in which the project leader runs the show from A to Z: the integral project team. In fact, one should not speak of a lateral linkage in the latter case, because the project group has become part of the 'line organization'. Our case studies have clearly demonstrated that most of the firms move into that direction when bridging inter-functional boundaries. DSM Andeno is a case in point. At the same time, knowledge clusters in most firms are given a more formal character because the tasks they are expected to fulfill are becoming increasingly heavy: from informal exchange of knowledge to development and safeguarding of professional knowledge for the organization as a whole.

The technology council is an example of a formal strategic lateral linkage with the emphasis on policy formation and policy assessment. The strategic lateral linkage nurtures the knowledge and technology policy. Experiences with this cluster are not altogether favourable because of its formal character. In our study enthusiasm about new opportunities for synergy alternated with complaints about superfluous paperwork even within one company. Practical experiences with the technology council (Wolff, 1993) in the French electronics conglomerate Schneider show that the council is particularly effective when:

- the council is sufficiently small to function well and sufficiently large to encompass the major knowledge domains;
- the council focuses on a limited number of critical subjects;
- the council's tasks and working method are laid down in a 'charter'.

Formalization of lateral linkages does not automatically imply replacement of informal cooperation by rules and procedures. Knowledge clusters with a strong formal status will continue to function well only when people manage to find each other outside the formal order. Formal structures are merely the visible top of the knowledge enterprise ship. The 'real' work is carried out beneath the water line: in the daily agreements made between managers and in the exchange of knowledge between and among project teams, departments and company components.

2. The Mission

Lateral linkages are difficult to manage. They run right across fields of tension, or right through unknown territory. The power they are able to develop is generally based on informal behavioural codes, for which sense of direction is highly important. The knowledge ambition is a good point of orientation. Lateral linkages must be able to compare their own course against the lines plotted for the firm as a whole. The overall lines of the knowledge enterprise should be recognisable for all members of the organization. It provides a common point of departure in day-to-day communication. This holds true particularly of cooperation efforts that will bear fruit only in the longer term. And for the synergy between knowledge domains that are relatively isolated from each other but may offer new perspectives by new combinations in the future. The knowledge ambition legitimizes rewards, but simultaneously risky activities that may create future opportunities. It would be wise to make the added value of the lateral linkage explicit, thereby also indicating both opportunities and risks.

3. Composition

The composition of lateral linkages is critically important. Knowledge clusters and technology councils must be able to discuss the contents of knowledge, even when policy issues are at stake. In other words, such lateral linkages should not be allowed to stick to purely arrange-type and coordinating activities, but should include discussions about such things as molecules, proteins, soil improvement, types of mortgage, computer configurations, and wheel suspension. In relation to the group composition this means that content-related expertise is an essential criterion for selection. Key scientists should take an important place in the lateral structures. However, more is required from participants than knowledge about the specific content. They should also be prepared and able to look beyond the boundaries of their profession. They must be open to the enthusiasm of others. Additionally, participants are expected to isolate from their own hobbies and interests in order to commit themselves to boundary-crossing policies. To put it differently, there is no room in lateral linkages for bureaucrats or narrow-minded people.

4. Embedding

It is important for lateral linkages in the knowledge enterprise to reinforce each other. Technology councils, knowledge clusters, and technology or knowledge managers are all of them links in a knowledge network. A technology council that estranges from the knowledge network in the business will quickly lose its added value. Technology councils that feel no connection with the knowledge content are bound to get bogged down in policy considerations nobody is interested in. Knowledge clusters that fail to get policy under control, will continue to get stuck in amateurism. The value of isolated lateral linkages is therefore limited. The firm that seeks to distinguish itself from other firms will have to possess a coherent structure in which the lateral linkages are mutually connected.

Box 6.4. Lateral structures management development at DSM.

Career development of the 'Top 200' or 'Top 500' is crucially important for all multinationals. Career development not only provides a firm with its own top managers and top specialists trained in-house, it also supplies the cement keeping the firm together as a coherent entity. This is particularly relevant to firms built on a strongly decentralized structure. The critical question raised here is how this corporate objective can be effectively united with the substantial degree of autonomy of divisions and business units. The lateral structures recently designed by DSM for this purpose seem to be highly promising. In the framework of a concern-wide decentralization programme ('Concern 2000'), DSM has transferred the majority of tasks of the corporate personnel department to the business groups (BGs). The corporate personnel department (CPD) thus slimmed down has now focused attention on activities providing synergy at corporate level.

The *integrating role* in this exercise is played by the CMD (Corporate Management Development) department. This small team including four senior staff member supports three types of lateral linkages established by the corporate MD policy:

A business group MD committee, presided by BG managers and consisting of all 13 business groups as well as the heads of their personnel departments, which meets eight times per year. In addition, the CMD staff are part of the MD committees of the business groups as 'linking officers'.

Branch committees for functional sectors such as marketing, technology and production, and personnel and organization, finance, economics and IT, which follow the developments in the subject areas in question and translate these into function profiles, and advise about appointments. These sector groups consist of business and functional managers from the business units and the corporate organization.

Countries groups whose aim is to generate synergy in personnel policy for the four major DSM countries (the USA, UK, Germany and France). The countries committees meet two to four times annually and is presided by a 'country manager'.

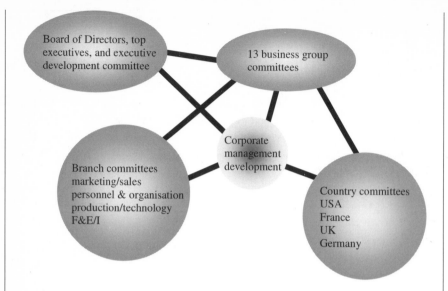

In this structure, the president of the corporation chairs the *top executive development* group, which prepares major top appointments. The director CPD presides the Executive Development Committee, which deals with the appointments directly beneath the top echelon. Additionally, this group acts as a steering group for the corporate MD policy. The remaining lateral linkages report to this group through CPD. In this way attention is devoted in an extremely light-weight decentralized structure to policy components that would otherwise have escaped from attention in the decentralized organization. This structure moreover provides a direct connection with strategic decision-making.

At Nationale Nederlanden, the formal knowledge structures were established as an integrated configuration in one stroke at a natural moment to do so (an organizational rotation). Similar extensive reorganizations often offer a good opening to set up an adequate structure for the knowledge enterprise. In other firms, such as Stork, this took place step by step, which may turn out well as long as the firm keeps in mind the aim of an integrated knowledge enterprise. In policy terms, such an approach is referred to as 'mixed scanning' (Etzioni, 1976). It focuses on a far-reaching change ('a big step'), which is carried out in small, incremental steps. As a precondition, the change of direction (the 'knowledge ambition', or 'mission') is clear to all policy makers and knowledge workers and the small steps are continuously tested for the big step aimed at.

5. Facilities

Establishing lateral linkages costs time and money, whether it be formal or informal groups. A lateral linkage does not become effective until it is provided with facilities enabling it to function. These may simply consist of time to partake in and prepare for discussions. Electronic means of communication are expected to play an increasingly important role here. Curiously, universities make highly intensive use of these world-wide. The limited funds available to universities force its employees to use cheap forms of communication. International co-operation in research, education and the organization of conferences is virtually inconceivable without email and the Internet.

Facilities may also include the *budgetary space* when a knowledge cluster comes up with new proposals. Or when the technology council reaches the conclusion that the knowledge ambition must be shifted. Providing lateral linkages with their own budgets is advised only when they are charged with a specific formal task that is better managed by the group than by a line organization unit. The principle of 'management by exception' should be applied as much as possible: 'in the line, unless...'. As we have seen previously, there may be sound reasons for such exceptions, for example when the firm has to catch up, or perhaps to take a knowledge lead. One cannot expect knowledge clusters, which discuss new developments in the business in their own time once in a while, to accomplish essential changes in the firm's core competencies. They might develop the ideas that way, but cannot set the driving wheel in motion.

6. Communicating at a Distance

The geographical dimension plays an increasingly important role in the knowledge enterprise. This holds true for both firms operating in a global market and service-providing firms employing many people working at the client's. Lateral linkages with strongly spread members will have to find other ways of exchanging knowledge. Electronic means of communication (Chapter 8) may be applied for the transport of explicit knowledge. The occasional personal contacts can be used for intensive exchange of tacit knowledge. It would be a waste to spend this time for matters that might just as well be confided to a computer.

7. Time Horizon

Lateral linkages are not established for eternity. Some firms reorganize their committees and special task groups every few years. In fact, this is too late; generally committees are not discontinued until they are near death. Just like the reorganization of government commissions, this provides only an optical saving. It would be wiser to set a fixed term for the lateral linkage's activities. The best criterion is the contribution made by the group to the knowledge enterprise. As a prerequisite, the lateral linkage must make their own performance transparent and ensure adequate report. Assessment by the clients of the knowledge outside the group should weigh most.

Chapter 7

Steering on People

Personnel work has become a true profession over the past 20 years, offering adequate training programmes and tested tools. When these tools are skilfully employed for business development we speak of 'personnel policy'. Personnel policy has a strategic meaning in the knowledge enterprise, because no single measure can be thought of that leaves the knowledge flows untouched. This chapter first addresses the interaction between personnel policy and the business strategy. Subsequently, it shows how the instruments of personnel policy can contribute to achieving the knowledge ambition, thereby touching upon the following aspects: recruitment and selection, coaching and assessment, training and education, and career policy. In the knowledge enterprise, the combined use of instruments is especially important. Finally, we will address the value of culture as a binding agent.

From Personnel Work to Personnel Policy

In the computer age people continue to be the most important carriers of knowledge in the organization. Every mutation in the workforce has an impact on the performance of the knowledge enterprise. When recruiting someone, new knowledge is brought in. When an employee is transferred, knowledge is moved from Department A to Department B. Thus, new combinations of knowledge can also come into existence. The knowledge gained in Department A can be combined with that in Department B. Finally, the dependency of the knowledge enterprise of its own human carriers of knowledge is shown when an experienced employee leaves the firm unexpectedly. Peter Drucker (1994, p. 8) uses the word 'knowledge worker' in this context: the employees 'who know how to allocate knowledge to productive use'. Drucker points out that this strongly growing group of employees require the organization to steer on other principles. A fundamental given here is that knowledge workers are the owners of their own production means: the knowledge they possess. The traditional contrast between the capital and labour factors lose value in this perspective, thus making personnel policy a powerful instrument in the knowledge enterprise. For such knowledge-intensive companies as IT firms it is without doubt even the most powerful instrument. Their product is tailored knowledge, which is developed (Box 7.1), maintained and transferred by the firm's employees. Their expertise directly determines the firm's value, especially in a growing market.

Box 7.1. Implicit knowledge as a means of production.

The software sector is a producer of an astronomical amount of explicit knowledge. This knowledge is given shape in different forms: software packages, programming languages, and software development tools. Examples are the new programming language JAVA, the SAP and BAAN systems, and the software development tools of Oracle or USoft. This explicit knowledge is not significant for the client until the human capacity is available to apply it. The majority of the software firms thrives upon that very market demand: the supply of high tech service-providing capacity. In fact, the operational knowledge is the primary means of production. In turn, software firms try to make part of this operational knowledge explicit to reduce their dependence of individual craftsmanship and keep their learning experiences at organizational level. Yet they are aware that they continue to rely largely on the implicit knowledge stored in the minds of their employees. The following

excerpt was taken from a brochure from the Dutch software firm
DPFinance:

> 'The operational continuity is fed by of DPFinance staff's motivation. Well-
> informed and motivated personnel are beneficial to the customer, it
> translates into low personnel turnover, extremely low absenteeism and thus
> maximum employability, productivity and continuity, based on extra
> attention and coaching.'

Personnel work is a well-developed discipline. It has become a
profession (Schuler and Jackson, 1996; Van Sluijs *et al.*, 1991) with its
own instruments, training and education, and behaviour codes. The
main instruments of personnel work are known as follows:

- Formation planning;
- Recruitment and selection;
- Performance appraisal;
- Career planning and guidance;
- Education and training; and
- Reward system.

The further development of these instruments is unmistakably
relevant to the knowledge enterprise. The toolkit for career planning
and coaching is less filled than that for performance appraisal and
rewarding. The field of education and training is constantly moving,
which is illustrated, among other things, by the application of computer-
supported learning programmes. The added value, however, lies not
so much in the instruments themselves, but in the way in which they
are utilized in the knowledge enterprise. This should be based on a
vision in which the labour factor is essentially viewed as an asset
rather than a cost, where personnel is seen (Barney, 1991) as a source
of added value. Human capital (Becker and Gerhart, 1996; Pfeffer,
1994) is difficult to copy and imitate and thus provides the basis for
a firm's competitive advantage. This vision is implied behind the
popular term 'human resource management' (HRM). HRM is highly

similar to the competence approach. Both approaches highlight the organization's knowledge sources and point to the business strategy's dependence of what the market demands and, particularly, what the firm *is able to* offer. HRM implies that personnel management not only responds to but also anticipates business development. Anticipation equals policy making. It is not simple to bring this philosophy in practice. In many firms (see Box. 7.2) the personnel function is still imprisoned in its reactive role (Van Sluijs and Den Hertog, 1993). The personnel manager settles the personnel matters ensuing from the decisions made by the management. Although (s)he does so professionally, basically it is still personnel *work*. Adopting the HRM philosophy is not enough. The crucial point is to utilize the existing tools in the knowledge enterprize proactively and in accordance with policy. In order to underline the importance of the policy-based utilization of personnel tools, the authors of this book prefer to use the old term 'personnel policy' rather than the modern phrase 'HRM'.

Box 7.2. Personnel work versus personnel policy: two extremes.

The personnel manager of a medium-sized printing Firm A has had a busy day. Management has decided to expand its IT department in order to enhance its services and add more value to its products. Recruiting programmers is not an easy job. At 4:30 p.m. the management's PA comes to visit the head of personnel, who asks him, on behalf of the manager, to contact the personnel manager of Firm B. Apparently Firm B was taken over by Firm A the previous day, the only thing remaining to be seen after being the labour conditions. This is an entirely new given to the personnel manager. He immediately contacts his colleague in Firm B and they manage to settle the matter within three days. Both the director and the trade unions are satisfied.

IT Firm C is also planning a take-over. Its personnel department has developed a scenario, which is followed up even before Firm D is taken over. A task group is formed consisting of representatives of both firms, which discuss the points of departures for personnel policy. A line manager and personnel manager of Firm C inform the employees of

Firm D about the intentions of Firm C and the procedure to be followed. They anticipate mistrust in personnel. Honest answers are given to tricky questions during the sessions. This is followed by intensive interviews with all key figures of Firm D, resulting in a scenario for personnel development which should first be discussed with the works council and later per department with the employees of Firm D. Those who feel they do not fit into the new set-up are assisted in finding a new job. The employees of Firm D are not accustomed to such openness and pragmatism, but feel like employees of Firm C even before the take-over contract is signed. The expected turnover of personnel failed to materialize.

This does not mean to say that the recent literature on HRM has failed to put forward some extremely valuable issues, especially concerning the involvement of line managers. This indicates (Devanna *et al.*, 1984) that it comes down to the way in which the day-to-day management practice 'steers on people'. Steering on people implies that personnel effects are weighed when important decisions are made. On the other hand, it means that the opportunities of personnel policy are also viewed as being a basis for business development. This vision has important implications for the way in which the personnel policy tools are utilized in the knowledge enterprise. Central to this is the connection between the various instruments. Personnel policy in the knowledge enterprise is not a loose collection of management techniques. The totality of instruments amounts to more than the sum of its subparts. Separate techniques add little value. In this sense, personnel policy is a *configuration* (Mohrman *et al.*, 1992) or a *system* (Becker and Gerhart, 1996) of elements. The relationship with the totality remains visible in each of these subparts. Performance appraisals, rewards, training programmes and career guidance complement each other in the strive to generate more value using the labour factor. This is the perspective from which we will elaborate upon the personnel policy tools below.

Strategic Personnel Policy

The idea that personnel policy (Becker and Gerhart, 1996; Kluytmans and Van Sluijs, 1995); Schuler and Jackson, 1996) has to fulfil a strategic role in business development is gaining recognition. There was a tendency in the past to translate this idea into hierarchical terms. It was imperative that the social policy be represented in the organization at the highest possible level. In recent years (Den Hertog *et al.*, 1990) the strategic meaning has also been translated into making formation and training plans based on business plans. The future personnel policy is derived in this approach from a chain of factors. Let's take an industrial firm as an example. Expectations for product/market

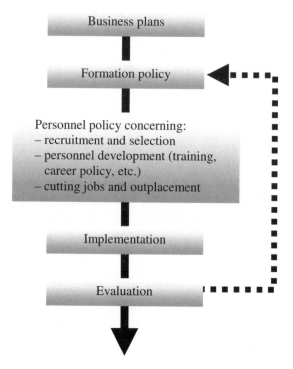

Figure 7.1. Linear personnel planning.

combinations are expressed on the basis of market research. In turn, these expectations are the point of departure for estimating production volumes. This is followed by decisions made about investments in means of production. It is not until the end of this chain that the resulting figures can be translated in terms of workforce: the size desired, the training desired, the demands for recruitment, and so on.

Two important objections can be made to this linear way of reasoning. First, the linear approach contradicts the strategy in which the core competencies (Hamel and Prahalad, 1994) are the starting point for business development. This approach takes the knowledge and skills of personnel as a starting point for the strategy rather than being its derivative. The second objection is concerned with the high degree of variability of a firm's business plans. Some plans need adjustment more than once per year. The dynamics of the market place is full of surprises and our possibilities to look into the technological future are limited. This is the reason why business planning (Rieken, 1995) has become a continuous process. Opposed to this variability of the market place and technology is the natural inertia of the workforce. It is impossible to essentially change the workforce (and thus the core competencies) in a large corporation within one or two years' time. A fundamental change in the workforce may last several years in duration both in quantitative and qualitative terms. Metaphorically spoken: one cannot slalom with a super-tanker (Van Assen, 1992).

Of course there exist large differences between organizations. Some markets and technologies are moving more than others. This observation is the argument to take the current workforce and the various scenarios of personnel development as point of departure when making business plans. This can only be done in an iterative process.

The personnel department collects policy information about the current workforce and the development of the workforce when the policy remains unchanged. The central question raised in this phase is: What are the possibilities and constraints of the workforce? The answer to this question is taken into consideration when designing the business plans, resulting in a guideline for personnel scenario formulation and consequence assessment. These are subsequently compared with the business plans in the making. In this process, the first question is set off to the second: What kind of workforce do we need to execute our plans? This will eventually lead to the choice of a personnel development scenario. As illustrated in Figure 7.2, the control loop between personnel policy and personnel work is also relevant. If the recruitment of a certain category of personnel fails to lead to results in practice, another policy must be pursued, for example, the training of personnel not directly qualified or subcontracting work. Closing these two control loops prevents the personnel function from becoming either encumbered with an impossible assignment or being behind the times. In order to simplify Figure 7.2 another important control loop has been left out: the control loop in which business plans are tested for their mission (including the knowledge ambition).

The observation that the life span of a business plan may be much shorter than the time needed to essentially adapt the workforce may lead to another conclusion. Personnel policy may also contribute to

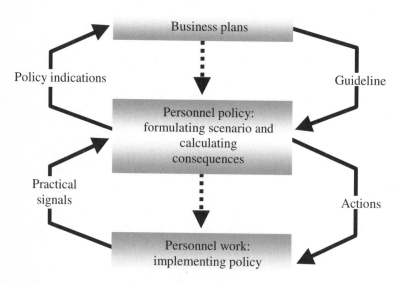

Figure 7.2. Cyclical personnel planning.

the workforce's capability of dealing with changes in the environment. This means that the organization's learning capacity is increased. This learning capacity is an effect of a complex of interventions: training programmes, career guidance, job rotation, task extension, and coaching. The strategic meaning of personnel policy is to be measured not only from the hierarchical level of the highest personnel manager. It is crucial that ideas, facts and policy interventions are constantly recycled both bottom up and top down. This also heavily enhances future personnel employability (Gaspersz and Ott, 1996). The resulting functional flexibility is entirely different from that resulting from numeric flexibilization. The latter term (Storey, 1992) particularly emphasizes temporary employability and job rotation. Flexible contracts, outsourcing and the use of common job pools may produce significant productivity advantages. The limitation of this strategy lies in the nature of the competencies concerned: they are exchangeable competencies. In the case of core competencies this type of flexibilization may prove to be extremely dangerous. Unique knowledge should not be thrown out. Unique knowledge that produces competitive advantage must be held on to.

Recruitment and Selection

Recruiting new employees is one of the most effective routes to underpin a firm's competencies. This holds true specifically for firms whose personnel are the primary means of production. Recruitment fulfils various functions for the firm. It is concerned not only with the replacement and expansion of capacity, but also with rejuvenating the workforce and enlivening the firm with new know-how and skills. Three different strategies can be distinguished in recruitment and selection:

1. Selection and placing: the right person in the right place

Thick manuals (see Casio, 1991) have been written about personnel selection. Selection has gradually become a grown-up discipline riddled with procedures and instruments. Job descriptions are central to the classical approach. Job demands are derived from the job description which appears in the personnel advertisement. This approach aims at a match between the task-imposed demands and the candidate's capacities and experience. It is a quest for 'the right man or woman in the right workplace'. Once this person is found, the machinery of the firm can go on as usual. Box 7.3 gives an example of a personnel advertisement which tries to reflect the job demands as accurately as possible.

Box 7.3. Clear job demands.

Municipality of Apeldoorn

[...]

1. The Function

The head of the Control Technical Infrastructure and PC support sub-department to be appointed:

- Is responsible for managing the sub-department, is a good team-builder and inspires its staff to achieve results;
- Ensures the development and realization of projects in the area of the municipal infrastructure;
- Develops and realizes plans to safeguard the continuity of the municipal information service;
- Ensures the formulation of tactical policy plans and their conversion into operational plans and projects;
- Is responsible for the management of external relations in aid of the purchase of IT equipment and subcontracting of the sub-department's tasks;
- Develops the strategic policy for technical infrastructures and partakes in the development of the I&A policy.

[...]

(Source, Intermediair, 6 September, 1996)

This method is based on two assumptions. First, that people are available in the labour market who comply with the profile given. In other words, that the demands imposed are not impossible and that the supply is expected to be large enough to ensure sufficient candidates responding to the advertisement. The second assumption is that the job demands can be described well. Thus, it is not difficult to recruit for a good history teacher along this way. It's clear who is needed for the job and the supply is sufficiently large. This strategy will generally be satisfactory in the case of clearly crystallized professions where educational programmes are fine-tuned to the work in a firm, for example: controllers with an MBA background, personnel managers with experience in government, and recently graduated biochemists with "electro-physiological patch clamp experience". These are concerned with jobs in which explicit knowledge plays an important role and experience paths can be adequately defined. In case the expected number of adequate candidates is small and the right people have jobs elsewhere, headhunters can be hired to complete the quest. But headhunters are more expensive than an advertisement, and, the firm in question will not exactly be popular amongst rival firms. Finally, the number of candidates needed plays a role. One white raven may be caught this way, but to catch a complete flight of them is far more difficult (cf. Boxes 7.3 and 7.4).

2. Training one's own employees

Recruitment focuses mainly on school-leavers and candidates with limited practical experience, and, when the labour market is tight, on people that do not possess the required education and experience. Recruitment and selection do not concentrate primarily on the things that people can *do*, but on the things they can *learn*: their development potential. This strategy implies (Box 7.4) an intensive training and career policy in the knowledge enterprise.

The choice to pursue this strategy is generally inspired by two factors: a tight labour market and the importance of firm-specific knowledge and experience. This is the case, for example, in the software

Box 7.4. We will train you.

[...]

We will train you to become a systems management specialist. Depending on the situation you will start as a Helpdesk operator and support users to work with their personal computers/work stations, or you will safeguard the data processing and output as an operator/system manager. The activities take place at the customer's offices spread all over the country. You will frequently work in a team and possibly in shifts. We will take care not only of the management of Information Technology in terms of technical content, but also the organizational and business administration aspects of this discipline. You are expected to grow into a technical, organizational or managerial function, for example project leader, consultant, or line manager. Of course this growth will depend upon your own input, development and possible participation in internal and external training programmes.

What we expect from you. You should be trained at higher professional or academic level at minimum. You possess a flexible attitude, good social and communication skills, you possess a service-minded attitude, a strong personality and you consciously aim at a career in Information Technology. Furthermore, you are prepared to work shifts. You are not older than 30 years of age, you possess a driver's licence and you preferably live in the Randstad. Like ourselves, you consider (continuous) education in addition to your job as a prerequisite.

What we offer. Pink Elephant is a young and successful company where quality goes hand in hand with progressiveness and integrity. We offer a fair, open working ambience and extensive opportunities for training at higher professional or university level. The careers are characterized by continuous growth of employees, who (have to) utilise the opportunities that present themselves at Pink Elephant. We apply a modern human resource policy in order to recognise, select and appropriately coach talent.

[...]

(Source: Intermediair, 6 September, 1996)

---

sector, which sometimes tries to attract school-leavers by jingling keys to the lease car without going into the job demands in the advertisement. The educational level is important, but the question as to what education one has followed seems to be of less relevance. The functional knowledge one brings from school is subordinate to the operational and contextual knowledge to be gained in the firm. This strategy may be inevitable, but it may also be risky due to its high risk of failure, high turnover, high training cost, and poor service. Firms that have decided to pursue this strategy know what they are doing (or at least they ought to know). They will have to take the career and training policy seriously and create workplaces in which employees can make mistakes that do not affect the client. Especially in growth situations one must avoid making unrealistic plans whic h recruit too many people too quickly. IT service firms which want to double profits through recruitment might do better taking over another firm. Or, like Pink Elephant does (Chapter 4), by investing heavily in training.

3. Recruiting networks

The third possibility of recruiting people is by investing in external knowledge networks, for example through close cooperation with educational institutions (Coombs and Rosse, 1992). This is referred to as 'campus recruitment' in the United States. Such cooperation can be far-reaching. Thus, Pink Elephant has set up a systems management course in conjunction with a college of advanced education. Such a cooperation provides a source of new personnel as well as a professional standard, which is beneficial to sales. A less heavy form is offering apprenticeship places and supplying part-time teachers, thus interesting, following and forming candidates before they leave school.

Cooperation can be effected also by funding research positions at universities (called AiOs, 'PhD students in training', in the Netherlands), which is done frequently by knowledge-intensive firms. The firm and the university set up a joint programme. 'Fundamental research should not be carried out in a firm, but at universities. By funding university research it will continue to be external, but within reach. We can determine priorities. Moreover, we can hold out the prospect of a job to the most promising researchers before they complete their dissertation.' This is briefly the guiding thought. Cooperation can also take the form of shared jobs. Thus, in the surroundings of the University of Louvain, Belgium, industrial laboratories have been created where the researchers work half of their time, while they are working at the university lab the other half.

Coaching and Performance Appraisal

Performance appraisals serve not only to determine the salary (see: career policy), but they are also an instrument used to give direction to personnel development. Performance appraisals force the boss and the employee to make explicit what's going well and what should be improved. In the services sector the client is often involved in this process, particularly when projects are completed. Performance appraisal must emphasize (Mohrman *et al.*, 1992) the employee's contribution to the performance of the team (s)he is part of. If this fails to happen, the appraisal may even have a negative effect on the group performance. Even more important than the formal appraisal which takes place on an annual basis, or after each project, is coaching in between appraisal moments. This applies especially to employees (Box 7.5) that work at a distance from their home base, such as programmers, maintenance engineers, and commercial field service staff, who work at the customer's premises most of their time.

Coaching has various functions. First, to develop skills. People that work 'outside of' the firm often think that their problems are unique. They don't tend to talk about their problems with the customer because they would then undermine their own and the company's positions. The second function is to spot gaps in the existing knowledge and experience. Employees are often absorbed by their own working situation to the extent that they lose insight into their environment and the future. Finally, the coach is also the link with the organization. This role is crucial in external service providers that are steered by

Box 7.5. Coaching.

A field manager in a medium-sized company which seconds IT personnel to client firms: 'In most IT firms the field manager is there just for the customer. The progress of projects is followed and new appointments are made. In our firm the field manager is also a coach, who supports our people, preferably of course before problems arise. But sometimes a problem manifests itself suddenly and then the field manager must be present immediately to assist our people. Like last week, when a big customer phoned. He didn't want our employee, Mr X, to come around any more and was about to throw out our entire team of six programmers. I got into my car at once. I took Mr X to a small pub where we talked for almost three hours. First, you have to make sure that he gets over the shock. If there's no trust, things will never get sorted out. After that we analyzed the situation step by step. We found that, soon after the team had started work at this client's, it appeared that the client had miscalculated the problems. The client kept putting off the problems we had warned them about months ago. Now they hired a new manager who is not familiar with the past history. The two of us thought about the best way of communicating this message and restoring the relationship. I left that to Mr X. Yesterday I got an enthusiastic phone call from the same client. He even gave us a compliment, because we were so straight.'

the client's management. Rather than the performance itself, the coach focuses on the way in which performances are made.

Education and Training

Comparatively, professional service-providing organizations spend large amounts of money on training. This is equally true of hospitals, insurance companies, IT and accountancy firms, and banks. Part of this training takes place according to the fixed pattern of the professional career ladder. These are training programmes that one must follow to be eligible for a job as insurance inspector, surgery nurse, accountant, or senior programmer. The risk related to these paved training paths is (Bentley, 1992) that they often have a conserving effect, that is to say, they reinforce the boundaries between disciplines and obstruct renewal. This is particularly so (Mohrman *et al.*, 1992) when training programmes focus merely on deepening rather than broadening competencies. However, a new approach is emerging in the training field in which training programmes are used as tools for renewal. This approach was discussed in Chapter 4 for the cases of Moret Ernst & Young, Pink Elephant, and Nationale Nederlanden. It is characterized by the following elements:

1. The knowledge ambition as point of departure

The aim of training programmes is not only to maintain a firm's own workforce, but also to accomplish the strategic knowledge objectives. Training programmes can stretch a firm's competencies (Chapter 2). The relationship with the knowledge ambition will have to be made explicit in the training plan of the firm.

2. Direct coupling of training and development

From the start of a development project the firm must take into account that the new knowledge must be disseminated in the organization effectively. This goes for the introduction of a new production technology as well as for the introduction of new knowledge in service provision. A direct organizational connection of developers and trainers has enormous advantages. In Chapter 4, this connection clearly came to the fore at Moret Ernst & Young, Pink Elephant and National Nederlanden.

3. Training the trainers

A significant part of the knowledge requires broad and constant dissemination in the organization. Additionally, this knowledge must often be embedded into the operation directly. The distance between school and training centres on the one hand and offices or factories on the other is often too big. Training the trainers is an alternative. Training and education are performed within the line organization. The training function makes sure this happens effectively. This route was discussed at Nationale Nederlanden (Chapter 4) and BFI (Chapter 1).

4. Computer-supported learning

Information technology (IT) opens up numerous opportunities for education and training. Examples are knowledge systems which can simulate specific tasks. Pink Elephant (Chapter 4) made use of such simulators to make its staff familiar with specific working conditions. The development of such systems is extremely costly, which is the reason why mainly the larger systems and tools suppliers have heavily invested in their development. In fact, computer-supported tools are part of their product. Chapter 8 will elaborate further upon the possibilities of IT for the knowledge enterprise.

Career Development and Guidance

The daily practice is the most significant source of knowledge and experience in organizations. The working experience gained so far largely determines one's future development possibilities. Nevertheless, experience in a certain discipline can also have a negative effect. Thus, an employee can be 'locked into' his own knowledge. Technologies can become outdated, such as analogous electronics, or markets may disappear altogether, for example the market for typewriters. Often operational knowledge and field knowledge are required to make a change-over. Staff officers who have been working at headquarters too long are no longer directly employable in other positions and, besides, they are often too expensive for a field function. The reverse can also happen. Successful project managers often run from project to project, only to find out after five years that their functional (professional) knowledge has run dry. In that case, possibilities for development are cut short.

In the majority of organizations it is customary to take account of employees' working experience when promoting or transferring them. Career policy goes further than that: it is led not only by today's needs and problems relating to occupancy, but by tomorrow's need for knowledge as well. Effective career policy is a top priority in the knowledge enterprise. This is illustrated by an example of the Belgian branch of the American chemical concern Raychem (Box 7.6).

Box 7.6. Raycherm: Managing personal growth.

Raychem is a knowledge-intensive forerunner. The firm is market leader in the area of heat-shrinking protective materials. These materials are used in all kinds of varieties in telecommunication, pipe systems and construction. The core of Raychem's technology consists of netted and conducting polymers, materials with shape memory, ceramics, adhesives, thin films, liquid crystals, optical glass fibres and electrochemicals. Obviously, the firm is concerned with an intelligent combination of chemical and physical disciplines, with material sciences at its centre. The company philosophy focuses on keeping the firm in motion, or as the former CEO of Raychem, Paul Cook (Taylor, 1990, p. 104) put it: 'For an organization to remain innovative it has to be willing — even eager — to obsolete itself as fast as it can'.

Raychem has a large subsidiary company in Belgium (Kessel-loo), which is responsible for its own R&D, manufacturing and marketing. The subsidiary employs 1,050 staff, including 250 academics. Like most other chemical companies, Raychem has gone through a difficult period in the market. This was related particularly to the dip in the defence industry and the construction sector. However, the firm has managed to recover from this economic slump and is once again the leading firm in its line of business. In 1993, the turnover in the Belgian branch was 10.3 billion Belgian francs, while its profit before taxes amounted to 1.2 billion francs.

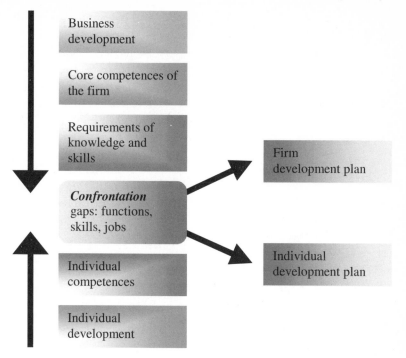

Raychem's personnel policy follows a dynamic perspective, which is clearly reflected at the individual level in career guidance. Two points of departure are at its base: first, the need for knowledge originating from business development, which serves as input for recruitment and personnel development. The focus is both on the firm's current and its future core competencies. The current and desired development of individual know-how and skills is the second point of departure. Interviews are conducted with all employees several times a year. This confrontation between the knowledge needs of the firm and those of the employees results in a gap analysis.

The gap analysis identifies current and future weaknesses in competencies. It takes place at different levels: the core competencies of the firm in its entirety, the competencies developed within and particularly those among departments, and the individual know-how and skills. The resulting image serves as the basis for making plans at the level of the firm, department, team and the individual; plans concerning recruitment, training programmes, career development, and rewards. Raychem aims to materialize these plans in terms of responsibilities, objectives and expected performance. Interviews are held with employees to adapt objectives, set norms, follow progress and make concrete arrangements. The latter are largely concerned with the ways in which employees' knowledge and experience can be broadened and deepened. These can be achieved through:

- Targeted training;
- Working under the supervision of a mentor for a specific time period;
- Plotting an experience path (projects enabling employees to gain experience);
- Seconding developers to the corporate R&D lab;
- Internships at other departments;
- Individual training programmes supervized by an internal coach;
- Visits to other companies, field trials, benchmarking activities;
- Break-out meetings of functional specialists in the entire organization and world-wide;
- Cross-divisional and cross-site project groups;
- Studying cross-divisional and cross-site state-of-art approaches.

(Source: Den Hertog and Van Sluijs, 1995b)

Raychem emphasizes the relevance of personnel movements beyond the boundaries of functional departments and business units. This relevance is also underlined in the MERIT study on innovation (Cobbenhagen *et al.*, 1994), which shows that innovative frontrunners focus more on extensive inter-functional mobility than pack members. This mobility underpins the organization's lateral processes. A lateral linkage (Chapter 6) will perform better when its members possess previous experience in various functions and units.

The most important components of knowledge-oriented career policy can be distilled from the Raychem example. The relationship with the knowledge ambition is once again the starting point. The issue is to translate company-level competencies into individual competencies. This may result in the description of *career trajectories*, which indicate the possible paths that lead to certain functions. Managers and staff are thus able to talk with each other about concrete knowledge areas, work experience, and training programmes. These career trajectories do not merely focus on careers in a hierarchical sense. In addition to the organizational management line, the philosophy of *dual careers* in R&D (Shephard, 1958) identifies a trajectory which is based on the development of professional knowledge and experience. Two arguments are typically given for dual careers: the decreased number of management positions due to the flattening of the organization, and the inappropriateness of many high-quality professionals for management tasks. The professional career offers a new perspective. Research (Allen and Katz, 1986) has shown that these two arguments are oversimplified. In practice there exist a variety of trajectories, which are highly specific to the knowledge domain concerned. Additionally, professional careers should focus both on depth *and* breadth. Career development is therefore also an instrument for strengthening lateral relations.

The *interview* is a next essential component of career policy. At least twice per year time should be made available to talk about the future with individual employees. This may be held with one's boss or, when the boss's field of perspective is too limited, with the career pilot (see Chapter 4: Pink Elephant). A career pilot is a senior who has no hierarchical relationship with the employee in question, and who supervises and follows the career development of a fixed number of employees for a number of years. These pilots may work in another unit (central or otherwise). They possess a 'helicopter view' and are coached and trained for this job. They are the 'godfathers' that employees can turn to when facing important career decisions. Employees themselves play an active role in this process. They are responsible for their own future within the opportunities offered by the company. In this perspective, the career is driven by persons rather than the organization.

When developing a career policy firms make increasing use of personnel information systems. These systems — referred to as skills maps, knowledge charts, and competence matrices — maintain the work experience, knowledge and skills, and education enjoyed by individual employees. In organizations where employees work in alternating project groups such skills and experience maps are virtually indispensable. Pink Elephant uses such a system for the allocation of employees to projects. This firm's service providersare expected to be able to work in various computer environments. The direct consequence of this is that the employees must gain experience in different environments and follow various training programmes. Meanwhile the firm has grown to the extent that it cannot do without a formal system. The same system can be used to discuss the farther future. It is moreover the basis for mapping the competencies at company level. In the Netherlands, researchers (Van Assen, 1992; Van Diepen, 1996) have introduced the idea to place the accent in these skills maps on the jobs that the employee has successively performed, thus identifying the breadth and depth of the knowledge and experience in completed work packages. This is particularly relevant to R&D personnel because the contents of the projects they worked on tells more about the knowledge they have acquired than their job descriptions. In addition, analyses of such learning paths indicate which paths work in practice and which don't. For example, it appears that changing over too quickly to another knowledge area, or alternatively, continuing to work in one single knowledge area, has a negative influence on future personnel employability.

Skills mapping is a personnel information system similar to a database. At the organizational level the system can be used for policy development, for example concerning recruitment, training and careers. It can also be applied in operational terms for peopling new projects. At the individual level, it can provide support in assessment, coaching and career interviews. The IT department of a large Dutch company uses the following categories:

- The resume which is updated by the employee;
- The functional competence (professional know-how, for example, packages, tools, proficiency in languages);

- The operational competence (for example, experience in logistic or financial projects);
- The contextual competence (for example, experience within a certain business unit, or experience in a certain country);
- The training programmes followed;
- The training programmes to be followed;
- The knowledge and experience desired;
- Performance appraisal, salary development;
- The agreements made between the employee and the firm over time.

Finally, career policy requires the willingness of managers to let go of well-performing employees and give the weaker colleagues from other units a new opportunity. This holds true particularly of advanced knowledge workers and senior managers. Career policy thus calls for responsibility that does not stop at the boundaries of one's own unit. The same applies to 'adverse' career steps, which purposefully deviate from well-paved career paths. Examples are the product developer who returns to research or the marketer who is employed in an IT firm as manager of a development project. Within large decentralized corporations, this often calls for an integrating role at corporate level (see Box 6.4). As previously pointed out in Chapter 6, the synergy between units often requires such an extra impulse.

Skill-Based Pay

Reward systems may play an important role in the knowledge enterprise. Recruiting and holding on to advanced knowledge workers relies not only upon salary size. The question how to stimulate knowledge development using different financial incentives is also of the essence. The introduction of skill-based pay is an important element here. The salary is based not only on the input delivered, but especially on the knowledge which is generated and added. In this way (Lawler and Ledford, 1985; Ledford, 1991) employees are encouraged to continue to develop themselves and they are better employable. In the majority of cases (compare Raychem) this is concerned with part of the reward. When skill-based pay is based mainly on experience time (= seniority) there is a risk that employees are encouraged to keep doing the things they're good at already. This does not stimulate them to take risks in new knowledge areas. The introduction of skill-based pay works particularly well when the knowledge and skills can be named. For example, formal certificates may be awarded when employees have proven to be familiar with certain knowledge and experience. More importantly, skill-based pay is not isolated from other aspects of personnel policy. American research (Ledford, 1992) has revealed that the diffusion of skill-based pay takes place especially in firms that also attach importance to: job rotation, team work, job enrichment, border-crossing training programmes, and adequate information supply. These are moreover firms that outperform their rivals in economic terms.

Research into the application of performance-based pay (Mohrman *et al.*, 1992) in high-tech companies demonstrate that this must be done with caution. Experiences with individual performance-based pay are negative rather than positive. The performance delivered is generally based on cooperation within and between groups. The risk of playing mutually dependent individuals and groups off against each other is huge. Additionally, performance-based pay typically places too much emphasis on short-term objectives. In any case, it is important to pick the right system level and the right moment. For example, by giving a team that succeeded in completing a project within the agreed period and budget part of the extra profit. On the basis of their research, Mohrman *et al.* (1992) advocate a combination of skill-based pay and profit sharing at business level. In the Netherlands, more even than in the United States, changes in the reward system obviously require thorough negotiation with the workers representatives.

Culture as a Binding Agent

Small firms are often idolized because all employees know and directly rely upon one another. They work together on a common task with a minimum of boundaries. When this 'we feeling' is strongly developed and commitment is high, we speak of a 'strong company culture'. Charismatic and enthusing entrepreneurs (Koene, 1996) can even strengthen this cultural bond. Larger organizations attempt to develop culture as a binding agent using all kinds of measures. This is particularly important when employees do not maintain a daily relationship with their own group or with the firm. An example is, once again, the IT firm that seconds its employees to customers. It tries to give new employees the feeling that they belong in the firm right from the start. These interventions often have a symbolic character: the manager is frequently present when new employees are introduced and the latter's partners receive flowers to show that the firm also holds them in high regard. Furthermore, social events are organized on a regular basis. Professional meetings may serve the same function. These measures are useful only when they are continued in the day-to-day working relationships. Otherwise employees tend to see through the shiny surface. The instruments available to personnel policy should therefore reinforce each other. This is illustrated especially by the examples in this study. Recruitment has direct consequences for training programmes. Training programmes must target today's and tomorrow's activities. Career policy does not become a reality until employees are able to continue to develop their competencies. In other words: a close-knit culture is realized only when the firm is a good place to work. To use Pink Elephant's ambitious objective: the best firm to work for.

Chapter 8

Information Technology

Information technology (IT) rapidly changes the working environment of the knowledge enterprise. However, the function of IT is not primarily to generate knowledge. At the operational level, IT creates an environment for the knowledge worker in which (s)he can operate far more effectively. It is an environment in which:

- routine operations are taken over by systems;
- the supply of information is booming;
- explicit knowledge can be better stored and transferred;
- communication is better and faster.

The knowledge worker plays an increasingly important role in this development. Better tools are at the disposal of the knowledge worker to develop and use knowledge, and make it accessible to and share with others. At the tactical level, IT thus contributes to facilitating knowledge flows. Improved knowledge development and knowledge transfer within and between organizational units add more value to the product or service. The strategic relevance of IT for the knowledge enterprise takes shape particularly in organizations in which IT is irretrievably linked to the primary process. For example: financial service providers, companies with a dominant logistic chain, and IT companies themselves.

This chapter discusses different IT applications for the knowledge enterprise using examples: databases, information systems, networks, expert systems, task-supporting systems (e.g. group ware), and knowledge banks. Finally, it is pointed out that the knowledge enterprise benefits from IT particularly when the applications are part of a coherent system: IT configurations, lateral connection, and human resource management.

The IT Environment

When the computer of the nine o'clock news breaks down, the newsreader will have to make do with reading text from a printout. Due to a train traffic system failure, alternative transport must be brought into action, and when the computer of a schoolbook publisher crashes, students in dozens of colleges will have to do without books for weeks. The role of data and information processing in companies and institutions has become dominant to the extent that their primary processes have become fully dependent on information and communication technologies. In a positive sense they can increasingly improve their competitive edge by strategically applying IT in their business. This holds true especially of firms with dominant logistic chains (for example, a retailer of car parts) and firms in which IT has become the basis for the primary process (for example, financial service providers). This chapter focuses on the question what IT specifically means for the knowledge enterprise. In order to answer this question we first have to return to the distinction between information and knowledge (Chapter 2). For example, are the conditions for risk acceptance from the knowledge bank at Nationale Nederlanden (Chapter 4) concerned with knowledge or information? Can an IT-based system generate knowledge, or is it the knowledge worker who builds knowledge using information, and what does he communicate? A concrete example from practice may assist us to keep this confusion of concepts within limits.

Indoor Airways constructs complex systems. The core competences of such firms mainly lie in harmonizing various technologies, which are supplied for the greater part by other firms. The combination itself,

Box 8.1. Indoor airways.

Indoor Airways Ltd. is a young and rapidly growing engineering firm employing 150 staff, which has developed in the past three years into a specialist in air treatment systems. The firm designs and installs tailored air treatment systems. As a senior project leader Henry is responsible for a museum renovation project. The customer is renovating and has turned an old cellar into a new exhibition hall. The museum wants to modernize the heating and ventilation installation to ensure the conservation of art collections and ceilings paintings. The project team is a week behind schedule and the completion date is approaching quickly. Each further delay would jeopardize the project. The opening exhibition might be cancelled if sound air conditioning cannot be assured. This particular customer is important to Indoor Airways because follow-up orders for other museums are in store if this project is delivered within the term stipulated and according to price and quality agreements. The core competence of Indoor Airways, project management and integration of technical disciplines, must therefore be substantiated.

Henry has just arrived at the firm and is looking for a workplace in the firm's open-plan office. He plugs in his notebook to the intranet and browses through his email messages. He opens the email that has just been sent by one of the staff working on location. When testing the system a failure was spotted in one of the ventilation system's components. Henry immediately contacts the employee and gets a detailed description of the problem. It seems to be a technical problem with a cooling component. Unless quick insight is gained into the component's specifications, the ventilation system cannot be connected to the air treatment channels.

The search for a solution begins in the knowledge bank in Indoor Airways' computer. Henry is looking for previous project experiences, product specifications and supplier information. He comes across the project description of a similar project and contacts Jim, the responsible project leader at the time. Henry tells Jim about the problem and meanwhile contacts the supplier in question through the internet. Jim explains how they fixed the problem. Henry checks the 'skills database', part of the knowledge bank, to see if one of his own project members possesses the skills to fix this technical problem. A technical specialist is available to support the team temporarily. The supplier's helpdesk sends the specifications of the cooling component by email and suggests possible solutions. An order is placed with the local supplier using the EDI (Electronic Data Interchange) connection and is delivered at the customer's on the same day and for which Indoor Airways is invoiced. Meanwhile, the new product specifications have been sent to the team on location by email in order for them to prepare the connection. A solution was found without any noticeable delay for the customer within a few hours. All internally and externally available data, information and knowledge had been used to ensure timely delivery of the project.

however, is still determined by the specific demands imposed by the customer. The firm's growth is based on the ability of quickly searching, coupling and communicating functional (technological), operational (project-related) and contextual (museum) knowledge and information. IT offers the indispensable working environment for the company's knowledge workers, it is not essentially concerned with generating knowledge. This function is primarily fulfilled by the knowledge workers and its customers and suppliers. IT allows for the effective storage, transport and retrieval of the *knowledge*. IT can be viewed as the logistic system of the knowledge enterprise fulfilling several functions: the storage of data, information and knowledge; communication of information and knowledge; to couple the various information and knowledge flows; and controlling the work process ('work flow').

The IT community speaks its own language. Each year new words are added to that language (the 'computer lingo'). The meaning behind a word is not always univocal. The glossary below explains the meaning given to the concepts used here by the authors.

Once again, we stress that the value of IT at this moment does not primarily lie in automation, but in the support of processes where knowledge is developed and used. This supportive role is reflected in Box 8.3 for the Indoor Airways example.

Box 8.2. Definitions.

Database

A storage facility for a collection of digitalized data. Databases are the heart of an information system.

Data warehouse

A database containing large quantities of data which had often been gathered previously for another purpose. The data in a data warehouse are 'integrated' ('data mining') in order to discover underlying relationships between data with the aim of becoming more familiar with one's own markets and processes.

Expert system

Knowledge technology-based system laying down the tacit working method of experts. The procedures, methods and experiences implicitly used by an expert are laid down in an expert system using argumentative rules and defined relationships.

Functionality

The potential of functions that can be carried out by a system.

Information system (IS)

The whole of components to collect data, process them into information, and order, store and transport information.

IT infrastructure

A coherent architecture of IS and networks. The infrastructure creates an environment in which knowledge workers are supported in executing work processes and in which knowledge workers are linked with other workers.

Knowledge bank

Technically speaking a database. A knowledge bank is a file which is specifically suitable to lay down descriptions of knowledge, experience and results of knowledge work and to identify the location of knowledge.

Networks

A range of connected IS for the exchange and communication of data, information and know-how. Technical forms of network structures are:

- local area networks (LAN): a group of linked computers which can communicate with each other, usually within one firm or company entity;
- wide area networks (WAN): a complex of LANs where communication is expanded outside the corporation;
- client server architecture (CS): a structure of systems and programs where functions are divided according to the components that the specific function can execute best: the personal computers ('clients') or the central server. The server often fulfills a central function of storage, processing, security, and transport of information.

Examples of network applications are:

- EDI: Electronic Data Interchange between the corporation and its suppliers and/or customers;
- Email: electronic data traffic, a network application for sending and receiving electronic mail;
- Internet: a worldwide collection of networks where people from all over the world can exchange on-line text, image and sound. Internet can be used, among other things, as a sales and distribution channel, a communication instrument, and is a quick method for searching and accessing information;
- Intranet: a company-internal internet connecting applications such as email, databanks, and search systems.

Task-supporting system

- Work flow support system (WFS): system supporting the knowledge worker in work processes. WFS is based on the organizational philosophy of work flow management and fulfils the logistic function within service-providing processes. Streamlining of work processes is expected to lead to productivity and quality improvement. The use of WFS, for example, allows for the joint control of working appointments (agenda sharing), direct customer service by supplying information, fast document transactions, and thus shortening the throughput time of work processes;
- Groupware: software specifically aimed at supporting and accelerating joint work groups activities. Groupware supplies a number of office functions such as electronic agenda control, email, document storage and control, and videoconferencing. Together with the sharing of a database in a network the use of groupware can ensure more effective cooperation, faster throughput time of processes, more team communication, and improved alignment of separate tasks in group processes.

Box 8.3. IT support in knowledge processes.

The knowledge enterprise Indoor Airways has created a workplace and network environment in which IT supports various work processes.

work process 1:　*searching data and information*
　　　　　　　　The engineering company possesses an electronic archive (knowledge bank), enabling Henry to search the supplier's contact address using a query system.

work process 2:　*obtaining data and information*
　　　　　　　　Henry can recover the supplier information from the knowledge bank, retrieve the supplier's address on his screen, and contact the supplier's helpdesk through the Internet.

work process 3:	*creating knowledge and making explicit knowledge accessible* Henry can create knowledge using the information flows and the presentation of information systems. Henry finds information in the knowledge bank related to the cooling-technical problems and where he can find it.
work process 4:	*exchanging knowledge* As an experienced project leader, Jim is familiar with the problem. The use of communication devices makes it easier for Henry to contact Jim and exchange project experience.
work process 5:	*securing and retrieving data, information and know-how* The project leader reports his project experience and stores the new information about the component and the supplier in the knowledge bank.
work process 6:	*transporting data, information and know-how* Communication and exchange of data between the project team, Henry, Jim and the supplier takes place via a network of information systems.

Towards a Strategic Implementation of IT

For an increasing number of companies, the Indoor Airways working method is not a future scenario, but part of reality. IT has radically transformed the landscape of the knowledge enterprise in recent years. The development of technological IT opportunities can be divided into three phases (Figure 8.1). However, the development of IT in organizations is also determined by the learning process that managers and users go through (Nolan, 1973; Nolan and Koot, 1992) when using IT. Figure 8.1 shows the five 'stages' in that learning process along the same time axis.

With the introduction of the computer in the 1950s and 1960s, IT was initially aimed (phase 1) at the 'mechanization' of labour-intensive

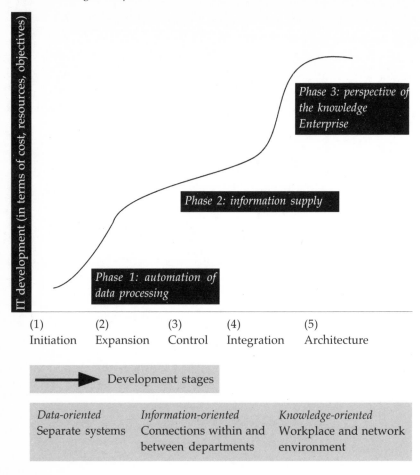

Figure 8.1. Development of information technology (based on Nolan and Koot, 1992).

tasks. The computer made it possible to execute complex calculations quickly and process large amounts of data more efficiently. Similar to the early mechanization in production, labour cost savings were the principal objective. As a result, the first large-scale applications of IT took place in organizations where *data processing* is a major activity, for example banks, public service corporations, and research institutions. The use of IT makes it possible to do things in a shorter time horizon, and execute data-intensive activities that were impossible in the past. During the next phase (phase 2; late 1970s and 1980s), IT was applied also to *control* production processes in services and industry. Emphasis was placed on information supply. Functional departments in the organization (for example: financial administration, planning, distribution and purchase) took the lead. In this way, a variety of functional systems was created which supplied information for the planning and control of functional activities. Yet the enormous growth of IT in this phase demonstrated how difficult it is to control the application of IT itself. In this period, automation had developed into a collection of loose functional systems. This situation led to a discontinuity in automation during the late 1980s. Costs were soaring and numerous projects jammed up at the implementation stages, as a result of which a large need was felt for better control of IT devices and processes. Integration of systems within and between functional departments was needed to allow for fine-tuning of primary process activities. Standardization was the technical key to coupling separate systems. Meanwhile, the rapid technological development has offered a new perspective of control. The application of IT has evolved into an architectural stage in which systems and networks are increasingly integrated. Due to this integration and the wide diffusion of personal computers in the workplace, the information supply of organizations has been greatly improved. It is quicker, better, cheaper and more reliable than ever before. This introduces a new phase for IT in which application is aimed at knowledge. We refer here to the *perspective of the knowledge enterprise*, where IT creates a workplace and network environment for the knowledge enterprise. Rather than being isolated, this phase is running in parallel with the development of information supply. IT is utilized on a broader scale: not only to make the primary process more effective, but also to add value to that same process. Value which is based on knowledge and information.

The literature on IT applications often distinguishes between the operational, tactical and strategic levels to identify how deeply IT is applied in the organization. In this chapter we will use this division in order to elaborate upon the third phase. The 'environment' plays a major role in the description of this phase. The environment accommodates a variety of instruments and facilities ('systems') to perform knowledge-related activities. The integration of systems ensures that these are targeted at the complex tasks that must be carried out. This might be compared to the dentist's 'workplace'. All instruments are grouped in such a way that the dentist can perform a broad range of operations from one point without having to go to another 'workplace'. When this appears to be necessary anyway, the client is referred to another organization (for example, the hospital) with another environment. The instruments and facilities in that environment are targeted to other competencies: those of the dental surgeon.

Let's return to the three levels at which IT can be implemented in the knowledge enterprise. The operational level is concerned with the use of IT instruments for the design of the workplace and network environment of the knowledge worker. The tactical level deals with organizing knowledge work and facilitating knowledge flows. Focusing

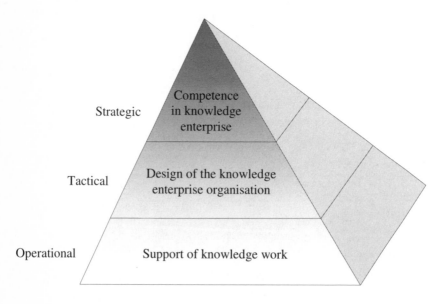

Figure 8.2. IT functions in the knowledge enterprise.

on the use of IT for the design of work processes and for information supply, this level aims at aligning the primary functions in the organization. IT becomes strategically relevant when it generates differentiating capacity (Porter, 1985). The application of IT in the company's primary process or the development of core competencies using IT makes it of strategic importance. A strategic role for IT is mainly directed towards:

- The design of processes superior to the competitor's (cost leadership); or
- The ability to differentiate from rival firms with other products and services (differentiation strategy).

Supporting the Knowledge Worker

As a form of work, knowledge work (Laudon and Laudon, 1996; 't Hart, 1995; Drucker, 1993) is distinguished from physical production work and routine service provision. Knowledge work consists of processing complex information and creating new information and knowledge (Laudon and Laudon, 1996). The knowledge worker makes use of data and information in order to develop new information and knowledge. The work is based on the knowledge possessed and used by an employee to perform activities. The knowledge worker can use the information available to him. He or she can also develop this information from the data available in or outside the organization. Knowledge work is present in virtually all aspects of business, for example: providing financial advice, making sales forecasts, introducing new machines, and supervising projects. Diagnosis, the formulation of problems, planning and decision making, control, presentation and communication are outstanding examples of tasks involving a great deal of knowledge work (Davis and Olson, 1984). Yet the knowledge worker does not merely carry out knowledge work. In general, data collection and information processing are part of the knowledge worker's task. Hence, it is difficult to tell exactly where the boundary is between knowledge work on the one hand and 'information work' and 'data work' on the other (Laudon and Laudon, 1996). By relieving the knowledge worker of data work or information work, IT can strongly increase productivity (Davis *et al.*, 1993). This will enable the knowledge worker to concentrate on the main issues: developing and applying knowledge in business processes, and creating added value.

Such support offers several IT capabilities (see Figure 8.3) (Davenport and Short, 1990) which enable the knowledge worker to process information more rapidly and simply and develop knowledge. An example about customer information may help picture how IT takes over parts of the knowledge work.

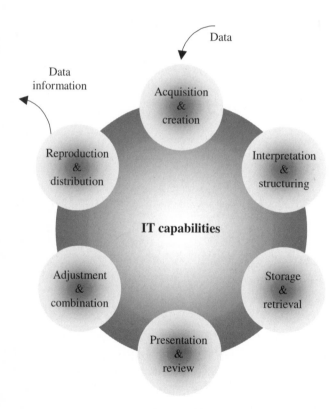

Figure 8.3. IT capabilities for knowledge management (after Zorkoczy, 1991, p. 53).

Box 8.4. From customer data to customer profile.

Companies increasingly recognize *who* their customers are. Yet they know relatively little about their customers and what they really want. The need for customer information and know-how does rise in order to target marketing and sales activities to individual customers and service each customer (one-to-one marketing). It also helps improve and develop products and services. Customer information and know-how is therefore essential to improve a firm's competitive edge. What can IT do to help here?

Customer knowledge is created by the knowledge worker. The knowledge worker is capable of structuring a complex set of data and information about customers into customer knowledge. Data are derived from various sources, such as customer contacts and transactions, which may be stored in a computer file. The marketer who wants to know more about a specific customer group can obtain loose customer data from the system, present it on his screen, and interpret and structure it into customer information. The collection can be filed in a separate customer file and is retrievable. Subsequently, the knowledge worker can graphically obtain and analyze more data about orders, prices, usage periods, repetition purchase, and such like using a worksheets on the computer screen. Word processing, calculation and data-filing programs are tools used by the knowledge worker to interpret the data and process it into customer information. The resulting customer information can be distributed and shared with other knowledge workers via a network. The customer information thus obtained is coupled with new data from other sources, thus resulting in a broader image of the customer group profile. This is used by the knowledge worker to develop customer knowledge: insight into the customer's motives and behaviour.

We have mainly come across a similar use of IT in the company case studies in the service-providing firms. In the direct contact with the customer by telephone or in the front office problems can be directly resolved using the screen. Experiences with specific customers can be introduced into the system immediately. The most striking example is the IT application at Nationale Nederlanden (Chapter 4). This company provides its employees with information systems and a knowledge bank containing manuals and guidelines for damages assessment and risk acceptance. In the field of tension between the service provider and the customer, a quick answer is an important motive to use the possibilities offered by IT. The helpdesk function of such firms and institutions is virtually inconceivable without modern IT applications. In industrial firms, this motive can be found in the need to quickly fix production problems, or to speed up development processes. With the current technological developments, an increasing number of tools become available for the knowledge worker and his environment. New technologies such as document imaging, groupware, email, and the Internet offer a range of applications for the support of knowledge work (Laudon and Laudon, 1996). Apart from 'support', two additional IT functions deserve attention: coding tacit knowledge and creating a learning environment.

1. Coding Tacit Knowledge

An important aspect of knowledge development is the conversion of tacit knowledge into explicit knowledge (see Chapter 2). In this way, knowledge gained by individuals can be effectively stored and shared with other people inside the organization. This might also be referred to as 'externalization' of knowledge (Nonaka, 1995). The precondition, and thus the limitation, is that one must be able to express implicit knowledge in words and numbers. The question is whether one needs the computer for that purpose, because it is mainly the knowledge worker who ensures the translation (or 'coding'). Nevertheless, IT may fulfill a major role here. By offering opportunities for storing, communicating and retrieving knowledge, employees are encouraged to introduce and use coded practical knowledge.

2. A Learning Environment

The knowledge enterprise is a learning organization (Chapter 3). The

Box 8.5. Coding tacit knowledge.

> In insurance companies, the acceptance of risks (the 'policy') is tied to a large extent to explicit rules and procedures. This applies to the large bulk standard insurance policies in particular. These rules and procedures can be determined by applying mathematics and statistics to damage cases. Actuarial mathematics does not only calculate the risks of the insurance policy, it also provides indications of the conditions under which the risks are acceptable. However, there exists a substantial category which is far more difficult to catch in mathematical formulas, for example risks that hardly ever occur, such as complex industrial transports. Additionally, it is often difficult to compare (mainly business) clients. Let's take the example of insuring discos. There may be huge differences per disco in terms of risk. In those cases, one relies on the employees who are familiar with the risks from experience. This is the reason why modern insurers have combined risk acceptance and damage claim assessment in one department. Nationale Nederlanden aims to store this contextual knowledge of its employees in the form of rules and advice in a knowledge bank. Employees are made less dependent in their operations on the physical presence of experts and can add their own experience.

organization provides the environment in which there is room for experimenting and making mistakes, and experiences can be shared. IT may be an important component in that learning environment. Examples are:

- intranets containing best practices and lessons learned
- computer-supported learning systems;
- facilities for simulation of practical situations, e.g. for training programmes;
- test environments for new services and products (Box 8.6).

In these "virtual" environments the direct feedback to employees' actions and decisions are the key to learning behaviour. The effect of

Box 8.6. IT as a learning environment component.

Pink Elephant has set up a simulation environment to develop routines and effectively transfer knowledge about new automation services. Computers play a major role in the training of staff. Using these systems, they are taught how they can best tackle the implementation of new and existing services. When new systems management tools and methods are introduced in the market, the staff are first intensively trained. New staff also learn, using computers, to resolve problems they may be faced with in the maintenance and control of calculation and information centres. Gaining practical experience and learning from mistakes in an environment thus enhances employability.

one's actions is directly visible to oneself and others. One discovers experiments and learns how to solve complex problems without paying the actual price for real mistakes or failures.

The Design of the Organization

IT application at the tactical level becomes visible in the design of work processes in the organization. The effectiveness and efficacy of the value chain in its entirety is central to the design. The knowledge transfer between the primary process stages and the innovation process must be assured. For example, the transfer of technical know-how of development to production, or from the field service to the back office. The knowledge flows between self-managing units are also important. How can business Unit A benefit from experiences gained in business Unit B? Similar to the lateral linkage, IT offers opportunities to underpin such knowledge flows. It is difficult to make a distinction between IT utilized in the primary process and IT aimed at knowledge objectives. In many firms, IT is strongly interwoven with the primary process. For example, data and information processing in financial services is a main component of the primary process. The same applies to industrial firms with a dominant logistic chain. In such firms, IT is no longer a tool, but a 'leverage instrument for business process improvement and redesign' (Hammer & Champy, 1993). In this way, operating and development processes can be accelerated, and the firm can be tied to the market more closely. With the use of IT the organization's reaction speed increases. The ability to redesign processes using IT depends on the ability (or 'capabilities', see Venkatraman, 1991; Davenport, 1993) to:

- automate data-intensive tasks;
- change a series of tasks in a work process;
- make a process independent of geographical and organization barriers;
- eliminate process steps.

Thus, the opportunities offered by IT not only change the primary process work patterns, but those in development, transfer and application of knowledge as well. In other words: IT makes it possible at the tactical level (Davenport and Short, 1990) to redesign knowledge flows in the organization. An effective design of the knowledge enterprise is based in this perspective on adequate information supply (Beek and Jager, 1993). In the Indoor Airways example, IT has influenced the work processes and information supply. All employees now possess internal and external data sources, whereas data and information used to be tied to one place, person or time previously. Transaction handling processes, such as ordering materials and financial settlements, are now automated. The set-up of a company network enables Indoor Airways to ensure sound communication in the project organization. The project teams can communicate with each other any time, regardless of physical workplace. This example shows that in general the utilization of IT at the operational level also has a tactical meaning in the knowledge enterprise.

Competence Development

It is increasingly recognized that IT often fulfills a strategic function in new business development (Laudon and Laudon, 1996; Venkatraman and Henderson, 1992; Scott Morgan, 1991). Firms are becoming increasingly aware that IT is part of the strategic development and can contribute to competitiveness. IT is a powerful medium to distinguish from rival firms through superior processes and/or new services and products. The strategic importance of IT is reflected in the development of IT competencies and the creation of new business.

Development of IT competencies

In many service sectors, the lack of IT in business is just inconceivable. Today, IT is a precondition in the primary processes of transport, travel business and financial services in order to be cost-effective and competitive. For its continuity, such firms are (Box 8.7) structurally dependent on the utilization of IT. Additionally, without IT they would be unable to develop differentiation capacity in the market place. IT is rooted in the core business because information is the service or product, or because the primary process relies on rapid data and information processing. For those firms, IT develops into a core competence itself. It becomes a strategic factor for competing. This does not imply that the firm has to take the development, management and maintenance of its IT system in its own hands. A basic condition remains that the firm is able to make its own decisions. Strategic policies cannot be 'outsourced' without losing core competencies.

The strategic significance of IT results from the capacity of:

- raising entrance barriers in the market place;
- introducing other products and services into the market;
- coupling the primary process of supplier and client's;
- limiting the distribution channels for others;

Box 8.7. IT as core competence of Holland Flower Auction.

A lot of Dutch companies operating in the flower trade have a website on the Internet. For this sector, the Internet is an excellent medium to provide information about flowers and plants. The Internet houses a flower database with 7,000 pictures of flowers and plants, as well as an overview of importers, exporters, and cultivators. One of these companies is the 'Bloemenveiling Holland' (Holland Flower Auction). This firm takes up a prominent place worldwide in the flower and plants trade with a turnover of more than Dfl. 2 billion, approximately 5,000 suppliers and 2,950 traders.

Quality is of paramount importance to the auction. Only the very best products are eligible for auction trading. IT has caused a radical change in this firm's auction process. Due to the application of IT in the primary process, the Flower Auction has been able to develop its core competencies in trade and logistics and has assumed the 'orchestration' role in the value chain. The use of IT has enabled the firm to trade its products rapidly and limit the cost of distribution. With these core competencies the traditional working methods have been abandoned and the auction firm has obtained an essentially different status. There is no longer a need for flower traders, suppliers, auctioneers and products to be brought together physically at one location. At the Flower Auction, products are now traded using auction clocks and screen trade takes place more and more often. The products are sold on the basis of product pictures shown on the monitors next to the auction clock. The need to supply all products at the auction itself before they are auctioned, no longer exists. Screen trade ensures efficient and more rapid trade and that products be sent by the cultivators to the traders directly. In this way, the distribution chain is significantly shortened. There is no need for the buyer to appear at the auction either because of tele-shopping now. Some clients are linked to the auction location on-line, allowing them to offer a price directly from behind their computer screen.

Source: http://www.flowerweb.nl

- reducing production and delivery costs;
- speeding up and simplifying delivery.

The strategic significance of IT is not limited to such 'data factories' as banks, public utilities, inland revenue and insurance companies. IT has the same meaning for firms with complex logistic chains, high-tech firms that deliver tailor-made products or services, as well as firms competing on the speed (Stalk and Hout, 1990) with which they can deliver services and products.

1. Creating new business

IT enables firms to introduce new products and services, and open up new distribution channels and new markets. Even information itself can become a product or service part of a product, thus providing a basis for business development. The developments surrounding the Internet, electronic commerce and banking, online auctioning, personalised informing and tele-shopping, online equity trading etc. illustrate this. The implication is that when formulating strategies in a firm IT should be seen not only as a derivative of the business portfolio. IT competencies (Earl, 1989) can open up new ways of marketing, sales and service, and competitors can be kept at a distance. From this vision, IT also generates — similar to personnel policy — conditions for strategic choices.

IT Tools

The IT sector makes ample use of the word 'tools'. The comparison with the carpenter's toolkit, however, falls short to a large extent. His toolkit contains instruments that clearly differ in shape and function. This does not apply to the toolkit of IT instruments, which are to be regarded as components of a Meccano construction set. They can be used in varying compositions. Furthermore, IT instruments are generally different in nature, ranging from colossal logistic information systems to relatively simple systems for electronic mail in a small network. Below we will take a closer look at the following important IT instruments and delve into their significance to the knowledge enterprise:

- databases;
- information systems;
- task-supporting systems;
- expert systems;
- knowledge banks.

Databases

Databases are the breeding ground for the development of knowledge. They contain a quantity of data that can be processed to form information. For example, management information which can be used in turn (Box 8.8) to plan and control production processes. The knowledge enterprise requires more and more data for its business activities. In addition, more and more data are becoming available. The number of electronic transactions and documents is many times larger than it used to be, and clients leave their marks everywhere when making electronic purchase and payment transactions. This data offers new possibilities for firms. A concept that zeroes in on that increase in volume and the associated need for a larger processing capacity is 'data warehousing'. The knowledge enterprise can derive consumer behaviour and preferences of individual clients by 'hacking', so to speak, their own large data files. For banks, the millions of financial transactions are a rich source of information about their clients' payment behaviour. Multiple retailers are now able to carry out thorough analyses of consumers' spending behaviour using a combination of chip cards, transaction systems and data warehouses. As a result, they are better able to target products and services to the changing needs of their clients.

Box 8.8. Database applications.

---

1. Rover's component database

Automobile manufacturer Rover aspires to a leading position in product innovation and in shortening the development time (time-to-market). The speed of product development is a critical success factor at Rover. In order to achieve this ambition, the firm makes heavy investments in IT. To support the product designers, a powerful component database has been established, providing access to an enormous amount of technical data concerning component technical performance, quality, and availability. Product designers are thus able to make the best material choices when making a new design for cooling, fuel injection, ABS, bodywork, or coating (Bird, 1993).

2. Ericsson's International Product Problem Database (IPPD)

Ericsson is an international firm whose development, production, marketing and sales are strongly spread in geographical terms. Its 'International Product Problem Database' contains detailed information about Ericsson's products and components sold worldwide. The database offers all its employees a first guide about the functioning of products and components. It provides access to product information resulting in the quick and adequate solution of specific problems. In this way, Ericsson has structured all production information, enabling its employees to communicate about products and production on a world-wide basis (Van Sluijs, 1995).

3. Data warehousing in the retail business

Possessing customer-specific knowledge provides a firm with competitive advantage. This certainly holds true of the retail business. Data warehousing enables a retailer to anticipate individual customer needs, thus targeting the product assortment, promotion and presentation to specific customer groups. For example, in the United

States data warehousing techniques revealed a link between the sales of beer and diapers. Apparently, married men often bought diapers before closure time and purchased a case of beer at the same time. This finding can be taken into account when designing the shopping floor and assortment presentation.

Information Systems

Information Systems (IS) bring the application of IT to the level of information management. Information management is concerned with the planning, organizing, and controlling of an organization's information flows (Earl, 1989). Information systems can be split up according to the task they are expected to fulfil or the application area (Figure 8.4) they are aimed at. The task of an IS is to supply and process information for efficient business management. An IS can be used for (Hartman, 1990):

- performing and coordinating (functional) knowledge work;
- steering and controlling processes;
- achieving strategic objectives.

Information systems are originally strongly focused on applications within one functional knowledge domain. The integration of information systems allows for the creating of cross-functional information flows. The processing of information can therefore take place irrespective of location and time.

Thus, in the production environment the integration of logistic and sales systems has been gradually realized using 'materials resource planning' (MRP I) and 'manufacturing requirements planning' (MRP II). Today, information systems are designed for specific business functions which can be coupled directly, with the aim of building up an integral system. Such systems are referred to as 'enterprise resource planning' (ERP) systems. ERP — for example the BAAN IV and SAP R/3 packages, focus on the support of business-critical processes. The application of ERP allows for streamlining of

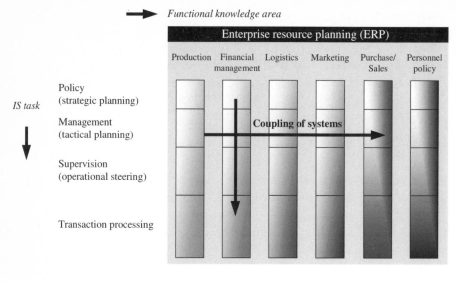

Figure 8.4. Functional information systems (after Hartman, 1990, p. 9).

Box 8.9. Examples of IS.

1. Information systems for the hotel and catering industry

The hotel and catering industry makes increasing use of IS to enhance the efficiency and speed of service. In hotels, restaurants and pubs, waiters directly introduce the orders at the client's table using a palmtop computer (point-of-sales computer). The order is automatically transferred to an order fulfillment system, which directs it to the kitchen and processes it for billing.

2. Planning of patient flows using MIS

The health care sector is confronted with the difficult task of constantly improving or at least maintaining the quality of patient care while facing an incessant budget pressure. This forces hospitals to utilize the available capacity at maximum. IS are increasingly used to streamline patient care. Logistic models appear to be invaluable in hospitals. It is in the interest of the patient as well as the health care insurer to reduce waiting and treatment times. In a factory this would be referred to as reduction of the throughput time, and the patients as 'work in progress'. Similar to a production process, waiting times can be shortened by better fine-tuning the treatment and nursing process: investigating and treating physicians, operating theatres, nursing capacity, rehabilitation facilities, and so on. Hospitals introducing such IS-based streamlining (Kaplinsky, 1995) soon discover how little they know about their own work processes.

production and distribution processes with the most important aim to improve forecasts, decrease stocks, and speed up deliveries.

Networks

Electronic networks offer new opportunities to reinforce knowledge flows. Their strength is based mainly on the ability to bridge distances, cross boundaries and eliminate time differences. Essentially, a network couples knowledge workers and can be extended to integrate teams, departments, business units, value chains, or business sectors.

The possibilities offered by networks for the improvement of the knowledge and information traffic are strongly determined by the technical characteristics of hardware and software. This might be compared with the traffic network. It is important not only that the roads connect, but also that common traffic rules are accepted. Such traffic rules ('protocols') also play a major role in the information and knowledge traffic. The scope of communication is determined increasingly by the degree of standardization.

However, networks also introduce a risk for the knowledge enterprise: the risk of unwanted visitors in the knowledge domains that one does not wish to share with others. Building in safety doors has therefore become a serious profession within IT.

Box 8.10. IT networks.

---

1. Assuring synergy in case of decentralization

It is in the interest of a decentralized company to have a good network for data communication. The correct data, information and know-how must be present at the right place at the right time. For a BU, the information flows with the corporate environment and with other BUs are important. Assuring the relationship of the BU DSM Andeno with its corporate environment means that IT must ensure the linkage between the internal computer network with that of the other business units (LAN LAN coupling). The transition to a DSM network (WAN) supports the interaction between Andeno and the other DSM BUs.

2. A network with intermediaries

Communication with intermediaries is crucial in the insurance sector. The intermediaries are the primary customers for a lot of insurance companies. In order to streamline communication with the intermediaries the relationship is laid down in a nation-wide electronic network (assurance date networks), insurer and intermediary, enabling to share policy-relevant information directly.

3. One-way traffic in relation to clients

Many service-providing firms make use of what is called 'bulletin boards', where clients can file a problem or defect, or a question about the use of a product. The limitation of bulletin boards is the lack of a dialogue with the customer. Another facility is needed for this, for example the online helpdesk which provides the customer with tailored support on the basis of incoming messages.

4. EDI: the firm contacts partners electronically

Company networks expand to the external environment by linking up with suppliers and customers. An important application in this area is

---

EDI (Electronic Data Interchange). EDI systems ensure electronic exchange of documents between firms. Documents such as orders invoices, product specifications and stock data are sent electronically and automatically stored in data files. These information flows between supplier and customer are transmitted by telephone lines, networks and computers using a standard protocol, thus eliminating communication obstacles between computers and safeguarding the document traffic. This direct communication and exchange of information leads to both a reduction in administrative activities and more efficient inventory management as well as a more rapid delivery process.

Expert Systems

More and more work processes call for the direct utilization of expertise. Direct access to the knowledge and know-how is particularly important in professional service provision when problems have to be solved 'on the spot'. One might think here of providing investment advice, fixing a crashed computer, or calculating the price in a business deal. An expert system enables people to carry out knowledge-intensive activities without possessing the necessary know-how themselves. The lack of knowledge and experience in younger staff is compensated by the possibility to apply an adequate expert method. They are thus able to help customers directly 'at the counter' without time-consuming consultation with specialists. This has a double advantage: the available knowledge is better used in daily operations, and more time is created for the supply of new tacit knowledge. Without this new supply, the wellspring of knowledge is bound to dry out sooner or later.

Task-Supporting Systems

Task-supporting systems focus on the support and improved control of work processes. Workflow support systems assist the individual knowledge worker, and 'groupware' supports a group of employees.

Groupware provides groups responsible for a common task with a common work environment. In this environment, information flows can be freely shared, group activities can be partly automated, and locally developed information and know-how is accessible and stored centrally.

A well-known application area of task-supporting systems is product development, where computer systems take over part of the analysis, design and development activities. The firm's specific design and development know-how is laid down in CAD (computer aided design) systems (Box 8.11). Later in the development process this know-how can be quickly retrieved and changes in specifications can be introduced relatively easily. By coupling the design know-how with a computer-aided production system (CAM) it can be immediately applied to the production process. Such a CAD/CAM system supplies the foundation for knowledge recycling.

Box 8.11. Task-supporting systems.

---

1. Construction work

CAD systems are frequently applied in construction. Architects use CAD to lay down design know-how. Thus, design specifications, plans, material descriptions and detail constructions are registered in a system. This enables the architect to adjust his construction designs and discuss them with customers, building contractors and project foremen more simply and rapidly.

2. Software engineering

Recycling of knowledge components is more and more widely accepted in software engineering. Software programs used to be developed rule by rule. In the development of each new software package the process was regarded as a unique and autonomous building process. This vision has changed with the emergence of new development methods (object orientation), programming languages (Java) and new software development tools. The development of software packages makes increasing use of standard components and CASE tools ('Computer-Aided Software Engineering'). IT firms speak of 'a development environment in which software codes are generated and the software know-how developed can be stored in a library'. Software components can be retrieved again from that library later and processed in other packages or systems. The recycling of software and software know-how can strongly increase the development productivity. Product (or system) development can moreover be accelerated and the time-to-market reduced.

3. The front office

In financial service provision, workplace automation takes place not only in the 'back office' but in the 'front office' as well. Customer interaction and quick communication are vitally important in the financial sector. The financial consultant of a bank or insurance company takes his workplace to the customer. Equipped with a mobile telephone and a laptop he is able to connect directly with the firm anywhere. In this way, the consultant can supply any information about personal credits, mortgages, or types of savings. Together with the customer he can directly negotiate a tailor-made contract.

Knowledge Banks

Knowledge banks are developed to make more efficient use of the available know-how. Yet the term 'knowledge bank' may be misleading because in actual practice knowledge banks tend to contain *information about* knowledge rather than knowledge itself, for example information about product, process or project knowledge (Boxes 8.1, 8.2, and 8.3). The knowledge bank enables the knowledge worker to quickly find out whether and where certain know-how and experience is available, and whether it can be used immediately. Organizations which tend to set up knowledge banks include those where:

- work is carried out in projects;
- process standardization allows for the recycling of know-how;
- the scale size calls for the broad availability of knowledge.

Box 8.12. Knowledge bank for project management.

Knowledge banks are also applied at project level, particularly to support project leaders and team members in project management and implementation. The contents of a project knowledge bank may range from tools for planning, budgeting, and cost calculation to project documentation, specifications and work procedures. Methodologies for

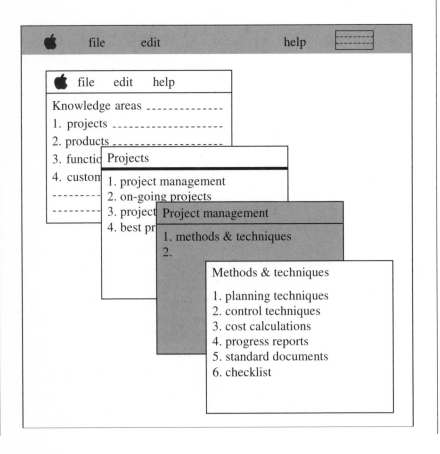

project implementation, controlling techniques, checklists and process criteria are made available to the knowledge worker for effective project management. A model for project management can thus be built up using different files containing:

- descriptions of methodologies and processes;
- reference material for techniques;
- industrial standards and procedures;
- best practices and research reports;
- project references and criteria;
- project experiences.

Knowledge banks are heavily subject to change. In many organizations they are initially introduced as separate instruments: as a digital card-index box or reference work. Yet knowledge banks can mature to become the basic facility supporting managerial control in all of its aspects: into a search system for the firm's competencies. It is crucial that the members of the organization want to use and feed the knowledge bank. Its contents must be useful, reliable and recognizable. This requires sound management of the knowledge bank as well as user commitment when designing the knowledge bank.

The Computer as an Ink Blot

Nobel prize winner Herbert Simon compared the computer with a psychiatrist's ink blot as early as 1977. Such a test consists of a series of ink stains on paper, which are created by applying a large ink drop on a sheet of paper and folding it. All kinds of fantastic shapes are thus produced. Everyone who looks at these ink blots sees whatever he wants to see: a fish or a boat, fighting dogs or a complex machine. The psychiatrist assumes that the patient projects his own hopes, fears and expectations in these ink blots. Therefore, patients' observations (Box 8.13) don't tell anything about the ink blots, but about the person observing them.

Box 8.13. 'Reading meanings into the shadows...'

'That is to say, like the psychiatrist's ink blot, they (computers) serve imagination as symbols for all that is mysterious, potential, portentous. For when man is faced with ambiguity, with complex shadows he partly understands, he rejects that ambiguity and reads meanings into the shadows. And when he lacks the knowledge and technical means to find the real meanings of the shadows, he reads into them the meanings in his own heart and mind, uses them to give external shape to his private hopes and fears. So the ambiguous stimulus, the ink blot, becomes a mirror. When man describes it, he depicts not some external reality, but himself' (Simon, 1977, p. 1).

This metaphor seems to be as useful today as it was in 1977. When reading the newspaper we are equally flooded with the images about the unbounded possibilities of tomorrow's information society as with the messages about the limitations and failures of today's information technology. The same holds true of IT applications within the knowledge enterprise. Suppliers enlarge upon the advantages of IT opportunities. A glance at actual practice reveals that the applications don't amount to more than a digitalization of what had been confided to paper. But one thing seems to be certain: the development of IT will continue. It is not a trend that will blow over. Regardless of the current transition problems, IT will increasingly influence the way we think and act. This makes it no less difficult to make predictions today about the place of IT in tomorrow's knowledge enterprise. Nevertheless, we shall make a careful attempt to do so.

A New Work Environment

So far IT has placed an emphasis upon information, and this will continue to be so for a long time. The possibilities to generate knowledge using IT will remain limited. Knowledge workers generate tacit knowledge using information and their own intellectual capacity. Once tacit knowledge is made explicit, it is ready to be committed to a computer. There is no doubt that knowledge technology will make progress and win ground here. Yet for all appearances the role of the knowledge worker will become more rather than less important. At the same time, the significance of IT to the knowledge worker will enhance considerably. Knowledge workers concentrate not only on the development and application of knowledge. The largest part of their time is spent on interpreting and processing data and information. Their output, too, often has more characteristics of information than of knowledge in many cases. Thus, the huge opportunities lying ahead of them in terms of productivity improvement and quality enhancement in knowledge work lie not so much in automating knowledge development tasks, but rather in automating information tasks. Let us look at an example from practice. A major task of welfare workers in the municipal social services is to ascertain the size of social security payments. A knowledge system enables him to carry out this task relatively simply. But the welfare worker has yet another task: working round together with the client to reach a situation allowing (re)entry into the labour market. This task requires social intelligence to such an extent that computers will never be able to play more than a limited role in that. Yet without IT applications it would be altogether impossible in present-day society to focus on that task at all.

Thus, IT has produced a change in the work environment of knowledge workers, and this change will not stall. Expectations are constantly adjusted to the possibilities at hand. The possibilities to communicate world-wide from every single location, filing documents on the Internet rather than in the cellar, and carrying along one's office in a briefcase. That is no longer a vague stain on a projection test.

IT and Organizational Renewal

IT is often presented as a tool that can 'break' the organization open. Clogged up communication channels can be pricked, superfluous chains can be 'out-automated', and managers are finally provided with the correct steering information. This line of thought is put forward in a lot of literature, mainly in the literature on Business Process Re-engineering (cf. Davenport, 1993; Hammer and Champy, 1993). IT is sketched in this literature as an adequate device fighting against the dysfunctions of the organization. The organization is expected to change as well, because automation and computerization are also a process of organizational renewal. Opposed to this is another vision (Van Ewijk *et al.*, 1995; De Sitter *et al.*, 1997), in which the roles of IT and organization are reversed. Increasing complexity and uncertainty in the environment put the organization under pressure. Internal processes are becoming too complex and increasingly difficult to control. In this line of thought, it is essentially wrong to turn to IT tools directly. When organizational processes are becoming too complicated, it would be wiser *first* to simplify these processes and thus reducing the control burden. What's the use of investing in additional control devices for an organization that is gratuitously complex and compartmentalized? This approach is mainly aimed at reducing the control burden. This can be achieved, first, by focusing the package of products and services. Streamlining of organizational processes (the 'production structure') is a second step. By dismantling the functional organization and the set-up of self-managing units, the number of interfaces within the organization can be greatly reduced. Finally, the new rule (or control) structure can be built up bottom up, following the principle that everything that *can* be performed close to the work processes *should* be performed right there. This is where the information structure comes in. The new streamlined organization is provided with modern IT tools to the optimum extent.

As the case study reports presented in Chapter 4 have shown, the writers of this book are adherents of the second ('sociotechnical') vision with one reservation. Most of the firms have begun streamlining, or rotating, the organization and have introduced new IT afterwards. Nationale Nederlanden was quick at establishing a link between IT and the organization. The redesign of IT processes at NN anticipated the renewal of the organization. IT has become a tool used to make the new organization effective. At DSM Andeno, the rotation of the organization has paved the way for the effective utilization of IT (which was, in fact, already available).

Our reservation is the following: IT is acquiring increasingly infra-structural characteristics. Machinery and systems are no longer autonomous, but provide access to a complex of joint facilities. The strength of infrastructure is its community relevance as well as its unit-crossing relevance. A sound IT infrastructure moreover offers more and more possibilities for choice concerning the design of primary processes. This holds true particularly of organizations where information processing dominates the primary process. In this way, the IT policy does not escape from the paradox of innovation (Chapter 5): ensuring local autonomy and overall synergy. This is an and/and decision rather than an and/or choice.

Chapter 9

Renovation of the Knowledge Enterprise

The knowledge enterprise is the product of a permanently learning organization. Like individuals, organizations must learn by trial and error. The question is how this learning process can be accelerated in such a way that business goes on as usual and the risks remain limited. Is it possible at all to make plans that show, step by step, when and where a specific tool should be used? This final chapter discusses the paradox between design and development. It addresses the risks of the knowledge enterprise. Finally, learning experiences from actual practice are put on a time scale.

The Permanently Learning Organization

When someone wants to build a house, he knows that he or she should begin by laying the foundation before building the walls. And that he cannot start with the roof until the walls are built. That order is straightforward. Managers facing complex problems like things to take place in a straightforward order: this comes first, followed by that. Complex problems are unravelled in small orderly pieces which are later put together like pieces in a Meccano construction set. 'We could learn a lot from project management in construction' sighs many a manager facing complex innovation projects. It hardly makes a difference whether these are concerned with technological, organizational or market-centred innovations. The 'construction metaphor' offers a new value basis for the controllability of complex processes. The IT sector is pervaded with complex processes. This becomes clear when just looking at the language used in the IT sector. System architecture, programmes of requirements, content management, building components have all become day-to-day terms used in IT. In addition, the IT revolution has provided us with tools to carry the construction metaphor further in the design of organizational processes. The most important instrument here is the study of systems, which enables us to describe, fractionate and reassemble complex processes. We are thus able to make a plan of steps, in which we seem to recognize a universally applicable order, derived from (Lewis, 1994, p. 19) 'systems engineering': the architecture of complex technical systems. The starting point is to find a solution to a given problem (Box 9.1).

Box 9.1. Systems engineering (Source: Lewis, 1994, p. 19).

Systems engineering, in common with other 'hard' systems approaches, is concerned with finding a solution to a given problem. For a structural engineer the problem may be to design a way of crossing a river with a bridge which is strong enough for some predicted use but cheap and easy to build. The engineer's work begins when the *need* for the river to be crossed has been *already identified*. Systems engineering too is concerned with the creation of a system to satisfy a defined need; the systems engineer knows (or at least proceeds upon the basis that they know) *what* must be done; their skill, craft and techniques are directed towards deciding *how* to do it. Because there may be many possible, alternative ways to do it, much attention must be given to the process by which to select the 'best' (variously interpreted as the most elegant, the most effective, most efficient or cheapest) way.

This basic pattern is found today in the design plan of virtually every business process, whether it be concerned with logistics, quality control, or the workforce. Therefore, it only seems logical to base the knowledge enterprise on such a pattern as well. In fact, this pattern has been identified in the first chapter (Figure 1.1), where definition of the knowledge ambition is the formal starting point. In that phase the direction and aim have been recognized. Yet a crucial phase precedes the formal start: the phase in which political forces are bundled and the sense of urgency is reinforced. After defining the knowledge ambition comes the avenue along which the knowledge ambition can be realized and, in the end, implemented. In practice we don't seem to be able to work without such step plans. Before going into the planning of the knowledge enterprise we will highlight the limitations of the construction metaphor.

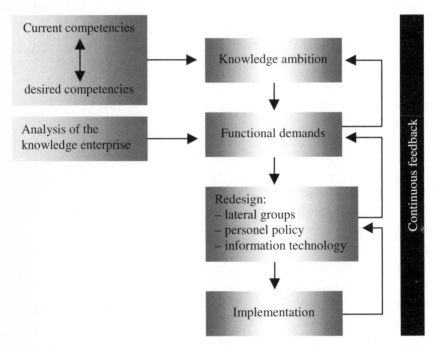

Figure 9.1. The knowledge enterprise as a construction process.

The first limitation is that the construction metaphor is derived primarily from a new construction. The designer has a white sheet of paper in front of him and needs to bother little about past structures. In contrast, the knowledge enterprise is generally concerned with 'renovation', 'reconstruction', and 'redesign'. A transition in which old structures are run down and new ones must be built up at the same time. The shop is reconstructed while business must go on as usual. This has two important consequences. First, the logical sequence of design steps is lost, or to continue the construction metaphor: sometimes the walls must stay erect when the fundament is subsiding, or the roof must remain intact when the frontage is in need of reconstruction. In other cases most of the exterior structure will remain the same, but the building fulfils another function: a textile factory becomes a hotel or a church becomes an exhibition hall. This happens a lot in organizations. The existing distribution system is used to market new products and services, or a firm's own production know-how is utilized to sell production systems elsewhere. The second consequence is concerned with the relationship between what exists and what is new. The redesign process always has an iterative character. When defining the knowledge ambition, one is always reliant upon the available potential. Wanting and being able are stuck to each other as by elastics. This argument was thoroughly discussed in Chapters 2 and 6.

This brings us to the second fundamental limitation of the construction metaphor. In construction work, the problem to be resolved is identified in advance. Let's take the building of a new bridge over the river Rhine as an example. The *functionality* and starting conditions (soil conditions) are known. The organization of the construction process seems to be mainly a matter of sound planning and applying existing knowledge. But also when building bridges one may be faced with unexpected problems. Or unexpected opportunities. In the knowledge enterprise, unpredictability of problems and opportunities plays a major role almost by definition. A recent example of new problems and new opportunities is the development of the programming language Java. Java was designed as a universal language for PDSs (small handy-sized computers). These devices were not initially successful in the market place. Nevertheless, the Internet offered a new perspective for Java because a strong need was felt for a kind of 'digital Esperanto'. This example shows that one can be mistaken in the starting conditions (the market) and how unexpectedly another functionality (the application possibilities) may present itself.

Unpredictability manifests itself particularly when there is a new demand for knowledge, or vice versa, when there is a supply of new knowledge. The organization can do nothing else in that case but make use of its own learning capacity. The organization mainly learns from its own mistakes. New solutions are thought of by reflecting upon the things that went wrong. This is the very paradox of the knowledge enterprise. On the one hand it is concerned with a process that requires steering, focus and planning, while it is based on trial and error on the other. The art is to learn at maximum from one's own experiences by trial and error, while the overall line remains visible. Illustrative in this context is the way in which we talk about 'lean production' in the west. It is a mistake to consider lean production merely as a radical slimming diet for the production organization on the basis of thorough system analysis, a sharp pruning hook and hierarchical power. Lean production is mainly the effect of a long-lived learning process. An organization becomes lean and mean by training labour. This learning process has taken the Japanese dozens of years. Fascinating in this connection is the discovery (Box 9.2) in the late 1940s and early 1950s by Toyota chief engineer Taiichi Ohno of the hidden and unused learning capacity of the firm's production workers.

The conclusion to be drawn here is that the knowledge enterprise has both characteristics of organization design and of organization development. This applies to every far-reaching renewal of the organization. It takes one or two weekends at maximum to read a challenging management book on BPR, knowledge management or 'empowerment'. Defining the policy does not need to be a matter of months. The essence, however, lies in the implementation. That is where that the commitment of all relevant players within (and outside

Box 9.2. Learning from mistakes.

'Quality does not come about by sieving out faulty products at the end of the production process, but by finding out what caused the errors during the process. This learning principle is important to the extent that the assembly line should be stopped if needed.' This message from the Japanese automobile industry was found in the well-known MIT study 'The Machine that Changed the World':

'When it came to 'rework', Ohno's thinking was truly inspired. He reasoned that the mass-production practice of passing on errors to keep the line running caused errors to multiply endlessly. Every worker could reasonably think that errors would be caught at the end of the line and that he was likely to be disciplined for any action that caused the line to stop. The initial error, whether a bad part or a good part improperly installed, was quickly compounded by assembly workers farther down the line. Once a defective part had become embedded in a complex vehicle, an enormous amount of rectification work might be needed to fix it. And because the problem would not be discovered until the very end of the line, a large number of similarly defective vehicles would have been built before the problem was found.

So, in striking contrast to the mass-production plant, where stopping the line was the responsibility of the senior line manager, Ohno placed a cord above every work station and instructed workers to stop the whole assembly line immediately if a problem emerged that they couldn't fix. Then the whole team would come over to work on the problem.

Ohno then went much further. In mass-production plants, problems tended to be treated as random events. The idea was simply to repair each error and hope that it didn't recur. Ohno instead instituted a system of problem-solving called 'the five why's'. Production workers were taught to trace systematically every error back to its ultimate cause (by asking 'why', as each layer of the problem was uncovered), then to devise a fix, so that it would never occur again.'

(Source: Womack, Jones and Roos, 1990, p. 56–57)

of) the organization is becoming crucial. This process is far more difficult to steer. Formal planning in that process works only when it is based on a guiding vision and common insight into the organization as a knowledge enterprise.

Risks

Setting up the knowledge enterprise is quite an enterprise. It is with this double meaning that we have used the term 'knowledge enterprise' throughout this book. Enterprising implies that risks must be taken. The risks inherent in the knowledge enterprise can be classified into two categories:

- risks that ensue from a wrong choice of competencies in the knowledge ambition;
- risks that are the consequence of a wrong approach.

Wrong Choices

1. No choice: too many things done badly

It is difficult to make choices and concede ground that yielded a lot of money in the past, especially if it has direct consequences for the positions of individuals and groups of people. This particularly applies to organizations that have stabilized or cut down. Established positions are automatically put under pressure. Yet the temptation to sit on the fence, run with the hare and hunt with the hounds is fatal. Too many things are badly managed in the course of time. Indications of this risk are the following:

- too many core competencies (> 4);
- changing priorities;
- chronic shortage of time and resources;

- competencies are 'neatly' divided over departments and company units;
- decisions mainly ensue from compromises;
- breakthroughs fail to occur;
- lack of overview.

2. No choice: no ambition

Especially in prosperous times, choices are often put on a back burner. The current turnover and returns are used as measurements of success. The firm's differentiation capacity does not seem relevant. Strategic innovation is regarded as a cost. Development capacity is to be used mainly to enhance quality and reduce costs. The firm is eroding its knowledge base without being aware of it. The risk here is that the distance between the firm and its pursuers becomes smaller or that it does not succeed in joining in with the group up front. Indications for this are:

- the same failures are used time and again as an argument not to invest;
- the development portfolio mainly consists of low-risk projects;
- market pull or cost control are the only sanctifying arguments;
- long-term projects are constantly suspended for the benefit of short-term activities;
- the Board of Directors fails to promote the importance of knowledge;
- when asking about the firm's differentiation know-how it refers to the competencies also used by rival firms to distinguish themselves.

3. Too narrow a choice: locked in one's own possibilities

Too narrow a knowledge base is equally dangerous as too wide a knowledge base. The firm takes the risk of being locked in its own know-how and no longer being able to digress when necessary. The following phenomena hint at this risk:

- too few risky projects in the development portfolio;
- incapacity to find adequate investment destinations for the money supplied by cash cows;
- a static and conservative customer pool;
- the firm is focusing on existing markets only;
- the end of the cash cows lifecycle is approaching;
- the same old success stories are recounted again and again;
- there is no need for external knowledge.

4. Badly founded choice: ignorance

Making sound choices presupposes that the organization has a good overview of the most relevant knowledge areas. Frontrunners have sensitive antennas and gatekeepers to spot and assess new developments. Yet pursuers too should possess the ability to absorb new knowledge (Chapter 3). They should be able to 'zoom out' and compare their own competencies with the knowledge areas they are part of. When firms don't possess that capacity they risk missing the boat, invest in competencies that exceed the power of the organization, or winding up in a dead end. These risks can be recognized as follows:

- there exist only few relationships with external knowledge centres;
- the firm is not aware of its competitors' competencies;
- the firm grimly closes its doors to pryers;
- sparse participation in conferences, visits to trade fairs, etc.;
- few or no apprentices or school-leavers are recruited;
- the contrary: there is a belief that all relevant know-how can be purchased when needed.

A Wrong Approach

1. Centralism

The knowledge enterprise is greatly driven by its concern for synergy of company entities within the larger whole. This concern for the whole is not allowed to legitimize restoration of the obsolete centralized order; an order where headquarters do the thinking and prescribing as to how the decentralized organization should behave. In this approach, discussions about competencies are often confined to elitist think-tanks operating in isolation from the rest of the firm. A risk involved here is the working of the self-fulfilling prophecy in the various company entities: one cooperates, but does so especially to be able to prove later that the centralized approach does not work. Indications of this are:

- central officers rule the roost;
- decisions are made in a small circle;
- measures are not targeted to the need;
- a unilateral top-down information flow.

2. Building up a paper knowledge structure

The formal measures described in this book meant to create conditions to foster the knowledge enterprise. Defining the knowledge ambition, designing lateral linkages, offering new electronic communication possibilities, and introducing a new career system are formal measures that can be taken in a comparatively short time period. These are all measures that can be entrusted to paper. They can even be copied to a large extent. Thus, the terms of reference of another firm's technology council can be easily adopted. Yet the risk will remain that organizations don't get any further than paper measures. Organizational changes do not add value to the company until people change their behaviour. This certainly applies to the design of the knowledge enterprise. The yields come from daily practice. From the way in which people work with each other, inform each other timely, make use of each other's knowledge and experience. Unless policy is translated into behaviour there will be investments, but no harvest. The accompanying symptoms are:

- meetings are difficult to arrange and are badly visited;
- instruments are badly used and maintained;

- plans are easily mothballed;
- endless flows of documents;
- measures are not visible at work level.

3. The lack of joint orchestration

Rejection of a centralized approach does not mean that one does not need any form of control or steering. One might use a theatre metaphor in this respect. The knowledge enterprise requires the stage to be set, rules to be clarified and players to be prepared for their roles. Without 'orchestration', there is no concerted action and the knowledge enterprise remains noncommittal and unfocused. Knowledge workers and more so their managers have a tendency, especially in the beginning, to continue to defend their own territory and safeguard the organizational boundaries. Priority is given to the individual task and performance to be produced today. The extra energy needed to bring about synergy across the boundaries of one's own unit is seldom summoned. Indications of this risk are:

- core competencies continue to be patchwork of local competencies;
- border-crossing projects are given low priority;
- although one wants to benefit from other people's knowledge, one is reluctant to make one's own knowledge available;
- rewarding though risky activities are passed on to others;
- there exists little willingness to lend and transfer one's own expertise;
- border-crossing discussions continue to be evasive.

The Road Map

Each plan of steps is due to fail on two accounts. First, the plan is always too rigid and inflexible. When designing technical systems one frequently faces *unexpected* problems and solutions along the way. When designing and developing social systems, this is even more true. The social character of the organizational system also gives rise to the second limitation of each step-wise approach: the *hiddenness* of problems and solutions. In social systems it is not only the visible formal objectives and rational arguments that count, but also hidden interests and powerful positions of individuals and groups. Steps in the road map are riddled with the 'unwritten rules of the game' (Scott Morgan, 1994).

Yet we cannot afford to do without plans: we cannot do without naming and timing activities and dividing the work load. Given the limitation of formal planning it is wise to delve into the political forces that may be instrumental during the process and into the interventions that may overcome obstacles. From this perspective, a number of important learning experiences are given below.

1. The knowledge enterprise begins with the formation of a 'Gideon Gang'

Each extensive organizational renewal is preceded by an extremely important phase, in which one must 'to blaze a trail and take up one's quarters'. A small close team must be set up to make preparatory arrangements. This is the 'Gideon Gang' which is expected to set the wheel in motion and break down the organizational boundaries. At the start, it is mainly the task of this group to bundle forces, introduce new ideas into the organization and convince the organization of the need for change. The composition of the group is highly important. A lateral linkage (Chapter 6) representing various hierarchical levels, functions and company units is most appropriate. Willingness to change, influence, communication skills and expertise are the most relevant criteria. The composition of this 'inner circle' is a sign that the knowledge enterprise is taken seriously. The inner circle is made familiar with the ideas relating to knowledge management. External orientation should not be underestimated here: How do other firms go about it? What are the different strategies used and what instruments are available? When composing the Gideon gang, one lays the foundation for underpinning the change management at key positions. In this sense, management development is a starting point in this operation rather than being at the bottom of the list.

2. Choose a natural starting point

In general, extensive changes come about only when there is a forceful need to move with the times. A firm can take advantage of such a need to start the knowledge enterprise. One may think of far-reaching processes which have been initiated recently such as:

- a strategic repositioning;
- the introduction of a unit structure;
- a merger or acquisition; or
- the introduction of a new IT infrastructure.

The starting point may also be an acute and existential problem, such as the loss of a big customer, or a project that has got snarled up. It may also be the confrontation with new technological possibilities or new unexpected opportunities in the market place. The advantage of such a starting point is that the urgency for change is clear. The organization's rusted bolts and nuts must be turned loose anyway because of various reasons.

3. If there is no sense of urgency, it must be evoked

Introvert and introspective organizations tend to shield themselves off from external influences. The willingness to change does not come about until the urgency is felt right across the organization. This feeling can be awoken by opening up rusted windows using force. For example by:

- taking up fresh blood in the management ranks;
- investing in benchmarking;
- critical self-investigation: why did Project X snarl up and why wasn't Product Y successful?

- seconding employees to other organizations;
- calling upon external experts;
- cooperating with other firms;
- focused training programmes;
- involving customers in the renewal process.

One might say in that case that the knowledge enterprise has got started even before the starting shot was given. No matter how one puts it: making plans without a powerful fighting team and without a sense of urgency is useless.

4. Ensure broad support in the organization when formulating the knowledge ambition

Once the inner circle is installed it must be widened for two reasons. First, when defining the knowledge ambition the organization must benefit maximally from the knowledge available in the entire business chain. Second, support must be created for the organizational change. One method to achieve this is organizing three one- or two-day workshops for a larger outer circle:

- Workshop 1 (*objective: involvement, 'unfreezing'*): the need for change and the approach to change are discussed. At the end of this workshop, work groups are composed for the analysis (home) work.
- Workshop 2 (*objective: formulating alternatives*): the analysis results are discussed and diagnosed. Work groups are assigned with the task of elaborating a number of options for the knowledge ambition.
- Workshop 3 (*objective: making decisions*): discussing the options for the knowledge ambition and making a choice.

It is self-evident that the form chosen for these workshops (or 'search conferences') is heavily dependent upon the nature of the organization. Thus, in a small firm the entrepreneur himself will generally play a central role and the analysis will probably be less complicated. The meetings may be shorter and more informal in character. Yet the line of thought will be the same. It is essential that things run swiftly. If the meetings are prepared well, the throughput time can be limited to three or four months. The outer circle is composed of key figures right across business units, functions and hierarchical echelons. They are not only a source of ideas, but also provide a link in the communication with the rest of the firm. They are given the explicit task of discussing the development with their own colleagues.

5. Design the knowledge enterprise from a broad outline to details

'Doing the right things right' is the objective of the third step in the knowledge enterprise. The organization is understood as a knowledge-developing and knowledge-processing system. In this phase, it is determined what improvements and renewals must be made in that system. It is important to first 'zoom out' to the company in its entirety, allowing for a map of its most important knowledge flows and bottlenecks. Only then does one 'zoom into' the lower system levels. In this way, the functional demands for the knowledge enterprise are finally formulated. The advantage of this design sequence is that insight into the coherence is thus maintained. When the reversed segmented avenue is chosen, one will get stuck sooner or later (Moss Kanter, 1983): the pieces will no longer fit the puzzle.

6. The strength of the tools lies in their coherence

The tools of the knowledge enterprise (Part 2) derive their strength from the coherence they are used with. Thus, an instrument such as the skills map (Chapter 2) will only work when there are good career coaching and training programmes. Communication systems reinforce organizational lateral linkages. Sound organizational lateral linkages allow for job rotation.

7. Work step by step on radical renewal

In the case of innovation the contrast between incremental and radical changes is often pointed out. The strategic character of the knowledge enterprise and the emphasis on integration leads one to suspect that innovation is concerned with radical rather than incremental changes. The question that rises immediately is whether radical change fits in the heavy control burden carried by managers in each complex organization. We advocate an approach referred to by public administration researchers (Etzioni, 1976) as 'mixed scanning'. This approach focuses on a radical objective. The knowledge ambition mirrors the radical objective for the knowledge enterprise. We have pointed out previously that a broad support base must be developed in the organization for that objective. However, this radical objective can be achieved only when taking small steps. As a precondition, (a) the thread of the knowledge ambition is constantly followed, and (b) the connection with other steps is constantly observed. For example:

- when adjusting assessment procedures, it is checked what stimuli are needed to encourage individual knowledge development;
- the development of a skills map database is focused on the composition of project teams and career development as well as competence development at organizational level;
- the introduction of intranet should be accompanied by pilot projects set up around the most relevant knowledge clusters, including discussion lists, newsletters and a knowledge bank;
- when the business units are screened once a year, it should be identified what new technology is introduced in service provision.

This once again underlines the importance of the knowledge ambition and the functional demands placed upon the organization. They are a constant standard measure.

8. Ensure constant feedback and 'feed forward'

Each change trajectory or programme can be regarded as a flow.

Upstream we find the plan makers and designers and downstream are the groups called upon in later stages, or the groups that are expected to work with the new processes and structures. It is vital in this process that the process steps overlap. This also applies to the knowledge enterprise. One begins with step b while step a is not as yet completed. Activities take place in parallel to a large extent to reduce the throughput time and better connect the steps. Upstream groups are thus given better insight into the feasibility of plans and downstream groups are better able to anticipate changes. Feedback and feed forward of information are crucial in this process. Preliminary plans must be discussed timely with the people that have to work with them, for example: How do we inform our customers before we start renovating? Furthermore, the effect of actions in actual practice must be constantly evaluated. Why are new systems badly used and why is the implementation of job rotation in business unit A so much better than in business unit B?

A New Start

European thinking about organizations throughout the past twenty years has been greatly inspired by developments in the United States and Japan. In North America, one is able to knock up greenfield sites at a high pace. Radical innovation fits in splendidly with a pioneering mentality. The consequence is, however, that when new opportunities and threats present themselves in that part of the world, one tends to decide to shut down an organization and rebuild it elsewhere. This often happens too quickly, because valuable things are lost as a result. The Japanese are masters of continuous improvement. In their country too, culture is the strength of progress. Zen and Kaizen provide the inspiration for organizational design. The recent comparison of the development of information and communication technology shows once again that Europe is lagging far behind in the beneficial introduction of new products and services. The question is whether we should keep concentrating upon the American and Japanese approaches. Isn't it about time that we look at our own strength, which is inherent in our European culture? Looking at the strength of one's own culture is hard, because culture is an implicit phenomenon. If we move about in another culture, the differences strike us immediately. In our own culture, things are self-evident. Yet by studying Japanese and American approaches, it becomes clear that it is useful to make that connection. And why wouldn't that hold true for Europe as well? This is the thought that crosses our mind at the end of this book. It fits in the reasoning built up in this book previously. But where should we start? What is specific to the European culture that might provide a source of renewal? Reflection upon this study brings up a concept that might be the starting point for a European approach: 'renovation', or innovation from existing structures. Providing established entities with new functionality. Revitalizing cultures that have fallen asleep. Rebuilding, while business goes on as usual. That is what we are constantly doing in our old cities. One needs only to travel to the old cities in the new German 'Länder' to witness what we are good at. Renovation does not infer falling back on the past, but using a rich past for the benefit of a profitable future. Looking back at this study, this may be the European essence of the knowledge enterprise. It is the stimulus that starts from the experiences from the seven companies central to this book: starting from one's own strength.

Appendix

Constant 'juggling' is part of each design process. Those who want to set out a course must know where to start. The same holds true of the knowledge enterprise. In general, one deals with a redesign because one does not start from scratch, but from an existing organization. Therefore, the analysis that serves as a preparation for the design focuses both on the existing situation ("IST") and on the desired situation ("SOLL"). This Appendix offers a number of well-known and new analysis instruments. These instruments are concerned with:

- identification of knowledge issues;
- ordering and assessment of knowledge areas;
- identification of knowledge flows; and
- formulation of functional demands.

Rather than being a "High Tech toolkit", this Appendix contains simple instruments that have proved their use in practice to the adept user. Most instruments are conceptual in nature, they are principles used to order and assess knowledge fields. Subjective assessment plays an important part here. The same applies to approaches that try to express knowledge in market or replacement value: these too continue to be subjective approaches. The user is advised to snoop around is this toolkit and pick out the tool that looks most useful at first sight. In some cases, the instrument must be adjusted. In any case, the toolkit represents the pioneering spirit that is required in the knowledge enterprise. The pioneer will have to manage without well-paved paths and proved standard recipes.

Indications of Knowledge Problems

A base for change cannot be developed until it is clear that something has to change. Powerful signals are needed at the beginning of a change process. Later, these signals appear to be the symptoms of an underlying syndrome. The table below lists a number of important signals.

Signal	Possible cause	Significance (S)	Intensity (I)	Urgency (= BxI)
Burnt-out knowledge workers	- Lack of new talent - Too high work pressure - Experts don't get an opportunity to rebuild their reserves - Experts stay in a fixed place too long			
Functional knowledge threatens to crumble off	Lack of lateral linkages			
Functional managers continually argue about using their workers in projects	- Project managers have too little influence - Priority setting is too noncommittal			
There are too many consultants	- Enabling competencies are subcontracted too often - Absorbing capacity is too low			
Own crucial patents threaten to expire	Lagging behind new competitors in technological terms			
The project portfolio has too few projects with a high risk/high reward profile	Management is not prepared to invest, the costs weigh more than the benefits			

(Continued)

Signal	Possible cause	Significance (S)	Intensity (I)	Urgency (= BxI)
The project porfolio has too few projects with a high short-term market expectancy	The projects in the pipeline are strongly dominated by the development department			
The project throughput times are far too long	- Internal fossilization, lack of multidisciplinary co-operation - Too little use is being made of IT			
Development projects must be continually stoked up	A lack of a sound project management system and management commitment			
Other firms zero in on new knowledge development much sooner	- The firm is at too far a distance from the technological source and the market place - Lack of good 'gatekeepers' - The firm's present customers are too conservative			
The value added of the well-known success stories is on a downward trend	The firm has failed to add new value (= knowledge) continuously			
An increasing number of potential assignments accounts are lost	The product, service or technology is becoming obsolete			
Until right before introduction in the factory or in the market, product and service specifications were still in need of adjustment	- Lack of early manufacturer and customer involvement - Specification definition is unsatisfactory - The time between specification and introduction is too long, as a result of which they become obsolete			

(Continued)

Signal	Possible cause	Significance (S)	Intensity (I)	Urgency (= BxI)
A limited number of experts become overburdened because the same people are continuously called upon	Lack of adequate knowledge transfer and human resource development			
Personnel turnover: knowledge workers at crucial places leave the firm	Too little attention for personnel development			
Solutions coming from outside of the firm are rejected in advance (the 'not-invented-here syndrome')	The organization is too introvert			
The wheel is reinvented time and time again	- Learning experiences from projects are not transferred - The firm's own know-how has not been stored well			
There is a constant shortage of resources to bring innovative projects onto the market in a qualitatively sound way	Lack of focus: too many things are done too badly			
Innovation fails to lead to new business	Business development is underdeveloped			
Recruitment: it is extremely difficult to hire knowledge workers with the right experience and training profile	- The work is not sufficiently attractive in terms of tasks, responsibilities, career opportunities, and reward - Many firms are fishing in the same pond			

Total Urgency Score

The checklist with indications can also be used as a test. In that case one jots down, for each signal, the relevance ('seriousness') for the organization and the intensity (frequency) of observation. The following scales can be used:

	1	2	3	4	5
Relevance	not relevant	hardly relevant	somewhat relevant	relevant	highly relevant
Intensity	never	seldom	sometimes	often	very often

The sum of the products of these scale values provides a total score.

System Boundaries

When analyzing knowledge areas and knowledge flows, it is wise to identify the organizational domain the analysis is concerned with. It may focus on the organization as a whole, or rather as part of a larger system. The organizational domain may, however, also be formed by a single department, a network of departments, or the interface between two departments. Whatever the case may be, the current and desired boundaries of the knowledge system must be identified. The criteria for demarcating system boundaries are as follows:

- a recognizable and identifiable value chain;
- knowledge developers and users must be brought together within the system boundary;
- the link between hierarchical levels;
- a closed control loop in the knowledge flow (important input/ output relationships within the system boundary);
- ample overlap with other functions and/or units.

The table below provides a number of system demarcations and their associate practical examples from practice.

System demarcation	Relevant actors
The firm in its environment	- *Internal*: the business functions and business entities adding value and maintaining links with the outside world (gatekeepers); - *External*: customers, suppliers, other knowledge centres (universities, institutes, consultants), government, interest groups
The business unit (or division)	- *Internal*: the business functions and entities adding value and maintaining links with the outside world (gatekeepers); - *External*: the corporate organization, other BUs, customers and suppliers, knowledge centres
Functional groups within a firm	*For example*: controllers in various BUs, personnel services, chemical analysis departments *External*: university sections, professional organizations, firms (e.g. consultant agencies) practising the function as a core activity
Various functional groups in one firm (along a value chain)	*For example*: an entire manufacturing or innovation chain, or links in that chain (R&D and production, the commercial field service and office service)
The firm and its fixed relationships	*For example*: the value chain the firm belongs to, or links from that chain (e.g. the BU and a number of lead users, the BU and the most important suppliers or OEMs)

Identification of Knowledge Areas

When defining the knowledge ambition, knowledge areas must be demarcated. The most relevant questions are:

- Ordering ('coding'): What types of knowledge can be distinguished and what is the connection between them?
- Assessment: what is the significance of the knowledge area for the firm (added value, strength/weakness, competitive advantage)?

Ordering precedes assessment. Ordering is heavily determined by the way in which knowledge is directly linked to products, services and processes. When the link is strong, one might use a schedule that tells where the knowledge in the different generations of products, services and processes are applied. Still, it will mostly be necessary to look at the very knowledge areas that go beyond existing divisions according to product, services, processes and markets. The assessment can be based on the following:

- subjective (with or without a judgement scale);
- estimating the contribution to turnover, profits and the added value of product/market combinations;
- comparison with other firms.

In the latter case, one speaks of benchmarking. Benchmarking is a performance and evaluation technique (Dence, 1995) that answers the question: does the firm do the right things and does it do so better or worse than others? This provides insight into the firm's differentiation capacity in the eyes of customers, suppliers, or competitors. Benchmarking may serve the following purposes (Zairi, 1996):

- it is used for defining performance standards;
- it is used for comparing one's own knowledge activities with best practice;
- it serves as a measure and steering instrument for process improvement;
- it maps customer demands;
- it is a device to motivate the firm's employees to perform better.

The technique can be used to measure the performance of knowledge usage by comparing one's own processes, products or services. Four types of benchmarking can be distinguished (Dence, 1995):

- *internal benchmarking*: this takes place within one organization and specifically between closely related divisions, units, or locations. This type of benchmarking focuses on common performance indicators and may, for example, be directed towards quality improvement.

- *functional benchmarking*: comparison of the performance and procedures of identical business functions in various organizational entities, organizations or business sectors. The purpose of a functional benchmark may be process improvement or cost reduction by comparing cost prices, throughput times, stock days, defect ratios, and so on.
- *competition benchmarking*: this is oriented towards comparing the firm's performance with that of direct competitors in the same sector, or with indirect competitors in related sectors or with the same business processes. Subjects may be price/performance relationships, service quality or customer satisfaction.
- *generic benchmarking*: aims at comparing firms from different sectors that are 'the best in class' for a specific aspect such as innovativeness, customer focus, or process control.

The assessment of competencies can also be carried out as part of a SWOT (Strength, Weakness, Opportunity, Threat) analysis. SWOT is a common method of analysis used for strategy formulation and planning (Learned *et al.*, 1965). It is a method of identifying the strengths and weaknesses of the firm in relation to its environment. Knowledge can be considered as an additional factor in this approach.

The following table provides insight into the applications of the instruments discussed below.

Instrument	Can be used for:	Particularly when:
Mind mapping (nominal group method)	making competencies and relation-ships between competencies explicit	- concerned with identification of competencies going beyond units and functions - the demarcation of competencies has a strongly implicit character
Product/ technology mapping	- establishing the link of knowl-edge in successive generations of products, services and processes - comparison with rival firms (benchmarking)	knowledge is strongly anchored in products and processes (e.g. in electronic engineering and chemi-cal firms, and in the case of stan-dard software)

(Continued)

Instrument	Can be used for:	Particularly when:
Knowledge triangle	- giving direction to business development - establishing the link between functional, contextual and operational knowledge as starting point for the development of new knowledge	concerned with processes with a strong service component
Core competencies and enabling competencies	- strategy formulation - recognizing differentiating competencies and/or - value-adding competencies	a clear focus in knowledge development is lacking
Project portfolio	- prioritizing - evaluation of ongoing development work (short and long-term, risks versus profits)	knowledge development is taking place within development projects or innovative application projects
Knowledge intensity matrix	identifying the knowledge intensity of products and services	the relationship between product (or services) and process knowledge is unclear
Process control	Optimizing processes	cost leadership is aimed at

'Mind Mapping'

'Mind mapping' is a simple technique whereby the connections between devices, concepts or phenomena can be mapped comparatively easily. The technique is highly appropriate to reach consensus on the definition of diffuse, hard to demarcate knowledge areas. It is an application of the 'nominal group method'.

Working method

A group is composed of employees that have a good overview of the organization's knowledge areas and their links with external knowledge areas. In a first round, each group member lists a core competence of the organization using one catchword on five cards at maximum, followed by oral explanation. The group facilitator pins all cards to a large notice board. In a discussion, the cards are rearranged until more or less univocal categories of connected knowledge areas are created. The discussion itself is highly important because it makes explicit the categories that the participants have at the back of their minds ('mind map'), and because it puts forward similarities and differences.

In the second round, the participants are asked to:

- name the categories;
- localize similarities and differences in the participants visions;
- add and delimit core competencies;
- identify relationship between competencies;
- define the competencies desired (knowledge ambition);
- identify any missing competencies.

This procedure can also be applied to the enabling competencies. It provides an initial ordering, which can be used by a small group to be tested with other employees and to be worked out in more detail and underpin it.

Product & Technology (P&T) Mapping

Product & Technology mapping is a technique whereby the knowledge development in generations of products, services and processes are (graphically) mapped. This development is represented in the shape of a tree (see Figure A1). In the case of composed discrete products, this technique is mainly concerned with the knowledge and the technology applied in subcomponents, such as process technology in the processing industry (e.g. the chemical industry). The technique can also be applied to projects in technical service provision. P&T mapping is also applied as a concept to map developments within one

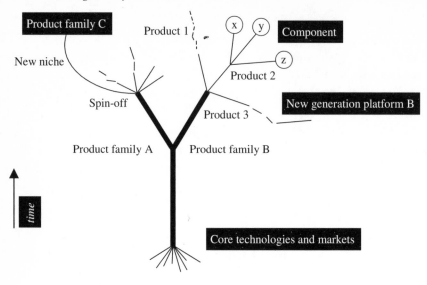

Figure A1. Product and technology mapping.

knowledge domain. Functional maps are thus created for engineering, production or marketing (Clark and Wheelwright, 1994).

The strength of P&T mapping lies in the development of integrated maps clarifying relationships between functional, process and product-linked knowledge. Comparison with other companies (benchmarking) provides insight into the firm's knowledge position as well as a basis for 'reverse engineering'. Reverse engineering takes the best elements of other firms' products and processes as starting point for one's own design practice.

P&T mapping has the following limitations:

- the knowledge development ('technological trajectories') is understood as a linear process making projections to the future from the past and the present;
- too little attention is generally paid to the lateral linkages between products, services and processes;
- there is a heavy emphasis on technology push, and far less on market pull.

The Knowledge Triangle

The knowledge triangle (see Sec. 2.2) is a tool for business development and for setting out the course for the development of new knowledge. The instrument is particularly useful for professional service provision and project-based companies, for example engineering and construction companies, software developers, and transport companies. The triangle's corners represent the three knowledge pillars of the organization: functional (professional) knowledge, operational (experience) knowledge, and contextual (environment) knowledge. When developing new business, or investing in new knowledge areas, the following rule is applied: *Always concentrate on two fixed pillars*. It is assumed here that the company will strain itself when two pillars are built up simultaneously. This can also be graphically represented (see Figure A2): by turning the triangle between two pillars, new knowledge can be developed from two existing knowledge areas.

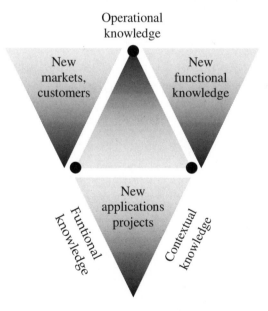

Figure A2. The knowledge triangle.

This enables the firm, for example, to serve new customer groups with existing functional knowledge and operational expertise. The firm's competencies can thus be built up from existing competencies step by step. The limitation of the triangle is that it fails to provide insight into the connection *within* each of the three pillars. Additionally, radical innovations are difficult to fit in, because they often involve the movement of more than one pillar.

Core Competencies, Enabling Competencies and Exchangeable Competencies

In Chapter 2, we discussed the various types of competencies. The table below lists the criteria for each of these three categories.

Core competencies	Enabling competencies	Exchangeable competencies
- Provide customers with essential advantage - Are difficult to imitate	- Are not unique and have no differentiation capacity - Add value	- Knowledge is exchangeable and not intertwined with core and enabling competencies
- Generate unique competitive advantage - Provide the basis for new products and new markets	- Are inextricably bound up with core competencies - Are not subcontracted, because the firm can do it itself cheaper or better	- Are mobile and not sustainable - Can be outsourced - Provide little or no added value
- Are sustainable and have been developed over time	- Are concerned with competition-sensitive know-how	
- Are hard to replace - Can be purchased only by acquisition and personnel recruitment	- Are embedded in the organization - Hiving them off leads to capital destruction and social problems	

Portfolio Analysis

Portfolio analysis is a commonly used instrument in strategy development. The underlying idea is that when assessing a firm's product package, one should not go by the separate products, but the whole of products available in the portfolio. What it comes down to is a balanced composition of the known successes that generate cashflow, and of new promises that safeguard the future. 'Worn-out products' that generate less and less money and cost more and more, must be timely removed from the portfolio. For this purpose, the Boston Consultancy Group (BCG) has developed a graphical representation of the product/matrix portfolio. In this matrix (Kotler, 1995), the products, product/market combinations, or business units are scored along two dimensions: market share and market growth. The technique can be used for a knowledge analysis by plotting the knowledge linked to products, markets or BUs in the matrix. Thus, the internal knowledge is measured using the market as a measure. The matrix shows the knowledge areas and in what phase of knowledge development (lifecycle) they find themselves. In other words, the matrix tells something about the health of the knowledge enterprise. Growth markets, declining business, or promising new products can thus be identified with the BCG matrix.

In terms of BCG, knowledge areas can be named question marks, stars, cash cows, or dogs. Each location in the matrix (Figure A3) identifies the market attractiveness and market growth of a knowledge area. The size of a field in the matrix is an indication of the relative importance in terms of competitive edge, contribution to turnover or returns. On the basis of the knowledge matrix, four strategies are possible:

- building: enhancing the market result of a knowledge areas;
- retaining: retaining the market share in order to generate cashflow;
- harvesting: squeezing the knowledge areas in the short term, regardless of the long-term effect;

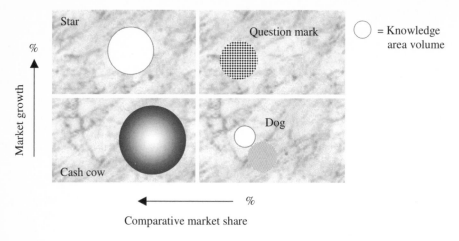

Figure A3. The BCG matrix.

• desinvesting: hiving off this knowledge area because the resources can be better spent.

The limitation of this matrix is that it only reflects the knowledge of products and services already introduced into the market.

1. Project portfolio analysis

The project portfolio analysis (Roussel *et al.*, 1991, see Chapter 2) is oriented primarily towards the knowledge which still is in development phase. This analysis is mainly appropriate for organizations where the knowledge development has a strongly process-like character: both firms with a solid R&D function and professional service providers, which build up their new knowledge especially in customer-oriented projects. The project portfolio is to be viewed as a representation of the firm's competence development. Similar to the BCG matrix, the leading idea is that the projects must not merely be assessed by their own value. Once again, what's important is the balanced composition of the portfolio. There should be a balance between the risky projects that offer a perspective of high returns, and less risky projects that reinforce or maintain the ongoing money flows. This project matrix can furthermore be used to check to see whether the resources are not fragmented too much and whether there exists sufficient synergy between projects in terms of content. Variables in the project matrix may be (see Chapter 2): newness of the knowledge (or technology) for the firm, newness for the market, the technological position of the firm, the technological risk (the 'makeability'), and the reward.

2. Knowledge intensity matrix

The information intensity model (Porter and Pillar, 1985) is at the basis of a matrix comparing the knowledge intensity of products and services with the knowledge intensity of the process. This matrix (see Figure 4) can be used to identify where the organization adds and should add most knowledge.

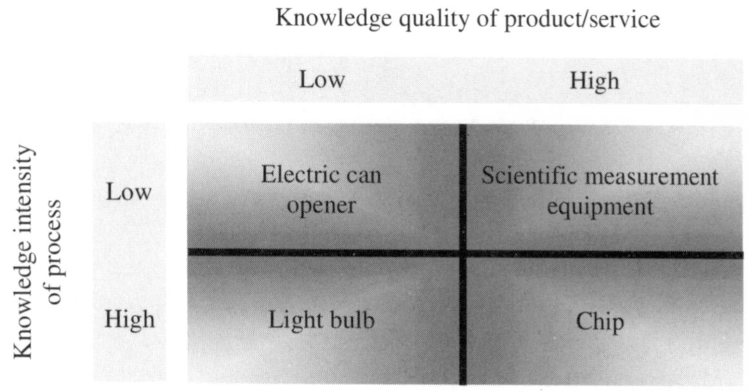

Knowledge quality of product/service

		Low	High
Knowledge intensity of process	Low	Electric can opener	Scientific measurement equipment
	High	Light bulb	Chip

Figure A4. The knowledge intensity matrix.

3. Limitations of portfolio analyses

The use of the portfolio analysis calls for some prudence:

- its strength lies in its simplicity, but generally speaking there are many more factors than just the two represented in the matrix;

Input (stock)	Throughput (flow)	Output (stock)
Aim: measuring investments in knowledge	*Aim*: measuring in the knowledge flow	*Aim*: measuring the use of knowledge
Financially	*Personnel*	*Financially*
- R&D intensity (R&D expenditure/turnover in %) - Product and process development budget	Time spent by R&D on fundamental research, process and product development	- Added value per employee - Increase in turnover and profits - Contribution to turnover/profits of new, improved and existing products - Growth of order portfolio - Market share according to product categories
Personnel - Employee training level - Training budget - Number of R&D employees according to projects - Number of employees according to function	*Product* - Product components developed - Growth of labour productivity *Process* - Ongoing work portfolio - Degree of process control of new business process (Bohn, 1994)	*Benchmarking* - Product performance - Service quality - Customer satisfaction - Patents and patents applications - Number of publications

- sometimes the matrix suggests unjustly that both dimensions are equally important;
- the matrix tells little or nothing about the connection in terms of content between the objects (projects, processes, products and services);
- the matrix does not show what rival firms are up to and what the market demands.

Input/Throughput/Output Measurements

Knowledge flows can be measured indirectly using a simple system model, measuring the resources that are used and the results yielded rather than the knowledge itself. Such an effort may be useful to screen the organization. Thus, it is observed (Hamel and Prahalad, 1994) that Japanese competitors develop comparable products much

Phase	Comment	Typical knowledge form	Example
1. Complete ignorance	We don't know that a certain phenomenon presents itself or is relevant	Nothing, nowhere	We are not aware that a certain packaging in a certain market deters customers
2. Awareness	We are becoming aware of the existence of the phenomenon and its relevance ('pure art')	Tacit human knowledge	We are starting to realize that the disappointing turnover might be related to the packaging
3. Measurement	Relevant variables can be measured. Interventions: trial and error ('pre-technical')	Documented	Through market research we have tracked the factors determining customer's perception of the packaging
4. Control of the average	The process can be controlled and stabilized within certain boundaries. Scientific measurement tools are available.	Documented and anchored in hardware (mechanized)	We are able to assess new packaging designs in advance to the extent that we will generally avoid future problems
5. Process control	The results of a process can be guaranteed. Knowledge embodied in a 'cookbook' or manual ('local recipe')	Mechanized, documented and partly computerized	We possess a manual containing the most important guidelines for packaging design
6. Know how	We know how variables influence the results of a process ('fine-tuning' in order to reduce costs)	Computerized, laid down in empirical comparisons	The packaging specifications can be retrieved using a knowledge system
7. Know why	We possess a scientific model and know how a phenomenon works in a broad range of circumstances. Simulation of the unknown situation is possible.	Laid down in scientific laws and formulas	Our knowledge of packaging has developed such that we can apply it to virtually any product (also outside of our sector)
8. Perfect knowledge	No new knowledge is needed ('Nirwana')	–	Nothing needs to be added to the packaging knowledge

faster and using fewer personnel. The table below provides an ordering of input, throughput and output factors. The limitation of this approach lies in the difficulty to allocate the effects of inputs to outputs. In many cases, it is concerned with spin-offs. New knowledge is particularly valuable for purposes other than the knowledge that had been developed for initially (for example: the walkman, the programming language JAVA).

Process Control as Measurement of Knowledge

Knowledge can also be translated into the degree to which a firm controls a process that is important to the firm. The division of Roger Bohn (1994, p. 63) is very useful here. Bohn's division is based on the development phases passed through when controlling a phenomenon in a production process. He gives 'grades' running from 1 to 8. '1' is 'complete ignorance', while '8' represents complete and utterly thorough knowledge. The following table shows the eight-phase model in the example of 'packaging knowledge'.

In a great number of business processes one will probably be happy, as in our packaging example, to reach phase five at all. Once this phase is reached, the conditions under which one has to work (the technology, consumer preferences, and so on) appear to have altered in such a way that one relapses into a previous phase. The phasing suggests moreover that the development always starts from tacit knowledge into the direction of explicit knowledge, yet the reverse is possible also: explicit knowledge can be converted into tacit knowledge. An example is the quality programme that the management wants to use to 'refresh' a company. Information and training are used to try and teach employees 'quality awareness' on the basis of rational arguments and rational techniques. Such a conversion is a type of internalization (Nonaka, 1994) because one aims at the adjustment to new standards and values.

Knowledge Flows

The Value Chain

Porter (1985) developed the value chain analysis as an instrument to analyze a firm's competitive advantage. The value chain analysis splits up the functions and activities carried out by an organization into activities within the primary process and the supporting processes, thus providing insight into:

- the organization's cost behaviour and cost structure;
- the locations creating added value;
- the locations possessing the firm's differentiating capacity;
- the way in which the competitive position can be improved.

Using the product flow, order flow or information flow, it is possible to identify value-creating functions and activities as well as supporting processes. The value chain (Figure A5) allows for identification of the relevance of knowledge to the creation of added value. As the AVEBE case shows (Chapter 4), it is possible to verify where knowledge input (for example, the development of new potato varieties) in the chain is expected to lead to adequate output (process optimization in processing).

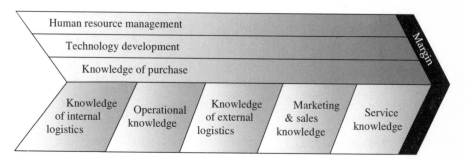

Figure A5. Value chain analysis.

Two other ordering instruments introduced by Porter (1985) for competition analysis purposes are the five-forces model and the value system. Both instruments can also be used for knowledge flows analysis.

Flow Analysis

The flow analysis graphically maps internal and external knowledge flows of (an) organizational unit(s). The working method has been described in Sec. 3.4. The most important knowledge suppliers (knowledge centres) and knowledge users are recognized and the flows between suppliers and users are named, on the understanding that knowledge suppliers are also knowledge users and vice versa. On the basis of this sketch bottlenecks can be identified. The word 'sketch' is used here with emphasis, because detailed flow analyses tend to make it impossible to see the wood for the trees.

1. Five-forces model

This competition model (Porter, 1985) shows the playing room of the knowledge enterprise by naming five forces: competitors, customers, suppliers, firms entering the market, and substitution products. The firm has a relationship with each of these forces, and knowledge can flow in each of these relationships (see Figure A6). The contents of the five forces and their accompanying knowledge flows is unique for each knowledge enterprise. The analysis can be applied to product, market and business level and provides a simple framework for discussions about the firm's course in the market. Furthermore the forces indicate where dominant obstacles to growth are located.

2. Value system

The value system is a continuation of the value chain. It looks into the position of the value chain (see Figure A7) in the total business

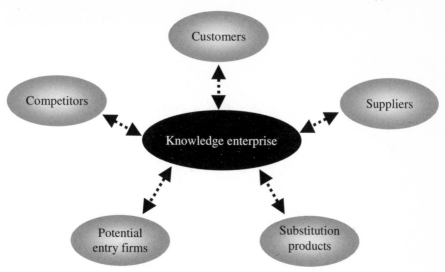

Figure A6. The five forces model.

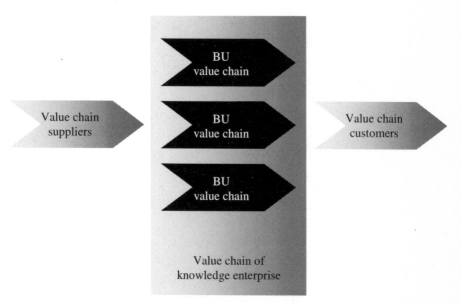

Figure A7. The value system.

chain. The value chain is coupled to the upstream and downstream knowledge activities in the business. The value system maps the knowledge flows between the business units in the firm, its customers and suppliers. It provides an integrated picture of total latitude of knowledge enterprises. Thus, it is made possible to determine hard to define interrelationships of product and process technologies or logistic links. Using the value system, the firm possesses a tool providing insight into cost structures, technology flows and product flows in the value system, and hence, discovering the direction of the knowledge flows.

Identifying Functional Demands

After defining the knowledge ambition ('doing the right things'), the demands are formulated that the organization must comply with to effectively being able to realize them ('doing the right things right'). In Sec. 3.3, this procedure has been outlined using an example. We will once again mention the most important steps here:

1. Sketching the map of most important knowledge flows

This map will identify:

- the knowledge centres (where is knowledge being developed, retrieved, or gained?);
- the knowledge flows (from where to where does the knowledge flow?);
- the most important control loops (where does feedback take place?);
- the knowledge development strategy (how is knowledge developed?).

2. The gap analysis, which identifies the gaps between IST and SOLL, with the knowledge ambition at the back of one's mind

The knowledge flows chart is 'coloured' after answering the following questions:

- Which knowledge centres must be reinforced?
- Which knowledge flows must be intensified?
- Which control loops must be better closed or shortened?
- Is a new knowledge development strategy needed?

3. The definition of functional demands, which identifies improvements as concretely as possible

In this process it is essential that the crucial knowledge flows are made visible as quickly as possible, working from general to detailed (Chapter 9). Simple graphical representations are highly suitable. One should not drown in overly detailed system analyses.

References

Allen, T.J. & Cohen, S., (1969). 'Information flow in R&D laboratories,' *Administrative Science Quarterly* **14**, 19–24.

Allen, T.J. & Katz, R., (1986). 'The dual ladder: Motivational solution or managerial delusion?,' *Research & Development Management,* **16**(2), 185–197.

Andreasen, L.E., Coriat, B., Hertog, J.F. den & Kaplinsky, R. (eds.), *Europe's Next Step: Organisational Innovation, Competition and Employment* (Cass Publishers, Ilford, Essex, 1995).

Arnold, R.H., (1992) 'Pitfalls of decentralization, or setting the fox to guard the chicken coop'. *Research & Technology Management,* **35**(3), 9–11.

Assen, A. van, 'Technologie en personeelsbeleid: De draad van Ariadne in het technisch labyrint' (Catholic University of Nijmegen, Nijmegen, inaugural speech, 1992).

Barney, J., (1991). Firm resources and sustained competitive advantage, *Journal of Management,* **17**, 99–120.

Bart, Ch.K., (1993). 'Controlling new R&D projects'. *R&D Management,* **23**(3), 187–197.

Becker, B. & Gerhart, B., (1996). 'The impact of human resource management on organizational performance. Progress and prospects,' *American Management Journal,* **39**(4), 779–802.

Beek, A. & Jager, J., *Hoofdlijnen Informatiekunde* (Wolters-Noordhoff, Groningen, 1993).

Bentley, J.C., Facing a future of "permanent white water". The challenge of training and development in high technology organizations, in *Human Resource Strategy in High Technology,* L.R. Gomez-Mejia, & M.W. Lawless, (eds.) (JAI Press, Greenwich, 1992).

Bird, J., (1993). 'The Rover Route to Computing'. *Management Today,* October, 92–96.

Boersma, S.K.Th., Kennismanagement. Een creatieve onderneming' (University of Groningen, Groningen, inaugural speech, 1995).

Bohn, R.E., (1994). Measuring and managing technical knowledge, *Sloan Management Review*, Fall, 61–73.

Brown, J.S. & Duguid, P., *Organising Knowledge* (Xerox Palo Alto Research Centre, Palo Alto, 1997).

Cameron, K., (1980). Critical questions in assessing organizational effectiveness, *Organizational Dynamics*, **9**, 66–80.

Casio, W.F., *Applied Psychology in Personnel Management* (Prentice Hall, Englewood Cliffs, 1991).

Clark, K.B. & Fujimoto, T., *Product Development Performance: Strategy, Organization and Management in the Auto Industry* (Harvard Business Press, Boston, MA, 1991)

Clark, K.B. & Wheelwright, S.C., *Managing New Product and Process Development* (The Free Press, New York, 1993).

Clark, K.B., Hayes, R.H. & Wheelright, S.C., *Dynamic manufacturing: Creating the Learning Organization* (The Free Press, New York, 1988).

Cobbenhagen, J., Hertog, J.F. den & Pennings, J., *Succesvol veranderen: Kerncompetenties en bedrijfsvernieuwing* (Kluwer, Deventer, 1994).

Cohen, W.M. & Levinthal, D.A., (1990). 'Absorptive capacity. New perspectives on learning and innovation,' *Administrative Science Quarterly*, **35**(2), 128–152.

Coombs, G. & Rosse, J.G., Recruiting and hiring the high technology professionals. Trends and future directions, in *Human Resource Strategy in High Technology*, eds. Gomez-Mejia, L.R. & Lawless, M.W. (JAI Press, Greenwich, 1992).

Cooper, R.G., (1994). 'Third generation new product processes,' *Journal of Product Innovation Management*, **11**(1), 3–15.

Davenport, T.H., *Process Innovation, Reengineering Work through Information Technology* (Harvard Business School Press, Boston MA).

Davenport, T.H. & Short, J.E., (1990). 'The New Industrial Engineering: Information Technology and Business Process Redesign,' *Sloan Management Review*, Summer.

Davis, G.B. et al., Productivity from Information Technology Investment in Knowledge Work, in *Strategic Information Technology Management*, eds. Banker, R., Kauffman, R. & Mahmood, M. (Idea Group Publishing, Harrisburg, PA, 1993).

David, G.B. & Olson, M.H., *Management Information Systems: Conceptual Foundations, Structure and Development* (McGraw-Hill, New York, 1984).

De Bono, E., *Serious Creativity: Using the Power of Lateral Thinking to Create New Ideas* (Harper Collins, London, 1994).

Dence, R., Best-Practice Benchmarking, in *Performance Measurement and Evaluation*, eds. Holloway J. et al. (Londen, Sage, 1995).

Devanna, M.A., Fombrum, C.J. & Tichy, M.A., A framework for strategic human resource management, in *Strategic Human Resource Management*, eds. Fombrun C.J., Tichy, N.M. & Devanna, M.A. (Wiley, New York, 1984)

Diepen, B. van, MD-beleid als instrument van kennisontwikkeling: Effecten van loopbanen, in *Management development. Ontwikkelingen en trends*, eds. von Grumbkov, J. & Jansen, P.G.W. (Kluwer Bedrijfswetenschappen, Deventer, 1996).

Dougherty, D., *Managing your Core Incompetencies for Product Innovation* (McGill, Montreal, 1993).

Drucker, P., *Post Capitalist Society* (Harper Business, New York, 1993).

Earl, M.J., *Management Strategies for Information Technology* (Prentice Hall, New York, 1989).

Elschot, W., Lijmen — Het been, in: Elschot, W., *Verzameld werk* (Querido, Amsterdam, 1980).

Etzioni, A. (1976). *Social Problems* (Prentice Hall, Englewood Cliffs N.Y, 1976).

Ewijk-Hoevenaars, A. van, Hertog, J.F. den Jaarsveld, J. van, *Naar eenvoud in organisaties. Werken met zelfsturende eenheden* (Deventer Kluwer, Bedrijfswetenschappen, 1995).

Florida, R. & Kenney, M., *The Breakthrough Illusion. Corporate America's Failure to Move from Innovation to Mass Production* (Basic Books, 1990).

Galbraith, J.R., *Designing Complex Organizations* (Addison Wesley, Reading, MA, 1973).

Galbraith, J.R., *Competing with Flexible Lateral Organizations* (2nd ed.) (Addison Wesley, Reading, 1994).

Gaspersz, J. & Ott, M., *Management van employability. Nieuwe kansen in arbeidsrelaties* (Van Gorcum, Assen, 1996).

Graham, R.J., (1984). 'Anthropology and OR: The Place of Observation in Management Science Process,' *Journal of Operations Research*, **35**(6), 527–536.

Gupta, A.K. & Govindarajan, V., (1991). 'Knowledge flows and the structure of control within multinational corporations,' *Academy of Management Review*, **16**(4), 768–792.

Gustavsen, B., *Dialogue and Development. Theory of Communication, Action Research, and the Restructuring of Working Life* (Van Gorcum, Assen, 1992).

Hamel, G. & Prahalad, C.K., *Competing for the Future* (Harvard Business School Press, Boston, MA, 1994).

Hammer, M. & Champy, J., *Reengineering the Corporation: A Manifesto for Business Revolution* (Harper Business, New York, 1993).

Hart, M.W., 't, De ondersteuning van kenniswerkers door informatietechnologie, in *Handboek Informatica: informatie-technologie voor informatici en managers* (Samson Bedrijfsinformatie, Alphen aan de Rijn, 1995).

Hartman, W., Een typologie van informatiesystemen, in *Handboek Informatica: informatietechnologie voor informatici en managers* (Samson Bedrijfsinformatie, Alphen aan den Rijn, 1990).

Hedlund, G., (1994). 'Knowledge management and the N-form corporation,' *Strategic Management Journal*, **15**, 73–90.

Hertog, J.F. den & van Sluijs, E., *Onderzoek in organisaties. Een methodologische reisgids* (Van Gorcum Assen, 1995a).

Hertog, J.F. den & van Sluijs, E., Managing knowledge flows: A key role for personnel management, in *Europe's Next Step: Organizational Innovation, Competition and Employment*, eds. Andreasen, L.E., Coriat, B., den Hertog, J.F. and Kaplinsky, R. (Frank Cass, Ilford, 1995b).

Hertog, J.F. den, Entrepreneurship on the shopfloor: Nationale Nederlanden, in *Europe's Next Step: Organizational Innovation, Competition and Employment*, eds. Andreasen, L.E., Coriat, B., den Hertog, J.F. and Kaplinsky, R. (Frank Cass, Ilford, 1995).

Hertog, J.F. den, 'Innovatie in een gestroomlijnde organisatie. Wat komt er na de business unit?' (MERIT, Maastricht, 1996).

Hertog, J.F. den, Philips, G. & Cobbenhagen, J., Paradox management: The fourth phase of innovation management, in *Paradoxes Management*, eds. Gutschelhofer, A. & Scheff, J. (Linder Verlag, Wien, 1996) 43–76.

Hertog, J.F. den, Sluijs, E. van, Diepen, B. van & Assen, A. van, (1992). 'Innovatie en personeelsbeleid. De beheersing van de kennishuishouding,' *Bedrijfskunde*, **63**(2), 58–67.

Hippel, E. von, (1986). 'Lead users: A source of novel product concepts,' *Management Science*, **32**(7), 1986.

Jaikumar, R. (1986). 'Postindustrial Manufacturing,' *Harvard Business Review*, **64**(6), 69–76.

Kaplinsky, R. (1995). 'Patients as work in progress: Organisational Reform in the Health Sector,' in *Europe's Next Step: Organizational Innovation, Competition and Employment*, eds. Andreasen, L.E., Coriat, B., den Hertog, J.F. and Kaplinsky, R. (Frank Cass, Ilford, 1995b).

Kiesche, E.S. (1993), 'CDA meeting: Honey and edge,' *Chemical Weekly*, **152**(11), 16–17.

Klimstra, P.D. & Potts J. (1988). 'What we've learned about managing R&D projects,' *Research & Technology Management*, May–June, 42–58.

Kluytmans, F. & Sluijs, E. van (1995). 'De relatie tussen bedrijfsbeleid en personeelsmanagement,' *Tijdschrift voor Arbeidsvraagstukken*, **1**, 34–44.

Koene, B., *Organizational Culture, Leadership and Performance in Contexts. Trust and Rationality in Organizations* (Datawyse, Maastricht, 1996).

Kogut, B. & Zander, U., (1992). 'Knowledge of the firm, combinative capabilities, and the replication of technology,' *Organization Science*, **3**(3), 383–397.

Kotler, P., *Marketing Management, Analysis, Planning, Implementation, and Control* (Prentice Hall, Englewood Cliffs, New Jersey, 1995).

Laudon, K.C. & Laudon, J.P., *Management Information Systems. Organization and Technology* (Prentice Hall, Englewood Cliffs, New Jersey, 1996).

Lawler, E.E. III & Ledford, G.E., (1985). 'Skill-Based Pay,' *Personnel*, **62**(9), 30–37.

Lawler, E.E. III, *Strategic Pay* (Jossey-Bass, San Francisco, 1990).

Lawrence, P.R. & Lorsch, J.W., *Organization and Environment: Managing Differentiation and Integration* (Irwin, Homewood, 1969).

Learned, E.P., Christensen, R.C., Andrews, K.R. & Gate, W.D. (1965). *Business Policy: Test and Cases*. (Irwin, Homewood, Ill., 1965).

Ledford, jr., G.E., *Skill-based pay: Results of a large-scale study* (University of South Carolina Los Angeles, 1992).

Ledford, G.E., (1991). 'Three case studies of skill-based pay: An overview,' *Compensation and Benefits Review*, **23**(2), 11–23.

Leonard-Barton, D., (1990). 'A Dual Methodology for Case Studies: Synergist Use of a Longitudinal Single Site with Replicated Multiple Sites,' *Organization Science*, **1**(3), 248–66.

Lewis, P., *Information-Systems Development* (Pitman Publishing, London, 1994).

Lewis, W.W & Linden, L.H., (1990). 'A new mission for corporate technology,' *Sloan Management Review*, **31**(4), 57–67

Maidique, M.A. & Zirger, B.J., (1985). 'The new product learning cycle,' *Research Policy*, **14**, 299–313.

Massier, C. & Boersma, S.K.Th., (1996). 'Pink Elephant: Over de geheimen van succesvol ondernemen,' *Bedrijfskunde*, **2**, 4–8.

Mintzberg, H., *The Structuring of Organizations* (Prentice Hall, Englewood Cliffs, N.Y., 1979).

Mohrman, S.A., Mohrman, A.M. & Cohen, S.G., Human resource strategies for lateral integration in high technology settings, in *Human Resource Strategy in High Technology*, Gomez-Mejia L.R. & Lawless, M.W. (JAI Press Greenwich, 1992).

Morgan, G., *Images of Organizations* (Beverly Hills: Sage, 1986).

Moss Kanter, R.M., *The Change Masters: Innovation for Productivity in the American Corporation* (New York: Simon and Schuster, 1983).

Nayak, P.R. & Ketteringham, J.M., *Breakthroughs* (Rawson Associates, New York, 1986).

Nolan, R. & Koot, W., (1992). 'De actualiteit van de Nolan fasentheorie,' *Holland Managament Review*, **31**, pp. 77–88.

Nolan, R., (1979). 'Managing the crises in data processing,' *Harvard Business Review*, **57**, pp. 115–126.

Nonaka, I., (1994). 'A dynamic theory of organizational knowledge creation,' *Organization Science*, **5**(1), 140–148.

Nonaka, I., & Takeuchi, H., *The Knowledge-Creating Company* (Oxford University Press, 1996).

Olie, R.L., *European Transnational Mergers* (Datawyse, Maastricht, 1996).

Pascale, R.T., *Managing on the Edge: How Successful Companies Use Conflict to Stay Ahead* (Viking Penguin, London, 1990).

Peters, T.J. & Waterman, R.H., *In Search of Excellence* (Harper & Row, New York, 1982).

Pfeffer, J., *Competitive Advantage through People* (Harvard Business Press, Boston, 1994).

Polanyi, K., *The Tacit Dimension* (Anchor Books, New York, 1966).

Porter, M.E., *Competitive Advantage* (The Free Press, New York, 1985).

Porter, M.E. & Millar V.E., (1985). How information gives you competitive advantage, *Harvard Business Review*, **63**, July/August.

Prahalad, C.K. & Hamel, G., (1990), The core competence of the corporation, *Harvard Business Review*, **68**(3), 79–91.

Reisman, A., (1988). On Alternative strategies for doing research in the management and social sciences, *IEEE Transactions on Engineering Management*, **35**(4), 215–220.

Rieken, J., Business planning op elk zelfsturend niveau, in *Naar eenvoud in organisaties. Werken met zelfsturende eenheden*, eds. Ewijk-Hoevenaars, A. van, Hertog, J.F. den & Jaarsveld, J. van (Deventer, Kluwer Bedrijfswetenschappen, 1995).

Roberts, E.B. & Berry, (1984). Managing the internal corporate venturing process, *Sloan Management Review*, Winter, 33–48.

Roberts, E.B., (1995). Benchmarking the Strategic Management of Technology, *Research & Technology Management*, **38**(1), 44–56.

Rotman, D., (1993). R&D: Searching for profits in tough times, *Chemical Weekly*, **152**(17), 31–32.

Roussel, Ph.A., Saad, K.N. & Erickson, T.M., *The third R&D generation, Managing the link to corporate strategy* (Harvard Business School Press, Boston, 1991).

Rubenstein, A.H., (1994). At the front end of R&D / innovation process: Idea development and entrepreneurship, *International Journal of Technology Management*, **9**(5,6,7), 652–677.

Schuler, R.S. & Jackson, S.E., *Human resource management, Positioning for the 21st century (6th ed.)* (West Publishing Company, Minneapolis, 1996).

Schumpeter, J.A., *Capitalism, socialism and democracy* (Harper and Row, New York, 1942).

Scott-Morgan, P., *The Unwritten Rules of the Game* (McGraw-Hill, New York, 1994).

Scott-Mortan, M. (ed.), *The Corporation of the 1990s, Information Technology and Organizational Transformation* (Oxford University Press, New York, 1991).

Senge, P.M., *The Fifth Discipline: The Art and Practice of the Learning Organization* (Century Business, London, 1990).

Shepard, H.A., (1958). 'The dual hierarchy in research,' *Research Management*, **1**, 177–187.

Simon, H.A., *The New Science of Management Decision* (Prentice-Hall, Englewood Cliffs, NJ, 1977).

Sitter, L.U. de, *Synergetisch produceren* (Van Gorcum, Assen, 1994).

Sitter, L.U. de, Hertog, J.F. den & Dankbaar, B., (1997). From complex organisations with simple jobs to simple organisations with complex jobs, *Human Relations* **50**(5), 497–534.

Sluijs, E. van, 'Ericsson Telecommunicatie: Het managen van competenties' (MERIT, Maastricht, 1995).

Sluijs, E. van, Assen A. van & Hertog J.F. den (1991). Personnel management and organizational change: A sociotechnical perspective, *European Work and Organizational Psychologist*, **1**(1), 27–51.

Sluijs, E. van & J.F. den Hertog, Praktijkverkenning Personeelswetenschappen, Deelrapporten Verkenning Personeelswetenschappen, Instituut voor Sociaal-wetenschappelijk onderzoek van de Katholieke Universiteit Brabant (IVA) Tilburg, 1993).

Stacey, R.D., *Strategic management & organisational dynamics* (2nd ed.) (Pitman, London, 1996).

Stalk, G. & Hout, T., *Competing Against Time: How Time-Based Strategies Deliver Superior Performance* (The Free Press, New York, 1990).

Storey, J., *Development in the Management of Human Resources* (Blackwell, Oxford, 1992).

Szakonyi, R., (1992). 'Follow these five steps to keep long-term R&D alive,' *R&D*, **34**(9), 53.

Takeuchi, H. en Nonaka, I., (1986). The new new product development game, *Harvard Business Review*, **64**(1), 137–146.

Thomson, J.D., *Organizations in Action: Social Science Basis of Administrative Theory* (McGraw Hill, New York, 1967).

Ven, A.H. van de (1988). Central problems in the management of innovation, *Management Science*, **32**(5), 590–607.

Venkatraman, N., IT-Induced Business Reconfiguration, in The Corporation of the 1990s, *Information Technology and Organizational Transformation*, ed. Scott Mortan M. (Oxford University Press, New York, 1991).

Venkatraman, N. & Henderson, J.C., Strategic Alignment: A Model for Organizational Transformation through Information Technology, in, *Transforming Organizations*, eds. Kochan, T.A. & Useem, M. (Oxford University Press Oxford, 1992).

Weick, K.E., (1993). 'Organisational redesign as improvisation,' in *Organisational Change and Redesign: Ideas and Insights for Improving Performance*, eds. Huber, G.P. & Glick, W.H. (Oxford University Press, New York

Womack, J.P., Jones, D.T. & Roos, D., *The Machine That Changed The World* (Macmillan, New York, 1990).

Zairi, M., *Benchmarking for Best Practice. Continuous Learning through Sustainable Innovation* (Butterworth-Heinemann, Oxford, 1996).

Zorkoczy, P., *Information Technology, An introduction* (Pitman Publishing, London, 1991).

Zuboff, S., *The Age of the Smart Machine, The Future of Work and Power* (Basic Books, New York, 1988).

GLOSSARY

Competence. Knowledge areas oriented towards fulfilling a function or task within the organisation.

Contextual knowledge. Experience knowledge about a specific environment (market, sector, culture, country).

Core competence. Competence yielding competitive advantage, which the firm can use to add value to the customer's chain, is difficult to imitate, and which is important to the various business units.

Dialogue. A type of communication for a team oriented towards a common objective, in which contradictions are accepted as being normal, openness prevails and hierarchic factors and power factors are eliminated to the maximum extent.

Enabling competencies. Knowledge intertwined with the core competencies, and which add value but do not yield differentiating capacity.

Exchangeable knowledge. Knowledge that is relatively separate from the enabling competencies and core competencies and can be purchased without much risk or acquired through outsourcing.

Explicit knowledge. Knowledge stored in material knowledge carriers (products, books, computers, programs, et cetera).

Functional knowledge. Knowledge about a specific subject area.

Data. The result of observations

Information. Ordered data with a more specific meaning.

Knowledge. A collection of information and rules used to fulfil a specific function.

Knowledge ambition. The objective of the knowledge enterprise: the choice for the competencies with which the organisation is able to achieve differentiating capacity in the environment in the future.

Knowledge area. Collection of mutually connecting knowledge elements.

Knowledge bank. An electronic or other system in which information and explicit knowledge are stored and in which information and knowledge can be quickly retrieved by users through effective search procedures.

Knowledge carrier. People or objects storing knowledge.

Knowledge centres. An organisational entity (a knowledge cluster, department, or firm) responsible for knowledge development and knowledge transfer.

Knowledge cluster. Group in the organisation exchanging specific knowledge and in special cases also responsible for its development, transfer and assurance.

Knowledge database. An electronic or paper file containing information about the knowledge, experience and knowledge objectives of the members of an organisation (synonyms: skills map, skill logs).

Knowledge domain. A knowledge area anchored in an organisational entity.

Knowledge element. The smallest completed entity of specific knowledge.